THE CAMBRIDGE COMPANION
TO *ULYSSES*

Few books in the English language seem to demand a companion more insistently than James Joyce's *Ulysses*, a work that at once entices and terrifies readers with its interwoven promises of pleasure, scandal, difficulty, and mastery. This volume offers fourteen concise and accessible essays by accomplished scholars that explore this masterpiece of world literature. Several essays examine specific aspects of *Ulysses*, ranging from its plot and characters to the questions it raises about the strangeness of the world and the density of human cultures. Others address how Joyce created this novel, why it became famous, and how it continues to shape both popular and literary culture. Like any good companion, this volume invites the reader to engage in an ongoing conversation about the novel and its lasting ability to entice, rankle, absorb, and enthrall.

Sean Latham is the Pauline Walter McFarlin Endowed Chair of English and Comparative Literature at the University of Tulsa, where he serves as editor of the *James Joyce Quarterly*, codirector of the Modernist Journals Project, and director of the Oklahoma Center for the Humanities. He is the author or editor of several books, including *Am I a Snob?: Modernism and the Novel* (2003); *Joyce's Modernism* (2004); *The Art of Scandal: Modernism, Libel Law, and the Roman a Clef* (2009); and *James Joyce: Visions and Revisions* (2009).

A complete list of books in the series is at the back of the book.

GW00580223

THE CAMBRIDGE COMPANION TO *ULYSSES*

THE CAMBRIDGE COMPANION TO *ULYSSES*

EDITED BY

SEAN LATHAM

University of Tulsa

CAMBRIDGE
UNIVERSITY PRESS

CAMBRIDGE
UNIVERSITY PRESS

University Printing House, Cambridge CB2 8BS, United Kingdom

One Liberty Plaza, 20th Floor, New York, NY 10006, USA

477 Williamstown Road, Port Melbourne, VIC 3207, Australia

4843/24, 2nd Floor, Ansari Road, Daryaganj, Delhi - 110002, India

79 Anson Road, #06-04/06, Singapore 079906

Cambridge University Press is part of the University of Cambridge.

It furthers the University's mission by disseminating knowledge in the pursuit of education, learning and research at the highest international levels of excellence.

www.cambridge.org
Information on this title: www.cambridge.org/9781107423909

© Cambridge University Press 2014

First published 2014

A catalogue record for this publication is available from the British Library

Library of Congress Cataloging in Publication data
The Cambridge Companion to Ulysses / edited by Sean Latham.
pages   cm. – (Cambridge Companions to Literature)
Includes bibliographical references and index.
ISBN 978-1-107-07390-6 (hardback) – ISBN 978-1-107-42390-9 (paperback)
1. Joyce, James, 1882–1941. Ulysses.   I. Latham, Sean, 1971– editor of compilation.
PR6019.09U6323   2014
823'.912–dc23   2014006003

ISBN 978-1-107-07390-6 Hardback
ISBN 978-1-107-42390-9 Paperback

Contents

PART III. READING *ULYSSES*

PART IV. CONTEMPORARY THEORY AND CRITICISM

Notes on Contributors

SCARLETT BARON is a Lecturer in Twentieth-Century British and American Literature at University College London. She is the author of *"Strandentwining Cable": Joyce, Flaubert, and Intertextuality*. Her current book project is *A Genealogy of Intertextuality*.

JOSEPH BROOKER is a Reader in Modern Literature at Birkbeck, University of London, where he is also the Director of the Centre for Contemporary Literature. He is the author of *Joyce's Critics*, *Flann O'Brien*, and *Literature of the 1980s*; he has edited special issues of *New Formations* and *Textual Practice*.

ENDA DUFFY is the author of *The Speed Handbook: Velocity, Pleasure, Modernism*, which won the Modernist Studies Book Prize, and of *The Subaltern "Ulysses."* In 2011, he coedited *Joyce, Benjamin and Magical Urbanism*. He teaches at the University of California at Santa Barbara. His new work is on energy.

MAUD ELLMANN is the Randy L. and Melvin R. Berlin Professor of the Development of the Novel in English at the University of Chicago. Her most recent book is *The Nets of Modernism*, a study of Woolf, James, Joyce, and Freud.

JONATHAN GOLDMAN teaches at the New York Institute of Technology, Manhattan, and is author of *The Modernist Author in the Age of Celebrity* and coeditor of *Modernist Star Maps: Celebrity, Modernity, Culture*. His writing appears in such publications as *James Joyce Quarterly*, *Novel*, and *Narrative*.

MICHAEL GRODEN Distinguished Professor at the University of Western Ontario, is the author of *"Ulysses" in Progress* and *"Ulysses" in Focus* and editor or coeditor of *The James Joyce Archive*, *James*

Joyce's Manuscripts, Genetic Criticism, Praharfeast, The Johns Hopkins Guide to Literary Theory and Criticism, and *Contemporary Literary and Cultural Theory.*

CHERYL TEMPLE HERR teaches at the University of Iowa. She has written widely on Joyce and Irish studies. At present, she is writing books on Joycean phenomenology and British rock culture.

MARJORIE HOWES teaches English at Boston College. She is the author of *Yeats's Nations: Gender, Class, and Irishness* and *Colonial Crossings: Figures in Irish Literary History* and the coeditor of *Semicolonial Joyce, The Cambridge Companion to W. B. Yeats,* and the forthcoming *Yeats and Afterwords.*

R. BRANDON KERSHNER is Alumni Professor of English at the University of Florida. Among other books, he is the author of *Joyce, Bakhtin, and Popular Literature* and *The Culture of Joyce's "Ulysses,"* as well as the editor of the Bedford Books edition of *A Portrait of the Artist as a Young Man.*

SEAN LATHAM is the Pauline McFarlin Walter Chair of English at the University of Tulsa, where he serves as editor of *James Joyce Quarterly,* codirector of the Modernist Journals Project, and coeditor of the *Journal of Modern Periodical Studies.* His most recent book is *The Art of Scandal.*

MARGOT NORRIS is the author of several books and numerous articles on the work of James Joyce. These include *The Decentered Universe of "Finnegans Wake," Joyce's Web: The Social Unraveling of Modernism, Suspicious Readings of Joyce's "Dubliners," Virgin and Veteran Readings of "Ulysses,"* and a study of the 1967 Joseph Strick film *Ulysses.*

VIKE MARTINA PLOCK is a Lecturer in English at the University of Exeter. She is the author of *Joyce, Medicine, and Modernity* and the editor of a special issue of *James Joyce Quarterly* on Joyce and physiology. She is currently writing a monograph on early twentieth-century women writers and fashion.

MICHAEL RUBENSTEIN is an Assistant Professor of English at Stony Brook University. His book, *Public Works: Infrastructure, Irish Modernism, and the Postcolonial,* received the American Conference for Irish Studies Robert Rhodes Prize for a book on literature and the Modernist Studies Association Prize for Most Distinguished Book.

PAUL K. SAINT-AMOUR is Associate Professor of English at the University of Pennsylvania and coeditor, with Jessica Berman, of the Modernist Latitudes series at Columbia University Press. The author of *The Copywrights: Intellectual Property and the Literary Imagination*, he is presently completing a book about modernist narrative and total war.

Preface: Why Read Ulysses?

A volume like this sets out, as its name suggests, to be companionable: to provide some useful guidance about how to read *Ulysses* – a book known in equal parts for its immense achievement and unnerving difficulty. To begin, let's address the most basic of questions: *Why* read *Ulysses*? Even the most devoted Joyce scholars ask themselves this on occasion, and every year or so news arrives of some iconoclast who dismisses the work as nonsense, condemns its complexity as elitist, or laments the way it has destroyed the fine traditions of the novel. Make no mistake, there is something to such grievances.

Reading *Ulysses* is a significant undertaking, one that will demand vast amounts of your time, attention, and patience – resources that will themselves often be repaid by frustration, confusion, and even an occasional sense of betrayal. First-time readers, in particular, might feel some kinship with the students we find in Stephen's classroom in the book's second chapter. Trying ineptly to make a joke, he tells the boys that a pier is "a disappointed bridge," a half-built edifice that never reaches its destination and instead leads only into deeper waters (*U* 2.39). *Ulysses* might seem an equally "disappointed" novel, in which the aesthetic attempt to bridge minds, construct a world, or even resolve a very basic marriage plot all end abruptly amid deep waters.

After all, even after working arduously through hundreds of pages, we do not learn if the Blooms' marriage has a future; and despite its epic allusions to the *Odyssey*, Stephen ends the book as he began it: alone, adrift, and without a home. Back in the classroom, the young teacher and aspiring author attempts to regain the attention of his class by offering them this riddle:

> *The cock crew,*
> *The sky was blue:*
> *The bells in heaven*

Were striking eleven.
'Tis time for this poor soul
To go to heaven.
                    (*U* 2.102–07)

The answer, "the fox burying his grandmother under a hollybush," is a nonsense joke (*U* 2.115). It cannot be divined in advance or deduced from the clue. No wonder the students barrel out of the room to recess as soon as the bell sounds.

So with such a warning in the opening pages, why don't we also head for the exits from a book that often seems equally solipsistic and elliptical? Can even the most pleasant of companions really justify a journey to the end of this narrative pier? Indeed, might we even end up like the children in one of Joyce's first short stories, "An Encounter," who set out on an adventure that leads first to boredom, then to mild titillation, and finally to a vague fear of punishment? Why, again, should we read *Ulysses*? Here are some possible answers:

- **Because it is there.** *Ulysses* towers over modern Western and now world culture as a lofty monument – albeit a monument whose meaning has changed considerably over the near-century since its first publication. In 1922, it was a banned book, famous as much for its alleged obscenity as for its aesthetic merit. Today, its sexual suggestiveness has largely paled, even if its sometimes baroque descriptions of the body's career – from outhouse to brothel to grave – can still unsettle a classroom. So *Ulysses* is no longer "there" in the way it once was, but it still looms on the shelves of literary people, in bookstores, on syllabi, in the annual Bloomsday celebrations around the world, and, of course, in Irish airport bookshops. It hails us as something worth trying, something modern, famous, and perhaps even beautiful.
- **Because it is a humane and intellectual challenge.** Part of the appeal also resides in what W. B. Yeats called the "fascination of what's difficult."[1] Generally speaking, *Ulysses* is not a difficult book to begin, but it is a very challenging book to finish. The opening episodes mix stream-of-consciousness with third-person narration to bring us into the overlapping worlds and minds of the characters. These sections are thick with plot and deeply structured by a set of mythic parallels to Homer's *Odyssey* – parallels that provide some guidance amid a welter of detail about workaday Dublin life on a warm summer day. At the midpoint of the book, however, such guideposts and even the mode of narration that had become customary fall away as Joyce sets out on

what Karen Lawrence calls a new "odyssey of style."[2] The epic plot, the shape of the characters, and even the book's representational strategies all shift as *Ulysses* becomes a book no longer just about a Dublin day in 1904, but about the very process of reading and interpretation itself. Difficulty, in short, becomes part of the book's point, and we test ourselves against it to uncover the challenges and mysteries that still shadow our lives and languages.

- **Because it celebrates everyday life.** Perhaps more than any other text, *Ulysses* lends weight and significance to objects, emotions, and experiences worn smooth by habit. It mystifies and even makes sacred the profane world around us. As Declan Kiberd argues, Joyce "believed that by recording the minutiae of a single day, he could release those elements of the marvelous latent in ordinary living, so that the familiar might astonish."[3] In the book, a key, a used bar of soap, a discarded newspaper, an empty biscuit tin, a cracked mirror, and even a simple kitchen tap all take on enormous consequence, becoming supercharged with meanings, histories, and even voices of their own. Watching the mundane world come vividly into being, we see into the dynamic complexity of our own everyday lives.

- **Because it puts hard and urgent questions to us.** In helping us see everyday life as an epic adventure, *Ulysses* also raises a complex series of ethical and political questions. Arguably the very first postcolonial novel – published just as Ireland achieved its independence – it inquires into some of modernity's most confounding concepts: race, nation, gender, class, and sexuality. In Stephen we encounter a colonial intellectual who wonders how to imagine – in a language not fully his own – an art, an identity, and a "conscience" for a country ruled from afar. Against this mournful figure destined for exile, the book poses Bloom, an uncertain Jew born in Ireland yet linked through family, religion, and culture to a larger exilic community itself on the brink of statehood. And these figures, in turn, are set against Molly, the daughter of a soldier, and herself not a native Dubliner, who nevertheless comes to symbolize the home toward which the narrative steadily drives its symbolic father and son. These cosmopolitan figures embody the complexity of a still unfolding modernity, their hybridity, mobility, and deep personal conflicts even more pressing now than they were a century ago.

- **Because it links us to communities of readers.** The very urgency of the ethical challenges *Ulysses* captures helps explain why a book so precisely (even obsessively) about Edwardian Ireland now commands a global audience of readers. It has been translated into dozens of languages and has spawned its own secular global holiday called Bloomsday. Across the world every June 16, people gather to celebrate the book by retracing the steps of entirely fictional characters around a very real Dublin, by reading the entire book in a marathon, by attending concerts of Joyce's favorite music, and by sometimes just enjoying Bloom's quiet lunch of cheese and wine. To read *Ulysses* is to become a part of this community, one that includes many literary scholars to be sure, but is by no means exclusive to them. (Indeed, Joyce offers his own ironic critique of scholarly reading both in the library episode of *Ulysses* and later in *Finnegans Wake*.) An example of what we now call global modernism, this extraordinary book explores and, with each successive reading, extends the network of connections between communities of readers who find new things in the book – new ways of fashioning a sense of self, new ways of articulating the peculiar valences of a nation, new ways of imagining erotic possibilities, and new ways of charting the connections between the past, the present, and the future.

- **Because it continues to be an extraordinary imaginative resource.** What can it mean that this book about a smallish colonial capital ran immediately to several editions and sold hundreds of thousands of copies when it was first translated into Chinese? What of the fact that it has been adapted into film; reimagined as a graphic novel; transformed into musical performances; made the subject of paintings; referenced in pop songs, commercials, and television shows; and otherwise imitated and reproduced through nearly every kind of cultural form imaginable? Put simply, *Ulysses* remains a tremendous imaginative wellspring of ideas that continues to challenge us with its difficulty, its cultural and now global resonance, its deep ethical engagement with modernity, its fascination with an everyday life shot through with staggering importance, and its ability to invoke and sustain a community of readers. Thanks to the unusual spelling of its title, *Ulysses* is already its own plural, and in each reading we add to its dazzling multitude.

These are some of my own reasons for reading *Ulysses*, and each of the authors who has contributed to this volume also provides a distinctive answer of his or her own. This *Cambridge Companion* has been designed to provide first an overview of the career of the cultural object we call *Ulysses*. The three essays in Part I, "Making *Ulysses*," describe the book's long journey from its earliest manuscript drafts through its historical circulation among readers and scholars to its final arrival as an icon. Part II, "The Story of *Ulysses*," then provides a more general overview of the book's major narrative features: its multiple beginnings, its basic plot and set-ting, and its equally diverse endings. Having provided these basics (and explained why there is actually nothing "basic" about them at all), Part III, "Reading *Ulysses*," offers four critical meditations on the most experi-mental episodes of the book. These chapters are thematically framed and thus rather than providing mere summaries, they instead offer exemplary interpretive lenses that refract some of *Ulysses'* central features. These have the virtue not only of offering one path through the complexity at the book's heart, but also of modeling basic questions about topics like the city, memory, interruption, and difficulty that resonate through all of *Ulysses*. Part IV, "Contemporary Theory and Criticism," then offers three more general readings of the novel; each synthesizes and exempli-fies some of the most innovative new work being done on *Ulysses*. Rather than mechanistically focusing on a single school or approach, these final chapters instead examine the book's dense intertextuality, its innovative exploration of the nature of a fully embodied life, and its fascination with the liveliness of the object world. The *Companion* then concludes with a bibliography designed to offer a brief guide to major critical and scholarly resources: a reader's toolbox rather than a scholar's compendium.

Depending on your own reasons for reading *Ulysses*, you might want to deviate from the path laid out here – something easily done since all the pieces can be read independently of one another. A reader curi-ous about Joyce's attempt to articulate what we now think of as a post-colonial or even post-national identity, for example, might want to skip the first section and begin instead with Enda Duffy's essay "Setting: Dublin 1904/1922" (Chapter 6), as well as those by Michael Rubenstein on the city (Chapter 8), Marjorie Howes on memory (Chapter 9), and my own on interruptions (Chapter 10). A focus on gender and sexuality might begin with Vike Martina Plock's "Bodies" (Chapter 13) and then turn to the pieces by Cheryl Temple Herr, Margot Norris, and Maud Ellmann (Chapters 11, 5, and 7, respectively). Alternatively, if you are looking simply for a clear narrative path through the book, you might want to read only Parts II and III. Or, for more experienced readers hoping to gain a sense of the history of scholarship on *Ulysses* and how our understanding of the book itself has changed in response to its greatest readers, the best place to start is Joseph Brooker's "Reception History" (Chapter 2) followed by the essays in Part IV. Finally, if you are interested in the question of how Joyce actually made *Ulysses* and what that, in turn, can teach us about the creative process more generally, then start with Michael Groden's essay (Chapter 1) and jump ahead to Part II to see how the book emerged from a loose series of drafts and notes into a tightly organized epic of the everyday.

There is, in short, no right way through this *Companion*, just as there is no right way through *Ulysses*. Regardless of whether you are attempting your first passage through *Ulysses* or if you have made the journey before, my hope is that this book will offer you a fit set of companions to assist rather than shape your encounter with one of the world's richest, most challenging, and most rewarding intellectual odysseys.

Notes

1 W. B. Yeats, "The Fascination of What's Difficult," in *The Collected Poems of W. B. Yeats*, ed. Richard J. Finneran, rev. 2nd ed. (New York: Scribner, 1996), p. 93.

2 Karen Lawrence, *The Odyssey of Style in "Ulysses"* (Princeton, NJ: Princeton University Press, 1981), n.p.

3 Declan Kiberd, *"Ulysses" and Us: The Art of Everyday Life in Joyce's Masterpiece* (New York: Norton, 2009), p. 11.

Acknowledgments

Let me close this introduction with a short word about some additional companions whose hands grew calloused in carrying this book to its Ithacan end. Omer Kazmi, Christian Howard, and Kent Emerson – all graduate students at the University of Tulsa – provided invaluable research assistance. They checked the accuracy of each quotation, proofed every word, and tested each essay against their own considerable critical intelligence. Their names do not appear on the cover or in the notes, but their work should not be invisible; they made this book stronger, more accurate, and more useful than it otherwise could have been. For that I am very grateful. And I owe a debt of gratitude as well to the book's contributors, all of whom enthusiastically accepted my invitation and patiently suffered my sometimes bluntly wielded editorial pencil even while holding to tight deadlines. Finally, I'd like to thank the University of Tulsa, the *James Joyce Quarterly*, and the Pauline McFarlin Walter Chair of English and Comparative Literature, all of which provided the time and resources needed to complete this book.

James Joyce Chronology

1882   February 2: James Augustine Joyce is born in the affluent Rathgar suburb of Dublin to John and Mary (née Murray) Joyce.

1888   Enters Clongowes Wood College, a prestigious Jesuit boarding school.

1891   The Joyce family finances begin a long decline, leading to James's withdrawal from Clongowes and a series of periodic moves to avoid creditors.

1893   James enrolls as a scholarship student at the prestigious Jesuit Belvedere College.

1898   After a successful secondary school career, James enters University College Dublin, gaining a command of French, Italian, and German in addition to Latin.

1900   Presents a paper on "Drama and Life" at the university and writes his first (now lost) play, *A Brilliant Career*. Also publishes a review of Ibsen's *When We Dead Awaken* in the prestigious *Fortnightly Review*, prompting a letter of thanks from the author.

1901   Publishes a pamphlet, "The Day of the Rabblement," which defends the Irish Literary Theatre against the perceived provincialism of Irish nationalists.

1902   Completes his degree and leaves for Paris in December to study medicine.

1903   Attends only a few medical lectures and instead spends a good deal of time in the Saint Geneviève Library, recording his notes and ideas in a series of notebooks. Returns home after a telegram arrives telling him that his mother has cancer. She dies in August.

1904   This is perhaps one of the most significant years in Joyce's life, and he later sets *Ulysses* on June 16 ("Bloomsday") – the same day that he likely goes on a first date with his future companion, Nora Barnacle. This same year, he publishes his first three stories – "The Sisters," "Eveline," and "After the Race" – in *The Irish Homestead*. He also teaches for a short time at a school in Dalkey and in August spends a few nights with Oliver St. John Gogarty and Samuel Chenevix Trench in a Martello tower. In October, he and Nora decide to leave Ireland and move first to Zurich and then to Pola (now Pula).

1905 In March, James and Nora move to Trieste, a cosmopolitan port city in the Austrian-Hungarian empire. Four months later, their first son, Giorgio, is born and they are shortly joined by James's younger brother Stanislaus who becomes a crucial (if often resentful) source of financial support. Joyce submits an early version of the story collection *Dubliners* to the Dublin publisher Grant Richards. The book raises a number of legal concerns about libel and obscenity; it will not appear in print for another nine years.

1906 The family moves briefly to Rome so James can take a job in a bank, only to return to Trieste after a few months. Work begins on "The Dead" and Joyce plans, though does not appear to write, a new story called "Ulysses."

1907 James publishes his first book, a collection of Symbolist-inspired poems entitled *Chamber Music*. Begins publishing articles on Ireland in a local Trieste paper, delivers a handful of lectures, and starts revising the autobiographical novel *Stephen Hero*. In July, the Joyces' second child, Lucia Anna, is born.

1909 Returns to Dublin twice during this year, the second time to open the city's first cinema – The Volta – with the backing of investors from Trieste.

1910 Returns to Trieste and is now caring for two of his sisters, Eva and Eileen. The girls help Nora care for the children, but the family remains poor and largely dependent on the steady financial support provided by Stanislaus. The Volta closes.

1912 Nora leaves Trieste for Ireland with Lucia; James and Giorgio soon follow. Reunited, the family leaves Dublin for what will prove the final time. After departing, Joyce writes and privately prints the crude broadside "Gas from a Burner," aimed at Dublin's printers and publishers.

1914   In a burst of creative activity, James finishes *A Portrait of the Artist as a Young Man*, writes a play about marriage entitled *Exiles*, and begins work on *Ulysses*. With the help of Ezra Pound, an avant-garde periodical in London called *The Egoist* begins to publish *A Portrait* serially. *Dubliners* appears later in the year, its reception blunted by the start of World War I.

1915   The politically active Stanislaus is detained as war begins; James and his family, however, win passage to neutral Switzerland and settle in Zurich.

1916   *A Portrait* is published in New York. The Easter Rising in Dublin is violently put down.

1917   *A Portrait* is published in England. Joyce receives anonymous gift of £200 from Harriet Shaw Weaver, a wealthy Englishwoman who will become his regular patron. In the summer, he undergoes the first of many painful eye operations.

1918   With the support of Pound, Joyce sends the first three episodes of *Ulysses* to *The Little Review*, an avant-garde New York periodical edited by Margaret Anderson and Jane Heap. Without Joyce's knowledge, some of the typescripts are edited to reduce the risk of suppression. The novel will continue to appear serially for the next three years, though four issues are seized for violating U.S. postal laws governing obscenity.

1920   The Joyce family moves to Paris, where James meets the city's famous artists and expatriates, forming close relationships with Adrienne Monnier, Valery Larbaud, and Sylvia Beach, the owner of the bookshop Shakespeare & Co. In September, the issue of *The Little Review* containing "Nausicaa" is seized for obscenity; a subsequent criminal trial of Anderson and Heap ends any chance of an American edition of *Ulysses*.

1921   Beach agrees to publish *Ulysses* in an initially limited edition of 1,000 copies by subscription only under the imprint of Shakespeare & Co. A French printer, Maurice Darantière, begins setting the proofs, which Joyce uses to introduce significant changes to the book.

1922   *Ulysses* is published on Joyce's birthday in February, but generally received as a difficult and deeply scandalous work. The Irish Civil War begins, and during a visit to Ireland, Nora and the children are forced to take cover when caught in a skirmish.

1923   Begins work on what will become *Finnegans Wake* but is known initially only as "Work in Progress" – a project that will absorb the next fifteen years of Joyce's life and conclude his career as a writer.

1924   The first section of "Work in Progress" appears in the *Transatlantic Review* but is generally seen even by Joyce's supporters as solipsistic and obscure.

1927   Portions of "Work in Progress" continue to appear, now in the journal *Transition*, edited in Paris by Eugène and Maria Jolas. Shakespeare & Co. publishes *Pomes Penyeach*.

1929   French translation of *Ulysses* appears. Lucia begins to show the first signs of a serious mental illness that will consume Joyce's energies and lead to her eventual institutionalization. In another setback, Samuel Roth begins publishing a pirated version of *Ulysses* in the United States.

1931   In March, James and Nora travel to London to obtain the marriage license necessary to protect the family's legal rights to inherit James's real and intellectual property. At the end of the year, John Joyce dies.

1932   Stephen James Joyce is born to Giorgio and his wife Helen (née Fleischman). Lucia's first hospitalization occurs.

1933   In the case of *The United States v. One Book Named "Ulysses,"* Judge John Woolsey lifts the American ban on the novel. Random House immediately publishes an American edition.

1936   Bodley Head publishes the first British edition of *Ulysses*.

1938   *Finnegans Wake* completed.

1939   *Finnegans Wake* is published in the United States and Britain, receiving mixed and often baffled reviews.

1940   As World War II rages, Joyce and Nora move to Zurich, leaving Lucia in a French sanitarium in Pornichet.

1941   After a troubled operation for a perforated duodenal ulcer, Joyce dies on January 13. He is buried in Zurich.

Abbreviations

Throughout this book, the following standard abbreviations are used for convenience. All other references are provided in endnotes following each chapter.

FW	Joyce, James. *Finnegans Wake*. New York: Viking Press, 1939. Cited by page and line number.
JJ	Ellmann, Richard. *James Joyce*. New and Revised Edition. New York: Oxford, 1982.
JJQ	*James Joyce Quarterly*. Cited by volume, year, and page number.
Letters I, II, III	Joyce, James. *Letters of James Joyce*. Vol. I. Edited by Stuart Gilbert. New York: Viking Press, 1966. Joyce, James. *Letters of James Joyce*. Vols. II and III. Edited by Richard Ellmann. New York: Viking Press, 1966.
P	Joyce, James. *A Portrait of the Artist as a Young Man*. Edited by Chester G. Anderson. New York: Viking Press, 1968.
SL	Joyce, James. *Selected Letters of James Joyce*. Edited by Richard Ellmann. New York: Viking Press, 1975.
U	Joyce, James. *Ulysses*. Edited by Hans Walter Gabler. New York: Garland, 1986. Cited by episode and line number.

PART I

Making Ulysses

CHAPTER I

Writing Ulysses

Michael Groden

As both product and process, writing pervades *Ulysses*. Characters read and respond to written texts ranging from the moral "Matcham's Masterstroke" to the erotic *Sweets of Sin*, from Milly Bloom's handwritten letter to Martha Clifford's typed one, from newspaper articles about horse races and funerals to a cryptic "U. P." (or maybe "U. p: up") postcard (*U* 4.502, 8.257–58). They think about possible sources of creative writing: "Invent a story for some proverb," Bloom ponders, and he recalls the "Time I used to try jotting down on my cuff what [Molly] said dressing" (*U* 4.518–20), while Molly wishes that she could remember Bloom's ideas "and write a book out of it the works of Master Poldy" (*U* 18.580). The characters pay attention to the paper on which a text is written (Bloom buys appropriate stationery for his response to Martha), the particulars of handwriting (he forms his letter e's in Greek style; Milly apologizes for her bad handwriting), and a newspaper's layout (the Plumtree's Potted Meat ad under the obituary notices). They also become textual critics as they note errors: Martha's typed "I do not like that other world" and "if you do not wrote" (*U* 5.245, 5.253), a newspaper article's "*L. Boom*" (*U* 16.1260), a telegram's "Nother" (*U* 3.199), Molly's handwritten "symphathy I always make that mistake and newphew with 2 double yous" (*U* 18.730–31).

Writing points to the future – someone sometime will presumably read the written words – but reading points to the past, as we take in what someone wrote and perhaps also make an imaginative leap into a novel's fictional past or consider the historical conditions under which the work was written. The writing also has a past. How did the work attain the form in which we encounter it? This question might imply the additional one: What went right and wrong as the work moved from the author's mind to a pen, typewriter, or word processor and then to print or screen? Scholars intrigued by this question are editors and textual critics. But the question can also involve the author's writing processes in themselves. Scholars who become fascinated by and study these processes are genetic critics.

More and more often in recent years, genetic criticism has moved from a fringe pursuit into the mainstream of Joyce criticism and scholarship. Every recent Bloomsday conference has prominently featured genetic issues, and essay collections providing overviews of approaches to Joyce's texts have included chapters on genetic criticism, Joyce's manuscripts, and Joyce at work. A recent book of essays is even devoted entirely to genetic analyses of the individual chapters of *Finnegans Wake*.[1] (Jean-Michel Rabaté has suggested that the *Wake*'s ideal reader is a genetic one who approaches the text "through the material evidence of the notebooks, drafts, and corrected proofs reproduced by the *James Joyce Archive*."[2]) Many books not primarily about manuscripts or genetic issues have turned to them to support diverse arguments. And newspaper and magazine articles and television's *The Colbert Report* have discussed manuscripts and sometimes even referred to genetic criticism by name.[3]

What can the *Ulysses* manuscripts say to us? Why should we listen?

Susan Sontag speculates about the attraction of writers' journals: even if they often provide little insight into published books, she suggests, they offer access to writers' daily lives, often in far less polished or self-conscious form than any finished works. The "rawness of the journal form" lets us encounter "the ego behind the masks of ego in an author's works."[4] A writer's manuscripts also take us behind the curtains but in a significantly different way. Rather than the human being in the process of living, they expose the writer in the process of writing. This is fine since, as Louis Menand has remarked about Joyce's life, "the writing is where the action is."[5]

As Joyce worked, he took notes ranging from focused thoughts and stray ideas to jottings from his readings. He listed events and characters, drafted passages, and made notations that made sense to himself (his manuscripts' only assumed reader) to indicate that he had used a note, inserted an addition, or copied a draft. He disposed of the pages as he saw fit. Whether by design or accident, not much has survived from his early efforts on *Ulysses*, but a great deal of evidence exists from the novel's later years in progress. We can look over Joyce's shoulder and follow him at work.

The surviving material covers an extraordinarily wide range. Major collections exist at the British Library, the University at Buffalo, the National Library of Ireland, and Cornell and Yale universities, with smaller collections at Harvard, Princeton, and Southern Illinois universities; the universities of Texas, Tulsa, and Wisconsin-Milwaukee; the Rosenbach Museum and Library; the Huntington Library; the New York

Public Library; and University College Dublin. Notes are extant in the British Library "notesheets" and eight notebooks. Early drafts survive for ten episodes: "Proteus," "Scylla and Charybdis," and everything from "Sirens" to "Penelope." The Rosenbach Library in Philadelphia owns a beginning-to-end manuscript (almost: it lacks the last "sentence" of "Penelope," and Joyce revised and augmented the episodes heavily before *Ulysses* was published as a book). Typescripts, fragmentary for the early episodes but complete for the last ones, are mostly at Buffalo, but scattered pages are elsewhere. The first set of proofs is at Harvard (for some pages there are up to nine sets), the middle sets are at Buffalo, and the final set is at Texas.

The Rosenbach Library published a facsimile of its manuscript in 1975, and volumes 12–27 of *The James Joyce Archive* contain photo-reproductions of all the other documents that were known to exist in the late 1970s. Phillip Herring has edited the British Library notesheets and, in a separate volume, two of Buffalo's notebooks and its drafts for "Cyclops" and "Circe." In 2012, the National Library of Ireland (NLI) put digital images of all its *Ulysses* manuscripts online, and Danis Rose has produced transcriptions of them. Book-length catalogs exist for the Buffalo and Cornell collections, with the Buffalo volume supplanted by a revised online catalog. I included a chart in *"Ulysses" in Focus* that lists and locates the extant documents for each episode up to the Rosenbach Manuscript.[6]

The manuscripts do not offer keys to unlock the kingdom that is *Ulysses*, nor do they open up avenues of reading and criticism that supersede or preclude others. However, knowledge about *Ulysses* coming into being can enrich the novel in the way that awareness of a friend's background and childhood lets us not only see the person in front of us but also perceive the shadow – the earlier layers – of the past. Joyce did not write his notes and drafts for genetic critics, but the documents survive to speak about *Ulysses'* earlier states, the childhood it both enjoyed and suffered through before Joyce gave it a public face and released it into the world. In Jed Deppman's clever phrase, genetic critics can use them to create a "Portrait of the Artwork as a Young Man."[7]

The object of study for genetic critics is called the *avant-texte*, a concept that involves the documents that precede a published text and implies that those documents can themselves be treated as a text.[8] The avant-texte of *Ulysses* does not necessarily include all the surviving documents. Does it include a note in a draft's margin that seems unrelated to *Ulysses*? A passage that Joyce never worked into any version of the text? The publication of *Ulysses* on February 2, 1922 provides a convenient end-date for the avant-texte, but when does it begin? In one sense, Joyce started working on *Ulysses* around 1914, after he finished *A Portrait of the Artist as a Young Man*. He first explicitly mentions the novel on June 16, 1915 (whether the month and day were by then the setting for the novel is uncertain), when he tells his brother that he is writing something called *Ulysses* and that he has completed the first episode (*SL* 209). In another sense, however, the beginnings can be traced to late 1906, when Joyce thought of an addition to *Dubliners* called "Ulysses" and quickly expanded the idea from a story into a short book before abandoning the project without writing any of it (*Letters II* 168, 190, 209; *JJ* 264–65). Or they can even go back to 1903 and Joyce's drafting of the first chapters of *Stephen Hero*. This starting point is consistent with Joyce's July 1915 description of *Ulysses* as a "continuation" of both *Portrait* and *Dubliners*.[9] Various scholars have shown how Joyce mined his earlier writings as he began to work on *Ulysses*, including a scene in the Martello tower, with *Ulysses'* Buck Mulligan called "Doherty," the *Giacomo Joyce* sketch, and various notebooks that he originally compiled for earlier works.[10]

Each genetic critic explicitly or implicitly constructs an avant-texte. Like other literary studies, genetic criticism involves individual judgment, choices, and preconceptions. Thus, even though "it deals with what Joyce thought *in so far as it can be shown in documents*," as Geert Lernout puts it,[11] those documents need to be interpreted, and different accounts of the genesis of *Ulysses* are not only possible but also inevitable and even desirable.

In a brief passage in an early copybook Joyce used to draft "Sirens," Father Cowley gossips about the Blooms. "There was an arrangement [revised to "a put up job"] between them," he says. "About ten she'd telephone down to the husband about the child and if Bloom had won anything, he was off," using a false excuse that something was wrong with his child. (Joyce revised this on the page to faintly suggest the voice of the presumably still unconceived "Cyclops" narrator: "About ten she'd ring up the hubby about the poor child and if Bloom had raked in the pool, begod, off with him.") Mat Dillon eventually figured out Bloom's con game, Cowley reports in conclusion.[12] A substantially altered version of this uncontextu-alized passage appears in *Ulysses*, not in "Sirens" but rather in "Cyclops." After Bloom leaves Barney Kiernan's to look for Martin Cunningham and after Lenehan tells the men in the pub that Bloom has won money on the horse Throwaway, the narrator leaves the room to pee:

> gob says I to myself I knew he was uneasy in his (two pints off of Joe and one in Slattery's off) in his mind to get off the mark to (hundred shillings is five quid) and when they were in the (dark horse) pisser Burke was telling me card party and letting on the child was sick (gob, must have done about a gallon) flabbyarse of a wife speaking down the tube *she's better or she's* (ow!) all a plan so he could vamoose with the pool if he won … (*U* 12.1563–69)

This passage about Bloom's card-game trick is hardly the only one that Joyce shortened or eliminated as he wrote. In other instances, an early "Cyclops" draft includes gossip involving Bloom and Molly's mother, anti-Semitic slurs about "buggy jews," and Stephen Dedalus as the man who quips that a Jew can love his country "when he's quite sure which country it is."[13] Why did Joyce – often depicted as a writer who expanded as he revised – rework or eliminate draft scenes like these? He never offered a reason, but in doing so he made the published *Ulysses* less specific in its derogatory gossip than the drafts, letting fewer examples of hostility towards Bloom or overt anti-Semitism make their point, and confining the bigoted remarks to the expected barflies. I am not suggesting that he weakened *Ulysses* – quite the opposite, in fact, as the language becomes more impressive and the gossip less credible in its reduced specificity – or that he should have retained the early versions. (Hugh Kenner cites Ernest Hemingway's remark that "a writer's omissions will show only when he omits things because he doesn't know them,"[14] and Joyce's deletions might be seen as evidence of his knowledge of the full details behind the scenes of *Ulysses*.) Once we know about the early versions, however, they are, in Stephen's words, "not to be thought away" (*U* 2.49). They constitute what Louis Hay calls "a kind of third dimension of the written work." The younger, alternate scenes lie behind the published ones as if in the text's memory, as its shadow, or in a palimpsest.[15]

Can events "have been possible seeing that they never were?" Stephen asks. "Or was that only possible which came to pass?" (*U* 2.51–52). His speculations about possibilities and actualities reverberate for genetic criticism, which has been described as "an esthetic of the possible" because "the work now stands out against a background, and a series, of potentialities."[16] This involves looking from two temporal vantage points, from the published work back to the drafts – "a retrospective vision" – and also from a particular draft to various future possibilities – "an anticipatory perspective."[17] The published text can't show the full range of possibilities that were in play at particular times in its past, or the ways in which Joyce responded to what was already written by retaining many of his words in an act of repetition but also by dropping, altering, and adding words in acts of invention. The published text comes to look like the last in a series of possible texts, even if a privileged one, "a necessary possibility."[18]

When I studied *Ulysses* in progress in the 1970s, I posited three stages in Joyce's work – an early one from "Telemachus" to "Scylla and Charybdis," a middle one from "Wandering Rocks" to "Oxen of the Sun," and a late one from "Circe" to the end – on the assumption that he wrote the episodes one at a time in sequence (*Progress* 4). The documents that the National Library of Ireland acquired in 2002, however, indicate something different. A very early "Sirens" draft – lacking any fugue-like elements, at first even lacking Bloom – suggests that Joyce worked on this middle-stage episode at least a year earlier than we had previously assumed; and passages in the manuscript's second part include early vestiges of "Cyclops."[19] For Luca Crispi, Joyce's experimentation with techniques that we now associate with *Ulysses'* middle stage while he was writing the early-stage episodes suggests that the concept of compositional "stages" should be replaced by one of "complex and nuanced incremental *phases*" and "a series of gradated innovations rather than distinct breaks with what Joyce had already accomplished" ("First Foray"). Readers of *Ulysses* might recognize stylistic and technical differences between, say, the first nine episodes and "Cyclops" or between "Cyclops" and "Circe," but these differences are not reflected in Joyce's writing processes in the way they once seemed to be. The new picture of Joyce at work is only beginning to be painted and, of course, if new documents come to light, the picture will again change.

One aspect of the new picture involves what I noted as Joyce's "habit of composing his material in blocks with only arbitrary attempts at transition or connection." I added that he "gives no indication of how he planned to connect" the scenes, "if he even knew at the time" (*Progress* 131). The only other drafts that Joyce apparently wrote out in this way were part of one for "Circe" and one for "Scylla and Charybdis," lost but described in a catalog. I concluded that the draft's unstructured fragmentary scenes indicated Joyce's uncertainty as he moved away from what he called the novel's "initial style" (*Letters I* 129) into what I termed its middle stage (*Progress* 124–39).

The new manuscripts have altered the outline of *Ulysses'* shadow and restored some of its memory. They include drafts of "Proteus" and (unexpectedly) "Sirens" from Joyce's early years of work on the novel, the second half of the University at Buffalo's "Cyclops" draft that I studied, and an early version of "Ithaca," all composed in unconnected textual units similar to those in the Buffalo "Cyclops" draft. Instead of seeming like an anomaly or an indication of his uncertainty, Joyce's method there has come to appear as his usual way of writing. Scholars now commonly refer to Joyce's piecemeal, mosaic, or epiphanic method of composition of *Ulysses* and talk about him writing in vignettes or fragments.[20]

Readers have often noted places in *Ulysses* where the transition from one paragraph to the next seems rather abrupt. For example, the "Cyclops" narrator's occasional use of "So anyhow" – as in "So anyhow in came John Wyse Nolan and Lenehan with him with a face on him as long as a late breakfast" (*U* 12.1178–79) – functions not only as a loquacious talker's verbal tic but also as Joyce's way of smoothing over a rough break. Several questions in "Ithaca" also seem unconnected to the previous answer, as in the series of questions and answers regarding Bloom's solution to a "domestic problem" sandwiched between Stephen's narration of "The Parable of the Plums" and Bloom's "examples of postexilic eminence" (*U* 17.657, 640–41,709–10). In these instances, the discrete units of Joyce's early drafts are faintly showing through in the palimpsest that is *Ulysses*. They are also apparent in Declan Kiberd's description of Joyce's novel as "a collection of stories bolted with some strain together, rather than a smoothly linear narrative."[21] If Joyce worked "like an assemblagist before he wrote continuous narrative drafts of episodes," as Crispi argues, a genetic study can call attention to the bolts, or the stitching, that readers sense as they experience *Ulysses* ("First Foray").[22]

Readers also often marvel at Joyce's use of paragraphs. He enlarged them incessantly as he revised. For example, the earliest surviving version of "Aeolus" includes Bloom's thoughts about J. J. O'Molloy:

> Practice dwindling. Losing heart. Used to get good retainers from D. and T. Fitzgerald. Believe he does some literary work for the *Express* with Gabriel Conroy. Wellread fellow. Crawford began on the *Independent*. Funny the way they veer about. Go for one another baldheaded in the papers and then hail fellow well met the next moment. (*Rosenbach* I "Aeolus" 9–10)

By the time Joyce published *Ulysses*, he had more than doubled Bloom's observations from these 56 manuscript words to 116, adding details about O'Molloy's gambling debts, the professional fickleness of newspaper men, and references to wind (*U* 7.303–12). He added to the lists in "Cyclops": the "Irish heroes and heroines of antiquity" grew from twelve to eighty-six

names and the "saints and martyrs, virgins and confessors" from twenty-
one (not counting the "eleven thousand virgins" at the end) to eighty-one
(*Rosenbach* I "Cyclops" 7, 52–53; *U* 12.176–99, 1689–1712). Many of Joyce's
paragraphs are like balloons filled almost to the bursting point. Did he
ever finish *Ulysses*? Molly Bloom's final "yes" ends it conclusively, but the
lists in the middles of paragraphs could easily have grown even larger.
Eighty-six Irish heroes? Why not 88? 188?[23]

Hans Walter Gabler has discussed Joyce's additions to a paragraph in
"Lestrygonians" in which Bloom looks at the shelves in Davy Byrne's pub
before he orders a cheese sandwich (*U* 8.741–56). The short passage in its
first surviving version reads:

> Sardines on the shelves. Potted meats. What is home without Plumtree's
> potted meat? Incomplete. What a stupid ad! [An interlinear addition:
> "Right under the obituary notices too. Dignam's potted meat."] With it an
> abode of bliss. Lord knows what concoction.
> –Have you a cheese sandwich? (*Rosenbach* I "Lestrygonians" 17–18)

Joyce enlarged the paragraph with Bloom's mental joke ("Ham and his
descendants musterred and bred there" *U* 8.742), the beginning of his
limerick about a cannibal, his thoughts about Yom Kippur, and his pun
on "[m]ity cheese" (*U* 7.55). Gabler shows Joyce returning to the paragraph over and over again, each time seeing *Ulysses* as a slightly different novel in progress: "Bloom's original slight hesitation over his order for
lunch has become transformed into a multidimensional acid sketch of a
hungry man's world view."[24] As Finn Fordham has suggested, genetic criticism should "correlate the thematics of the text with the processes of the
text's production,"[25] and Gabler demonstrates that Bloom's hesitation and
a hungry man's mind are both visible in the published "Lestrygonians"
paragraph and also in Joyce's work producing the paragraph over several
years.

Genetic studies tend to show Joyce preserving the various states
Ulysses went through – its several presents – as he moved the text
toward its various futures. For example, "Aeolus" existed in a "finished" beginning-to-end form, published in *The Little Review*, before
Joyce added the headlines to it on the proofs; and (we now know from
the National Library of Ireland's documents) he drafted "Sirens" and
then imposed on it what he called "the eight regular parts of a *fuga per
canonem*" – or, more accurately, just a fugue (*Letters I* 129).[26] Daniel
Ferrer writes about Joyce's "layering" of his different kinds of writing during the several time periods in *Ulysses'* development. Almost

inevitably, genetic studies that discuss changes in *Ulysses* through time end up using spatial metaphors as well.[27]

Joyce worked on *Ulysses* in space as well as time. "The space that Joyce had before his eyes most of the day, the space he spent most time exploring," Ferrer notes, "was the space of a rectangular sheet of white paper, written on or in the process of being written on" ("Writing Space" 203). Dirk Van Hulle refers to Joyce's "paper studio" ("Genetic Joyce Criticism" 117).[28] Joyce inscribed his "[s]igns on a white field" (*U* 3.415) in an idiosyncratic way. In most – but by no means all – cases, he wrote on the right-hand pages (rectos), leaving the margins at the left and the left-hand pages (versos) for revisions and additions. The left-hand margin widened as he moved down the page. Some margins and versos are blank, but Joyce filled many others with additions, which he usually connected to the main body of the text by a line or a superscript letter. Sometimes he wrote the main text in ink and revised in pencil, sometimes he reversed this procedure, and sometimes he wrote both the main text and the revisions with the same implement. He crossed out passages and full pages that he had used in the next stage with red, blue, and green crayons. Occasionally, as in a "Eumaeus" draft that came to light in 2001 and is now owned by a private collector, he wrote his additions in red and green ink as well as pencil.[29]

Joyce's pages are marvels to behold, especially the more cluttered ones with many additions that are nearly illegible and lack clear indications regarding their placement in the text. Joyce obviously had relatively little problem working with the pages he created, even if observers now have to learn how to read them. With his vision impaired by iritis, uveitis, glaucoma, and hyperopia, he might have been able to see not entire pages but rather only individual parts of them. Maybe, that is, he saw the text's body, the margins, and the versos as separate units.[30] Whatever the case, Joyce's margins have proved to be fertile spaces for genetic critics. Jacques Neefs discusses a writer's page as "a work-surface given depth, one might say, by successive returns to it" as the writer alters and augments the text in the margins; for Ferrer, reversing the temporal orientation, different times of writing are visible on the page as "[i]t is in the margin that the text is faced with its own future" since "the draft page is the locus of a dialog between the writer and his later self or selves."[31] If the page's main body of text is for the most part copied from past versions, the words in the margin point to the next one.

A draft's margins and a page's spaces can function in unexpected ways. The "Cyclops" draft that Buffalo has possessed since 1950 includes a note

Joyce wrote to himself at the end of some barroom gossip about Molly to see page 28, indicating a continuation of the surviving 48-page (24-leaf) copybook. The verso to the left of the page that Joyce numbered 28 in the second copybook (one of the manuscripts that the National Library of Ireland acquired in 2002) reveals what Joyce was noting to himself: an early version of the "Marion of the bountiful bosoms" paragraph, a passage of what he called "gigantism," to follow the conversational gossip (*U* 12.1003–07; Buffalo MS V.A.8, p. 43; *JJA* 13.127).[32]

The National Library draft includes a delightful example of Joyce's use of his pages' empty spaces. At the bottom of the first verso, he wrote a note to someone comically demanding a loan of ten francs (revised to five) for liquor he has just "stood you." Then, on page 8, a respondent – the handwriting belongs to his partner, Nora – regrets with mock formality that she cannot lend him "the maximum sum" but offers to loan him fifteen francs (revised to five). Joyce counters by adapting a phrase that appears as an addition on one of Buffalo's copybook pages – "[t]he curse of a lopsided God light sideways on the bloody thicklugged sons of whores' gets" (with "lopsided" revised to "goodfornothing," the phrase appears intact in *Ulysses* 12.1197–99) – to make Nora the recipient of the curse: "The curse of a lopsided God light sideways on your inebriated and unbalanced personality. Yours affectionately, JJ." Finally, Nora ends the exchange by modifying a note that Joyce had written a year earlier when the British Consul in Switzerland suggested that he enlist in the British Army: "James Joyce presents his compliments to the B. M. Consul General and returns a document addressed to him in error." She even substituted the name of Joyce's arch-enemy of the moment as she wrote "Sir Horace Rumbold presents his compliments to Mr Joyce and suggests that he shall go to Hell" (Buffalo MS V.A.8, p. 19; *JJA* 13.103).[33]

The exchange, like a series of refrigerator sticky notes, is a fascinating glimpse into the ways Joyce and Nora could communicate with each other. Just as Joyce's note to himself to see page 28 sets up a dialogue between two "Cyclops" copybooks, one that has ended up in Buffalo and one in Dublin, the written conversation speaks across several pages of a manuscript. The exchange indicates that Nora had access to Joyce's drafts and felt free to write in their empty spaces. It also shows how well she could play along with Joyce, in the process mocking and puncturing his obsessions.

The curse Joyce hurled at Nora is interesting genetically as well as biographically. Did he adapt words he had already added to "Cyclops" to insult her? Or did he create his fanciful invective and then realize that he could rework his words in "Cyclops," resulting in an addition to a scene he had already written for the episode? Two notes on the "Cyclops" notesheets – "lopsided God" and a fuller one with the entire copybook addition – make the former scenario more likely, tantalizing as the second one might be.[34]

Genetic study can be quite formalist due to the fact that it often pays attention to a text's words in isolation from other contexts. It is also author-centered and, explicitly or implicitly, concerned with both authorial activity and intention. Ferrer has argued that the vexed issue of intention is both an inevitability and an opportunity for genetic criticism, which highlights changes in intention over time and presents authorial intention as "a fluctuating, time-bound transaction between a series of writing events and a series of external constraints."[35] The idea of external constraints reminds us that Joyce didn't produce his manuscripts in isolation. Until a New York court in early 1921 declared *Ulysses* obscene, he worked under time constraints as he needed to complete each episode on schedule so that *The Little Review* could publish it. Conversely, once the magazine was prohibited from serializing the novel, he lacked such constraints, and there is probably a link between the length of the last episodes and the absence of deadlines. Paul Vanderham has argued further that Joyce's writing of the last episodes of *Ulysses* might have been affected by the court decision and his awareness of possible further censorship. His efforts at defining *Ulysses* through his schemas – highlighting each episode's art, color, technic, symbols, and correspondences – and his involvement in early critical studies of the novel might also spring at least in part from his responses to the obscenity conviction.[36]

Also, Joyce lived in several different cities in particular times – fraught ones, with the First World War and the Anglo-Irish war raging. He suffered from various physical ailments, especially with his eyes, and lived with a great deal of emotional turmoil, much of which he brought on himself. The external constraints of the contexts in which he worked can include his several periods of short and lengthy inactivity because of eye attacks and the limitations on his vision. I have speculated about the role of these and several other contexts in Joyce's ongoing work: his role in the English Players theater company in Zurich and his involvement in the lawsuit against Henry Carr over the cost of a suit of clothes Carr wore in a production of *The Importance of Being Earnest*, his infatuation with Marthe Fleischmann, his concerns over money, and Harriet Shaw Weaver's gift of a monthly stipend. Broader contexts – what Henri Mitterand has called "culture's thought," leading to a possible "cultural genetics" – need to be taken into account, as well as the impact of such legal issues as copyright on Joyce's work.[37]

In his authorized biography, Herbert Gorman pictures a Joyce sublimely indifferent to the turbulent life going on around him: his "existence ran parallel with the Great War" as he lived "in a city that was fearfully like a boiling cauldron and with the *brouhaha* of mad days about him but walking through it with his mind intent upon an olive-faced man whom he had created and set peregrinating through the streets of the Dublin of 1904."[38] However much Joyce might have wanted to project the image that Gorman conveys, he was more like authors as depicted by Virginia Woolf: creators of spider webs that are "attached ever so lightly perhaps, but still attached to life at all four corners." Woolf argues that "these webs are not spun in mid-air by incorporeal creatures, but are the work of suffering human beings, and are attached to grossly material things, like health and money and the houses we live in."[39] Much work is waiting to be done to reattach Joyce's writing to the four corners of life.

In "Lestrygonians," Bloom envisions girls writing in a showcart, with human curiosity leading people both to read and to shop: "[A] transparent showcart with two smart girls sitting inside writing letters, copybooks, envelopes, blottingpaper. I bet that would have caught on. Smart girls writing something catch the eye at once. Everyone dying to know what she's writing" (*U* 8.131–35).

Bloom's boss rejected his idea, so he, and we, can't know if his assumption about the writing scene's appeal was correct. But if we imagine Joyce at work exposed in Bloom's showcart, is "everyone dying to know" not only what he is writing but how he works? In many ways, the answer has obviously been "yes," and the story of Joyce writing *Ulysses* remains very much a narrative in progress. Despite great advances, genetic critics are still learning how to tell it, both for its own sake and to make it meaningful to a wide range of readers and critics of *Ulysses*. The stories are dependent on the availability of documents, and new ones can quickly alter the picture. Joyce and his manuscripts are in their own showcart for everyone to see: it has caught on.

Notes

1 See Richard Brown, ed., *A Companion to James Joyce* (Malden, MA and Oxford: Wiley-Blackwell, 2008); John McCourt, ed., *James Joyce in Context* (Cambridge: Cambridge University Press, 2009); and Sam Slote and Luca Crispi, eds., *How Joyce Wrote "Finnegans Wake"* (Madison: University of Wisconsin Press, 2007).

2 Jean-Michel Rabaté, *James Joyce and the Politics of Egoism* (Cambridge: Cambridge University Press, 2001), p. 196.

3 Julie Bosman, "To Use and Use Not: New Edition of 'A Farewell to Arms' Includes Alternate Endings," *New York Times*, July 5, 2012, C6; Terence Killeen, "Joycean Joy After Library Says 'Yes,'" *Irish Times*, May 7, 2012, http://www.irishtimes.com/newspaper/features/2012/0507/1224315686035. html (accessed, like all the online texts cited here, July 31, 2012); D. T. Max, "The Carver Chronicles," *New York Times Magazine*, August 9, 1998, 51; Alex Ross, "Deceptive Picture: How Oscar Wilde Painted Over 'Dorian Gray,'" *New Yorker*, August 8, 2011, 67–69. The "Who's Honoring Me Now?" segment of *The Colbert Report* on July 17, 2012 featured the Rosenbach Museum and Library's acquisition of the manuscript of Stephen Colbert's book *I Am A Pole (and So Can You)* and its display of that document next to the opening page of its *Ulysses* manuscript.

4 Susan Sontag, *"Against Interpretation" and Other Essays* (1966; rpt. New York: Picador USA, 2001), p. 41.

5 Louis Menand, "Silent, Exile, Punning," *New Yorker*, July 2, 2012, 72.

6 James Joyce, *Ulysses: A Facsimile of the Manuscript*, 3 vols., ed. Clive Driver (New York: Octagon and Philadelphia: Philip H. and A. S. W. Rosenbach Foundation, 1975); further references will be cited parenthetically as *Rosenbach*, followed by the volume, episode, and page numbers); Phillip F. Herring, ed., *Joyce's "Ulysses" Notesheets in the British Museum* (Charlottesville: University Press of Virginia, 1972) and *Joyce's Notes and Early Drafts for "Ulysses": Selections from the Buffalo Collection* (Charlottesville: University Press of Virginia, 1977); the National Library of Ireland online catalogue: http://catalogue.nli.ie/Search/ Results?lookfor=&filter[]=digitised%3A%22Digitised%22&filter[]=authorStr% 3A%22Joyce%2C+James%2C+1882–1941%22; Danis Rose, ed., *James Joyce: The Dublin "Ulysses" Papers*, 6 vols. (East Lansing, MI: House of Breathings, 2012; 2nd ed., 2013); Peter Spielberg, comp., *James Joyce's Manuscripts and Letters at the University of Buffalo: A Catalogue* (Buffalo: University of Buffalo, 1962); Robert E. Scholes, comp., *The Cornell Joyce Collection: A Catalogue* (Ithaca, NY: Cornell University Press, 1961); "The UB James Joyce Catalog": http://library. buffalo.edu/pl/collections/jamesjoyce/catalog; Michael Groden, *"Ulysses" in Focus: Genetic, Textual, and Personal Views* (Gainesville: University Press of Florida, 2010), pp. 200–01.

7 Jed Deppman, "Joyce and the Case for Genetic Criticism," *Genetic Joyce Studies* 6 (2006), www.geneticjoycestudies.org.

8 The term was coined by Jean Bellemin-Noël, *Le Texte et l'avant-texte: Les Brouillons d'un poème de Milosz* (Paris: Larousse, 1972). Attempts to render "avant-texte" in English – "pre-text," "fore-text" – have been unattractive and misleading, and so, as Jed Deppman, Daniel Ferrer, and I did in *Genetic Criticism: Texts and Avant-textes* (Philadelphia: University of Pennsylvania Press, 2004) – our collection of translated French essays – I have retained the French term and not italicized it. Further references to this text will be cited as *Genetic Criticism*.

9 See *Letters I* 83; see also Hans Walter Gabler, *The Rocky Road to "Ulysses"* (Dublin: National Library of Ireland, 2004), pp. 1–6ff. Further references to Gabler's text will be cited as *Rocky Road*.

10 For example, Gabler, *Rocky Road*; A. Walton Litz, *The Art of James Joyce: Method and Design in "Ulysses" and "Finnegans Wake"* (New York: Oxford University Press, 1961), pp. 132–41; Rodney Wilson Owen, *James Joyce and the Beginnings of "Ulysses"* (Ann Arbor, MI: UMI Research Press, 1983); and two articles in Zack Bowen and James F. Carens, eds., *A Companion to Joyce Studies* (Westport, CT: Greenwood Press, 1984): Vicki Mahaffey, "*Giacomo Joyce*," pp. 387–420 and Michael Groden, "A Textual and Publishing History," esp. p. 92.

11 Geert Lernout, "and yes i said yes Fritz but," in Ruth Frehner and Ursula Zeller, eds., *A Collideorscape of Joyce: Festschrift for Fritz Senn* (Dublin: Lilliput Press, 1998), p. 302 (Lernout's italics).

12 National Library of Ireland manuscript 36,639/7/B, p. 20, http://catalogue. nli.ie/Record/vtls000357771/HierarchyTree#page/11/, transcribed in Rose, ed., *Dublin "Ulysses" Papers*, 1:55.

13 Poetry Collection, University at Buffalo MS V.A.8, p. 21–23, 41–42; reproduced in Michael Groden et al., eds., *The James Joyce Archive*, 63 vols. (New York and London: Garland Publishing, 1977–79), 13.126, 105–07, 125 (further references will be cited parenthetically as *JJA*, followed by the volume and page numbers); transcribed in Herring, *Joyce's Notes and Early Drafts for "Ulysses,"* pp. 161–62, 170–71. Cf. *U* 12.1630. An early discussion of these passages is in Michael Groden, *"Ulysses" in Progress* (Princeton, NJ: Princeton University Press, 1977), pp. 126–28, 135–37, 147–48. Further references to my book will be cited parenthetically in the text as *Progress*.

14 Hugh Kenner, *Ulysses* (1980; rev. ed., Baltimore: Johns Hopkins University Press, 1987), p. 15.

15 Louis Hay, "Does 'Text' Exist?" (1985), trans. Matthew Jocelyn and Hans Walter Gabler, *Studies in Bibliography* 41 (1988): 75; memory: Daniel Ferrer, "Writing Space," in Valérie Bénéjam and John Bishop, eds., *Making Space in the Works of James Joyce* (New York: Routledge, 2011), p. 211 (further references to this text will be cited as "Writing Space"); shadow: Dirk Van Hulle, "Genetic Joyce Criticism," in McCourt, *James Joyce in Context*, p. 112 (further references to this text will be cited as "Genetic Joyce Criticism"); palimpsest: Groden, *Progress*, p. 4.

16 Michel Contat, Denis Hollier, and Jacques Neefs, "Editors' Preface," *Drafts, Yale French Studies* 89 (1996): 2. Further references to this text will be cited as *Drafts*. Genetic criticism lets us "see what *Ulysses* actually *was* in process at various stages" and "also explores what the work *could have been*," according to Luca Crispi in "A First Foray into the National Library of Ireland's Joyce Manuscripts: Bloomsday 2011," *Genetic Joyce Studies* 11 (2011), www.geneticjoycestudies.org/ (Crispi's italics). Further references to Crispi's essay will be cited parenthetically in the text as "First Foray."

17 Daniel Ferrer, "Clementis's Cap: Retroaction and Persistence in the Genetic Process" (1994), trans. Marlena C. Corcoran, in *Drafts*, p. 225. Dirk van Hulle talks about genetic criticism's "counterclockwise" and "clockwise" approaches to the study of authors at work in "Genetic Joyce Criticism," p. 121.

18 "[W]hat genetic criticism is actually confronted with is a dialectic of invention and repetition." Daniel Ferrer, "Production, Invention, and Reproduction: Genetic vs. Textual Criticism," in Elizabeth Bergmann Loizeaux and Neil Fraistat, eds., *Reimagining Textuality: Textual Studies in the Late Age of Print* (Madison: University of Wisconsin Press, 2002), p. 54; "necessary possibility": Hay, "Does 'Text' Exist?," p. 75 (Hay italicizes the words).

19 Ferrer, "What Song the Sirens Sang ... Is No Longer Beyond All Conjecture: A Preliminary Description of the New 'Proteus' and 'Sirens' Manuscripts," *JJQ* 39 (Fall 2001): 57–60. Further references will be cited as "What Song."

20 For example, Crispi, "First Foray"; Sam Slote, "Epiphanic 'Proteus,'" *Genetic Joyce Studies* 5 (2005), www.geneticjoycestudies.org; Gabler, *Rocky Road*, pp. 31–37; Ferrer, "What Song," pp. 54–56. See also Ronan Crowley's speculations at the end of "'The Hand that Wrote *Ulysses*' and the *Avant-Texte* of 'Wandering Rocks,'" *Genetic Joyce Studies* 7 (2007), www.geneticjoycestudies.org.

21 Declan Kiberd, *Irish Classics* (2000; London: Granta Books, 2001), p. 467.

22 In "Male Maturity or the *Pub*lic Rise and Private Decline of HC Earwicker" (in Slote and Crispi, *How Joyce Wrote "Finnegans Wake,"* pp. 288–89), David Hayman discusses "discrete but powerful transitions" in *Finnegans Wake* in ways that can usefully be extrapolated to *Ulysses*.

23 See Daniel Ferrer and Jean-Michel Rabaté, "Paragraphs in Expansion (James Joyce)" in Deppman et al., *Genetic Criticism*, pp. 132–51 for a wide-ranging and brilliant treatment of Joyce's paragraphs. Further references to this text will be cited as "Paragraphs."

24 Hans Walter Gabler, "The Synchrony and Diachrony of Texts: Practice and Theory of the Critical Edition of James Joyce's *Ulysses*," *Text: Transactions of the Society for Textual Scholarship* 1 (1984): 323.

25 Finn Fordham, *I Do I Undo I Redo: The Textual Genesis of Modernist Selves* (Oxford: Oxford University Press, 2010), p. 229.

26 See also Susan Brown, "The Mystery of the *Fuga per Canonem* Solved," *Genetic Joyce Studies* 7 (Spring 2007), www.geneticjoycestudies.org; Michelle Witen, "The Mystery of the *Fuga per Canonem* Reopened?" *Genetic Joyce Studies* 10 (Spring 2010), www.geneticjoycestudies.org.

27 Daniel Ferrer, "The Joyce of Manuscripts," in Brown, *A Companion to James Joyce*, p. 292. Further references to this text will be cited as "Joyce of Manuscripts."

28 Hans Walter Gabler discusses the "zones" of Joyce's writing on his manuscript pages in "Explorations in Spaces of Writing" (1998), http://www.edkomp.uni-muenchen.de/hwgabler/hwg-explorations.html.

29 Sam Slote, "Preliminary Comments on Two Newly Discovered *Ulysses* Manuscripts," *JJQ* 39 (Fall 2001): 21.

30 Groden, *"Ulysses" in Focus*, pp. 134–37; Francisco J. Ascaso and Jan L. van Velze, "Was James Joyce Myopic or Hyperopic?" *British Medical Journal* 343 (2011): d7464.

31 Jacques Neefs, "Margins" (1989), trans. Stephen A. Noble, in *Genetic Criticism*, ed. Claire Bustarret, special issue of *Word and Image* 13 (1997): 149; Ferrer, "Writing Space," pp. 205–06, "The Open Space of the Draft Page: James Joyce and Modern Manuscripts," in George Bornstein and Theresa Tinkle, eds., *The Iconic Page in Manuscript, Print, and Digital Culture* (Ann Arbor: University of Michigan Press, 1998), p. 257.

32 See also Herring, *Joyce's Notes and Early Drafts*, pp. 171, 177n58 and NLI MS 36,639/10, p. 6, http://catalogue.nli.ie/Record/vtls000357792/ HierarchyTree#page/5; *Dublin "Ulysses" Papers*, 1:85.

33 Herring, *Joyce's Notes and Early Drafts*, p. 160 and NLI MS 36,639/10, pp. 2, 8; online: http://catalogue.nli.ie/Record/vtls000357792/HierarchyTree#page/3/ and .../HierarchyTree#page/6/. Joyce's note to the B. M. Consul General is quoted in *JJ* 441. I thank Luca Crispi (who also discusses the exchange in "First Foray") for identifying the handwriting on the draft page as Nora's. See also Groden, *"Ulysses" in Focus*, pp. 141–42.

34 Herring, *Joyce's "Ulysses" Notesheets*, notes 1:43 and 7:47–48, pp. 82, 110.

35 Ferrer, "Joyce of Manuscripts," p. 290 and "Production," p. 56.

36 Groden, *Progress*, pp. 169–70; Paul Vanderham, *James Joyce and Censorship: The Trials of "Ulysses"* (New York: New York University Press, 1998), pp. 58–59, 71–82.

37 Groden, *"Ulysses" in Focus*, pp. 125–43; Henri Mitterand, "Genetic Criticism and Cultural History: Zola's *Rougon-Macquart* Dossiers" (1989), in Deppman et al., *Genetic Criticism*, p. 117; Paul Saint-Amour, *The Copywrights: Intellectual Property and the Literary Imagination* (Ithaca, NY: Cornell University Press, 2003), pp. 159–98.

38 Herbert Gorman, *James Joyce* (1939; rev. ed., New York: Rinehart, 1948), pp. 239, 241.

39 Virginia Woolf, *A Room of One's Own*, ed. Susan Gubar (Orlando, FL: Harcourt, 2005), pp. 41–42.

CHAPTER 2

Reception History

Joseph Brooker

A reception history is centrally a history of reading. That history is known to us mainly through acts of writing, including reviews and essays, letters and diary entries. This essay first traces the precondition of such reading: the worldly fortunes of Joyce's text itself. It then considers a number of significant ways in which *Ulysses* was read in the first two decades of its existence. Finally, it offers a brief, contextualized history of the academic work produced on *Ulysses* since the end of Joyce's life.

The Adventures of *Ulysses*

Ulysses was first published in serial form in two magazines. *The Little Review*, based in New York, published *Ulysses* irregularly across twenty-two issues from March 1918 to August 1920. Publication commenced with the first episode and reached a single instalment of the fourteenth. The later and longer of these episodes extended over as many as four issues each. Three issues of the magazine containing the serial were seized and burned by the United States Post Office before a full-scale legal confrontation took place over episode thirteen. Meanwhile, the London-based *Egoist* magazine published only four early episodes of *Ulysses* in 1919, in part because the London printers refused to set certain episodes in type altogether. In both cases, publication was enabled and encouraged by the American poet and literary impresario Ezra Pound, Joyce's greatest promoter in the years of the book's composition.

Those who encountered *Ulysses* in serial form experienced not only a leaner text, but also a particular context. In *The Egoist*, Joyce's writing appeared alongside the philosophical disquisitions of the magazine's editor Dora Marsden, and in *The Little Review* he was heralded by the sometime anarchist editor Margaret Anderson. In both magazines, Joyce's text nestled alongside remarkable works – by such writers as W. B. Yeats, T. S. Eliot and Wyndham Lewis – that have become part of modernism's canon, as well as letters and debate. *Ulysses* was thus first encountered piecemeal, amid a jostling array of texts which confirmed each other's place in the advanced literature and thought of the era.

That context for *Ulysses* vanished in 1920 when *The Little Review* was prosecuted for sending the final instalment of "Nausicaa" through the United States mail. Attorney John Quinn, a consistent patron of modernism, led the defence in a New York court, but without success. Serialization of *Ulysses* ended and publication of the whole book in the United States now appeared impossible. The first editions appeared instead in Paris, published by Sylvia Beach's Shakespeare & Company. They were strictly limited: 1,000 in February and 2,000 in October 1922 (of which up to 500 were reportedly burned by the U.S. Post Office), and 500 numbered copies in January 1923 (of which 499 were seized by customs at Folkestone). "After that," Harriet Shaw Weaver concluded, "the book was banned in England" (*JJ* 506n). Yet a considerable amount of discussion of *Ulysses* had already taken place in the Anglophone press by this point, and it would continue. *Ulysses* became known to many only indirectly, in the form of commentary about it. To a very unusual degree, in this first decade, critical reception actually became a surrogate for the work itself. As Hugh Kenner states: "All the early discussions have this curious property, that readers who had never seen a copy were required to assume Joyce's book was what the protagonist of the moment said it was."[1]

This was also true of the first authorized, extensive account of the novel, produced by Joyce's associate Stuart Gilbert in 1930. Gilbert quoted extensively, giving the reader a kind of fragmentary miniature of the novel as well as his own detailed, chapter-by-chapter account. Gilbert's book exemplified Joyce's recurrent attempt to direct the reception of his own work. In 1921 the novelist had given French critic Valéry Larbaud access to the Homeric "key" to *Ulysses*, to be announced in a lecture at Sylvia Beach's Paris bookshop. Gilbert in turn published a schema of Homeric correspondences, and devoted much space to their explication. Gilbert's account was heavily prompted by Joyce. So was that of Frank Budgen, whose *James Joyce and the Making of "Ulysses"* (1934) promoted a more realist view of *Ulysses* centred on the character of Leopold Bloom.[2]

Gilbert's book had one distinction that Budgen's by 1934 could not: It contributed to the unbanning of *Ulysses*. In 1933, Random House imported a copy of the novel to New York with the aim of testing the justice system and securing the book's legal status. Morris Ernst, the lawyer arguing the case for *Ulysses* against the United States, argued that a full understanding of the novel ran deeper than a superficial response – for instance, sexual arousal – to a given sentence, involving instead an apprehension of the book's complex unity. Ernst drew on Gilbert's book to propose that *Ulysses* was a "coherent artistic whole," not a piece of pornography.[3] Justice John M. Woolsey accordingly pronounced that the book was not obscene and could legally be imported into the United States. The judgement was upheld by Justice Learned Hand in a court of appeal. In 1934, Random House produced the first American edition, hence securing U.S. copyright, with Woolsey's judgement printed on the book's endpapers. Two years later, the Bodley Head followed suit in Britain. *Ulysses* was henceforth legal across the Anglophone world, though still hard to procure in Ireland.

For five decades, further editions of *Ulysses* appeared without significant controversy. The Bodley Head issued a revised text in 1960, which Random House drew on for an elegant new edition the following year. Penguin Books published an easily affordable paperback in its Modern Classics series in 1969. Owing to the complicated history of the novel's composition, these texts produced and reproduced divergences from each other and from the original 1922 edition. Yet the question of textual rectitude did not generate notable public controversy until the 1980s. In the late 1970s, the James Joyce Estate enlisted German scholar Hans Walter Gabler to produce a new edition that would correct prevailing textual errors. In 1984, the American press Garland issued the resulting three-volume synoptic and critical edition. Gabler and his team had extensively re-examined manuscripts and notes in accordance with current European editorial theory. On this basis, a "corrected text" was issued in a single volume in 1986 by the Bodley Head, Vintage and Penguin. A "student's edition" added the line numbers that most Joyce scholars (and this Companion) now use in citing the book.

English novelist Martin Amis reviewed Gabler's edition in 1986 with the assurance that no ordinary reader would notice the difference.[4] Yet some less ordinary readers did. Gabler's work was attacked by American scholar John Kidd: most publicly in the *New York Review of Books* in 1988, then in the sustained critique "An Inquiry into *Ulysses: The Corrected Text*."[5] Kidd alleged the presence of numerous particular errors and demanded the withdrawal of the corrected text and its replacement by an earlier edition. Gabler's principles consistently favoured a return to drafts, rather than beginning from any extant printed text. Kidd demonstrated that some errors could only be resolved by historical research into the reality that the book refracted. Yet in earning the bombastic label "The Joyce Wars," the debate became immensely polemical and personalized, which hardly helped clarify the substantive issues involved.[6] Despite these wide-ranging debates, the corrected text has nevertheless remained the authoritative reference point for most professional Joycean scholars.

Beyond the academy, however, the corrected text has lost prominence since the early 1990s, when several publishers responded to the confusion of "The Joyce Wars" by simply retreating to earlier stages of textual history. The Bodley Head and Random House both reverted to their texts from the early 1960s. Oxford University Press reissued the original 1922 text, with a fine introduction and notes from Jeri Johnson that made the edition useful to students. Penguin reissued all Joyce's major works in 1992; in a gently political gesture, each book was assigned an editor who was also a major figure in Irish studies. Declan Kiberd, who had done much to develop Irish criticism from a base at University College Dublin, thus took the opportunity to reframe *Ulysses* anew; but the text he framed was another reprint of the 1960 Bodley Head edition. While new introductions and notes were providing valuable contextual material for readers, publishers seemed to give up on the search for a more accurate text than those already issued.

In 2012, the works that Joyce published in his lifetime emerged from copyright in Europe, while his unpublished works also emerged from copyright in the United States. New editions in print and digital form have thus begun to proliferate. The complete text of *Ulysses* has been online for years. More elaborate forms of electronic presentation, involving images, music and a wealth of subsidiary information, are likely to be refined during the twenty-first century. Already, a reader with the appropriate mobile device can casually search the text for a given word while walking down a street anywhere in the world. The situation in which readers of *Ulysses* must rely on its commentators for clues about it has virtually been reversed: One need no longer even pick up the book to consult it. We are far from the days when *Ulysses* was, for most who wished to read it, more rumour than reality.

ABC of Reading *Ulysses*

Two things are widely believed about *Ulysses*: that it is difficult, and that it is obscene. Both were major issues from the start. Obscenity was the more urgent, as it jeopardized the book's availability. The trials of *Ulysses* raised numerous ideas about the relation of art to the erotic. One line of argument was simply that literature and pornography were mutually exclusive, and if *Ulysses* was art it could not be banned as obscene. This view finally won the day for *Ulysses* in 1933, and hence in principle still subtends our reading of it today. But John Quinn opportunistically tried other avenues at the *Little Review* trial in 1921.

One was to entangle obscenity in obscurity. Textual difficulty and sexual daring in one sense are aligned, since both are signs of the work's troubling, wilful modernity. In another sense, they appear to confound one another. John Cowper Powys, a witness called by Quinn, proposed that *Ulysses* was "too obscure and philosophical a work to be in any sense corrupting" (*Censorship* 48). The novel, Quinn argued, could not corrupt anyone because no one would be able to understand it. He even stated that he himself did not understand "Nausicaa," because "Joyce has carried his method too far in this experiment" (*Censorship* 49). "Experiment" here is the enemy of obscenity: If a text is too experimental, any obscene content will be irretrievable.

Quinn's other tack stated that "there was filth in literature and art, but ... it was not filth that would corrupt, but rather that would brace and deter" (*Censorship* 44). According to this model, literature could have moral implications, but only through an artistic recontextualization of "filth" to reverse the effect that it would have outside literature. "Nausicaa," in short, would produce nausea. "Joyce's treatment of sex," Quinn argued, "would not drive men to whore houses or into the arms of lewd women but would drive them away from them" (*Censorship* 45). *Ulysses* might also cause rage – again a wholesome reaction compared to lust. Quinn's last protest was to point to Assistant District Attorney Joseph Forrester as an exhibit for the defence: "Just look at him, still gasping for breath at the conclusion of his denunciation, his face distorted with rage, his whole aspect apoplectic. Is he filled with lewd desires? Does a reading of the chapter want to send him to the arms of a whore? ... Not at all.... He is my chief exhibit as to the effect of *Ulysses*" (*Censorship* 52).

"Effect" is an operative word. Meaning and interpretation might be at stake in the decades to come, but in this inaugural, highly charged scene of reading, it was the book's capacity to cause reactions and events that was at stake. Even outside the legal context, other readers responding to the first edition in 1922 tended to describe their reactions in visceral terms. Several reported disgust. Even the reviewer of the *Sporting Times* declared the "emetic" book "enough to make a Hottentot sick."[7] The sympathetic Holbrook Jackson described a reader "bored, drowsed, bewildered" in Joyce's "ocean of prose."[8] Contrastingly, the popular novelist Arnold Bennett reported that "The code is smashed to bits. Many persons could not continue reading *Ulysses*; they would be obliged, by mere

shock, to drop it."⁹ "The Scandal of *Ulysses*" was the *Sporting Times* headline that Sylvia Beach mischievously displayed in her shop. For numerous
early respondents, that scandal involved the book's troubling materiality –
whether in its effects on a reader, its sheer bulk, or the strange qualities of
its prose. More than one reviewer compared *Ulysses* to a telephone directory. The comparison responded to the book's blue-bound bulk, but also
to its obsessive all-inclusiveness. Readers also reached for metaphors from
the natural world: "Dead Seas," "a country without roads," "a Sahara that
is as dry as it is stinking," "the wide waters and the illimitable stars of this
universe." Less equivocally, the book was simply likened to a sewer. The
Sporting Times dubbed it "the literature of the latrine."¹⁰

If the mainstream press, literary world, and legal system had difficulty
appreciating *Ulysses*, this only confirmed Ezra Pound's contempt for them.
His review in June 1922 declared that "all serious men of letters, whether
they write out a critique [of *Ulysses*] or not, will certainly have to make
one for their own use."¹¹ Pound himself celebrated *Ulysses* as a vast satire
of contemporary society – of "the whole occident under the domination
of capital" – which reprised the encyclopedia of imbecilities undertaken
in Flaubert's *Bouvard et Pécuchet* (*Pound/Joyce* 198). Other writers echoed
Pound in making "critiques" for "their own use": In their varying responses
to *Ulysses*, several major modernists displayed their own preoccupations.
Virginia Woolf veered between reluctant admiration and ready disdain,
alternately granting Joyce's genius and dismissing *Ulysses* as "illiterate,
underbred," the "raw, striking" outburst of a "self taught working man."¹²
Her diary's response can be considered Woolf's "critique": one that was of
use to her in composing her next novel, *Mrs Dalloway* (1925).

T. S. Eliot's "*Ulysses*, Order and Myth," published in the *Dial* of
November 1923, would be widely cited and reprinted. Eliot discussed
Ulysses in the most abstract terms possible, focusing solely on the Odyssean
parallel. His memorable declaration that a "mythical method" had allowed
Joyce to find an order amid "the immense panorama of futility and
anarchy which is contemporary history" has gone down as one founding
statement of modernist aesthetics.¹³ Its "rage for order," to borrow Wallace
Stevens' phrase, became paradigmatic for subsequent decades of American
New Criticism with its attraction to well-wrought equipoise.¹⁴ Yet it has
become a truism that Eliot's apocalyptic view of history explains his own
work more directly than it does *Ulysses*. Wyndham Lewis, finally, fulfilled
Pound's injunction to "write out a critique" by publishing a lengthy, frequently mocking analysis of Joyce in 1927.¹⁵ Lewis's critique was idiosyncratic, but many of its sideswipes – about Joyce's Proustian immersion in

the past, his amassing of Irish detail, his privileging of technical experiment over ideas – remain suggestive decades later.

By the 1930s, *Ulysses* was increasingly comprehensible. These years in which Joyce's own attention was on *Work in Progress* were a period of assimilation: legalization, clarification, and a degree of respectability unsuspected by the *Sporting Times*. The accusations of formlessness made in 1922 increasingly had less purchase. *Ulysses* became the subject of extended essays and chapters – like those of New York journalist Edmund Wilson, whose *Axel's Castle* (1931), with characteristic bravura, managed to name and situate an entire pantheon of modernist writing – and of whole books. Gilbert's mythic emphasis and Budgen's emphasis on character and setting covered two bases – making the book intricately patterned and susceptible to painstaking exegesis, yet also an exemplar of humane realism.[16] A new generation of writers openly learned from *Ulysses*: from George Orwell's recasting of Nighttown in Trafalgar Square in *A Clergyman's Daughter* (1935) to Jorge Luis Borges's "Funes the Memorious," the story he pointedly included in his 1941 obituary of Joyce. Still more intensively – partly because of Joyce's still scandalous status in his homeland – Irish writers engaged with him. From the early Samuel Beckett and Flann O'Brien to Seamus Heaney and Paul Muldoon, it would hardly be an exaggeration to say that every major Irish writer since Joyce has negotiated with his legacy.[17] Many have done so explicitly in essays and commentary, as well as in their creative works.

The Joyce Industry

The single largest subsequent development was the transfer of the bulk of reception from journalists, poets, and novelists to academics. If one book signalled this, it was Harry Levin's economical, elegant, and erudite *Critical Introduction* (1941). Looking back in a postscript from 1960, Levin could already trace the emergence of what was now called a "Joyce Industry." "For his original readers," he reflected, "Joyce was a heretic, for many of them an emancipating force. The shift of values at mid-century has recast him in a priestly role, the patriarch of a neo-orthodox cult."[18] The industry's base was the United States. The American academy was rapidly expanding in student numbers. Major American universities – not least the Ivy League institutions where influential Joyceans were employed – were wealthier than most of their overseas rivals, and from the 1940s strategically bought up much of the surviving archive of drafts, notes and letters. By the end of the 1950s, such texts were held at the universities of

Buffalo, Philadelphia, Cornell, Harvard and Yale. The U.S. academy supported a professionalized network of commentary and publication: centrally and enduringly in the *James Joyce Quarterly*, founded by Thomas Staley at the University of Tulsa in 1963.[19] Others eventually followed, in and beyond the United States. They included the *Joyce Studies Annual*, which Staley founded at the University of Texas in 1990, and the slim *James Joyce Broadsheet* – primarily a space for book reviews – founded in London in 1980. The emergence of periodicals devoted to Joyce – metronomically guaranteeing a given amount of new work on him year after year – was as strong a sign as any book of his status in the contemporary academy. It was no longer just acceptable to read Joyce; it was imperative to understand and explicate him in the smallest detail.

This was also the implication of the regular events which emerged as counterparts to the printed periodicals. Preeminent among these is the International James Joyce Symposium: initially, from the late 1960s, held in Dublin, but subsequently a biennial, peripatetic event that has roamed the cities of Europe and expanded to fill a week. Other conferences would spring up to fill the time not occupied by the Symposium, including a biennial North American conference and an irregular gathering on Joyce's birthday in Miami since the 1990s. Towards the end of the twentieth century, it became possible for an academic to be a Joycean not merely as one emphasis among others, but almost as a job description in itself – part of a guild with its own gatherings, publications, shared memories and private jokes.

From the 1940s onwards, without significant interruption, reams of commentary rolled out: in books, in Joycean journals and indeed in every other academic literary outlet open to work on modern literature. It was easy enough for freelance Irish penmen to scorn the professionalism and pedantry of the Americans, but the latter could justifiably retort that it was they who had taken Joyce seriously and done most to maintain his legacy, while *Ulysses* remained absent from the shelves of Irish bookshops. No Joycean would defend all that has been published on *Ulysses*. Much from mid-century to the present has been superfluous. Much has simply followed the prevailing trends of the academic moment, from New Criticism on, and looked flimsily derivative when the wind has changed. Some arguments have been made with the appearance of authority, yet look factitious with a given amount of hindsight. Solemn statements of the devout religiosity of *Ulysses*, regularly offered by Catholics in the 1950s, are a case in point.[20] It is plausible to assume that some of what has been published in the twenty-first century will meet a like fate. And

much criticism, while worthy enough, has expended many words repeating things already said: an occupational hazard in an industry so heavily
staffed.

Yet insight has been offered, and some critical interventions have
attained special status for their rare acuity or their provision of hitherto
unknown information. None provided more than Richard Ellmann, the
most influential Joycean of all. Reviewing his hefty biography *James Joyce*
(1959), Frank Kermode reckoned that it had "fix[ed] Joyce's image for a
generation."[21] He probably underestimated. Five decades later, Ellmann's
would remain the central scholarly work in Joyce studies, present in
the bibliography of literally every work published on Joyce and unique
among scholarly works in retaining its own abbreviation in the *James Joyce
Quarterly*. Ellmann's efforts naturally encouraged biographical criticism,
making it easier for the events of *Ulysses* to be related to those of Joyce's life.
Alongside this, he also encouraged a certain view of Joyce, and of *Ulysses*
in particular. Ellmann's fundamental principle was unity. He sought a
continuity between experience and art, and his own shapely syntax tended
to achieve in style the harmony he valued. One thing his work did not do,
however, was register the shock, perversity and dislocation that others –
including the earliest readers – had found in *Ulysses*. Ellmann was Joyce's
greatest assimilator. He also presented the world with a humanist Joyce,
for whom "the ordinary is the extraordinary" and whose hero, Bloom,
allowed him to celebrate kindness and love (*JJ* 5). Ellmann's immense
intervention was thus a major event in what Emer Nolan has described
as "Joyce's canonization as the most congenial of early twentieth-century
writers."[22]

Modernism's most gifted critic took another tack. Hugh Kenner, a
Catholic Canadian mentored by Marshall McLuhan, spent most of his life
employed by prestigious U.S. universities. A critical prodigy, while still in
his mid-twenties he befriended Ezra Pound, followed by Eliot, Lewis and
Beckett. Only Joyce was personally unavailable. Kenner's PhD thesis was
published as *Dublin's Joyce* (1956): a crowded book whose cranky uneven-
ness and lapses into theological hectoring make it a poor guide to Kenner's
true quality. That quality would be clearer in his eventual return to Joyce,
when with *Joyce's Voices* (1978) and *"Ulysses"* (1980) he fired out in swift
succession two of the most coruscating readings of *Ulysses* ever offered.
Kenner was a profoundly close reader, able and willing to discern multiple
sets of invisible quotation marks around a sentence in "Telemachus."[23]
But his mind was also extra-literary, trained in mathematics and suffi-
ciently steeped in science to write books on Buckminster Fuller's geodesic

domes. Alongside Ellmann's humanist Joyce, Kenner offered a counter-humanism, which in diverse ways refused that seductive harmony.[24] He was apt to pursue disjunction where Ellmann settled for harmony, seeking ironies and ambiguities imperceptible to many, and conveying his insights in a style to startle and sway the reader. Profoundly at home with text, Kenner saw Joyce's language as a play with print that foregrounded modern mechanism. The brief, brilliant study *Flaubert, Joyce and Beckett: The Stoic Comedians* (1962) seems decades ahead of its time, grasping language as an intransigent material to be organized and the book as an informatic machine. Kenner saw in Joyce's formalism, pedantry and stylistic excesses the lineaments of a new poetics.

The Joyce Industry might be seen as a site of production-line professionalism, but one of its peculiarities was in fact the strong contribution made by non-academics – who in the terms of post-war criticism thus counted as "amateurs." This applied especially to *Finnegans Wake*, but the most enduringly insightful non-academic was more insistently a reader of *Ulysses*. Fritz Senn discovered the work in the mid-twentieth century and has spent much of his life rereading it, whether in his native Switzerland where he became director of the Zurich James Joyce Foundation or at countless international conferences. Among his distinctions was to turn his foreignness from an apparent weakness into a strength. For Senn, reading Joyce involved a kind of translation: The quizzical eye of the translator, he proposed, was precisely the attitude towards language that Joyce's work sought to foster. A stranger in English might be most at home in *Ulysses*. From such a premise, Senn has issued dozens of essays surprising *Ulysses* from different angles, showing himself perhaps the only reader who could outdo Kenner in his ear for the waywardness of words.

The arrival of theory transformed most areas of literary study from the 1970s onwards, as structuralism and post-structuralism were imported from Paris to the Anglophone academy. The work of Jacques Derrida, Roland Barthes, Jacques Lacan, Michel Foucault, Julia Kristeva and others was used to produce new frameworks and methods of reading. Lacan himself addressed the Joyce Symposium in Paris in 1975, and Derrida and Kristeva followed in Frankfurt in 1984.[25] In such thinkers' wake, a new emphasis fell pervasively on discontinuity, fragmentation and the instability of meaning, in what has been described as a reprise of modernism at the level of theory. In this respect, theory corroborated Kenner and Senn more than Gilbert and Ellmann, although those mavericks were unimpressed by what they saw as an invasion of jargon. Another result was the politicization of criticism, with leftist assumptions increasingly pervasive.

In Joyce studies, the giddy high point was Colin MacCabe's *James Joyce and the Revolution of the Word* (1979), a cocktail of psychoanalysis, post-structuralist linguistics and Leninist politics. Most subsequent criticism was more temperate, as memories of revolutionary Paris in 1968 were dimmed in the age of the New Right. Yet most criticism tinctured by contemporary theory, even when it was not politically explicit, tended intuitively against authority and in favour of the marginal or subversive. The age of theory was also the era in which the academic humanities in Britain and the United States became heavily tilted toward the liberal left, in the wake of educational expansion, the New Left and counterculture. By century's end it would be entirely commonplace among Joyceans to talk of *Ulysses*'s resistance to or (less often) complicity with power, or its subversion or reinforcement of ideological norms, and assume that the values implied were consensually accepted. This could hardly have been contemplated, let alone taken for granted, by an earlier generation of post-war critics.

Criticism after theory, as in earlier eras, involved industrial quantities of overproduction and work that would swiftly show its age. But its best exponents, like Maud Ellmann, combined new insights with abiding scholarship. The era's most exemplary Joycean was Derek Attridge. A globetrotting South African, friend to Derrida as Kenner had been to Pound, Attridge combined a patient, probing attention to Joyce's text with a theorist's questions about what such reading involved. A cautious writer, Attridge shunned heady political claims. But his constantly diligent reading opened up areas of worldly concern, as in his thorough examination of the relation of gender to literary form in "Penelope."[26] Feminism, indeed, made a substantial advance in this period. Joyceans became attentive as never before to the idea that the representation of gender might be an ethical issue. From Bonnie Kime Scott's *Joyce and Feminism* (1984) through an entire volume of essays on Molly Bloom ten years later, work proliferated. Anthologies or guides to *Ulysses*, including the present volume, now automatically devote a section to questions of gender. In the Joyce Industry, women gained more prominence. Dublin's first dedicated Professor of James Joyce Studies, appointed in 2006, was an Irishwoman, Ann Fogarty.

Fogarty's own work joined the largest critical development of the previous two decades: the rise of historical readings situating Joyce's work in its Irish context. Given Ireland's contentious history under and rebellion against British rule, this meant a continuation of the political tendencies already mentioned, but often in a concretely specified way. This "Irish

turn" had more poignant origins than most academic trends. Its wellspring
was the attempt of Irish scholars – Seamus Deane, Declan Kiberd and
Richard Kearney among them – to seek a new critical idiom and cultural
history in the face of the violence that had flared in Northern Ireland
since the late 1960s. By the twenty-first century, Joyce was central to Irish
criticism as well as Irish tourism, and his alma mater founded a centre for
Joycean research. But the historical study of Joyce could thrive elsewhere
too. It was London-based scholar Andrew Gibson who set a new standard
for the historical contextualization of *Ulysses* in his painstakingly detailed
study, *Joyce's Revenge* (2002).

Ulysses is proverbially a book more bought than read, with a reputation that still intimidates some. A writer can claim a day's headlines by
ignorantly disparaging it. But Joyce's importance in the academy has not
retarded the growth of his readership: On the contrary, given the immense
expansion of literary higher education since his lifetime, it has profoundly
encouraged it. The book endures and thrives through time, respected from
a distance but also closely read by a growing and now global audience. In
1922, Ezra Pound concluded that *Ulysses* "furnishes matter for a symposium rather than for a single letter, essay, or review" (*Pound/Joyce* 200).
Nine decades since have produced all those things by the score, but have
never yet made Joyce's book look out of date.

Notes

1 Hugh Kenner, *Joyce's Voices* (London: Faber and Faber, 1978), p. 1.
2 See Stuart Gilbert, *James Joyce's "Ulysses"*, rev. ed. (Harmondsworth: Peregrine,
   1963); Valéry Larbaud, "James Joyce," *Nouvelle Revue Francaise* xviii (April
   1922), pp. 385–405, in *James Joyce: The Critical Heritage* ed. Robert H. Deming
   (London: Routledge and Kegan Paul, 1970), pp. 252–62, henceforth referred to
   as *Critical Heritage*; and Frank Budgen, *James Joyce and the Making of "Ulysses"*
   (London: Grayson and Grayson, 1934).
3 Paul Vanderham, *James Joyce and Censorship: The Trials of "Ulysses"* (Basingstoke:
   Macmillan, 1998), 101. Also see chapters 4–6. Further references will be cited
   parenthetically in the text as *Censorship*.
4 Martin Amis, *The War Against Cliché: Essays and Reviews 1971–2000* (London:
   Jonathan Cape, 2001), p. 441.
5 See John Kidd, "The Scandal of *Ulysses*," *New York Review of Books*, 30 June 1988;
   and "An Inquiry into *Ulysses: The Corrected Text*," *Papers of the Bibliographical
   Society of America* 82:4 (December 1988), 411–584. In 1989, Kidd's James Joyce
   Research Center at Boston University published "Inquiry" in book format
   and on floppy disk. It is now available online at https://sites.google.com/site/
   textology/inquiry_1.

6 For an intelligent overview see Julie Sloan Brannon, *Who Reads "Ulysses"? The Rhetoric of the Joyce Wars and the Common Reader* (London: Routledge, 2003).

7 "Aramis," "The Scandal of *Ulysses,*" *Sporting Times*, 1 April 1922, in *Critical Heritage*, p. 193.

8 Holbrook Jackson, "Ulysses a la Joyce," *To-Day* (June 1922), in *Critical Heritage*, p. 199.

9 Arnold Bennett, "James Joyce's *Ulysses,*" *Outlook*, 29 April 1922, in *Critical Heritage*, p. 221.

10 Jackson, "Ulysses a la Joyce," pp. 199–200; "Domini Canis" (Shane Leslie), "*Ulysses*" (September 1922), in *Critical Heritage*, p. 202; George Slocombe, *Daily Herald*, 17 March 1922, in *Critical Heritage*, p. 218; "Aramis," "The Scandal of *Ulysses,*" p. 192.

11 Ezra Pound, "Paris Letter," in *Pound/Joyce: The Letters of Ezra Pound to James Joyce*, ed. Forrest Read (New York: New Directions, 1967), p. 194. Further references will be cited parenthetically in the text as *Pound/Joyce*.

12 Virginia Woolf, *A Moment's Liberty: The Shorter Diary*, ed. Anne Olivier Bell (London: Hogarth Press, 1977), pp. 145–46.

13 T. S. Eliot, *Selected Prose,* ed. Frank Kermode (London: Faber and Faber, 1975), pp. 177–78.

14 See Astradur Eysteinsson, *The Concept of Modernism* (Ithaca, NY: Cornell University Press, 1990), pp. 9–11.

15 See Wyndham Lewis, *Time and Western Man* (Santa Rosa: Black Sparrow Press, 1993 [1927]), chapter 16.

16 A. Walton Litz has suggested that *Ulysses* criticism from the start may be divided into such a "myth / fact" dichotomy: See "Pound and Eliot on *Ulysses*: The Critical Tradition," in *Fifty Years "Ulysses,"* ed. Thomas F. Staley (Bloomington: Indiana University Press, 1974), pp. 16–17.

17 The full story of Ireland's reception of Joyce remains to be published. John Ryan's *A Bash in the Tunnel: James Joyce by the Irish* (Brighton: Clifton Books, 1970) is a valuable anthology of its era. See also Dillon Johnston, *Irish Poetry after Joyce* (Mountrath: Dolmen Press, 1985).

18 Harry Levin, *James Joyce: A Critical Introduction* (London: Faber and Faber, 1960), p. 198.

19 On the development of the Joyce Industry, including the *JJQ* and international symposia, see Joseph Kelly's fascinating study *Our Joyce: From Outcast to Icon* (Austin: University of Texas Press, 1998), ch. 5.

20 See Jeffrey Segall, *Joyce in America: Cultural Politics and the Trials of "Ulysses"* (Berkeley: University of California Press, 1993), ch. 5. For a recent consideration of this issue see Geert Lernout, *Help My Unbelief: James Joyce and Religion* (London: Continuum, 2010).

21 Frank Kermode, "Puzzles and Epiphanies," *Spectator*, 13 November 1959, p. 675.

22 Emer Nolan, *James Joyce and Nationalism* (London: Routledge, 1995), p. 1.

23 Hugh Kenner, *"Ulysses,"* rev. ed. (Baltimore and London: Johns Hopkins University Press, 1987), p. 35.

24 See Joseph Brooker, *Joyce's Critics: Transitions in Reading and Culture* (Madison: University of Wisconsin Press, 2004), pp. 119–30.

25 For more on the ways Kristeva and Derrida shaped major rereadings of *Ulysses*, see Chapter 12.

26 See Derek Attridge, "Molly's Flow: The Writing of 'Penelope' and the Question of Women's Language" in *Joyce Effects: On Language, Theory, and History* (Cambridge: Cambridge University Press, 2000), pp. 93–116.

CHAPTER 3

Afterlife *

Jonathan Goldman

And the head coach
Wants no sissies
So he reads to us from something called Ulysses.
                                – Alan Sherman, "Hello Muddah, Hello Fadduh" (1965)[1]

Ulysses T-shirt

Since its 1922 publication, *Ulysses* has been repeatedly reincarnated, adapted across numerous media in works of all sorts. These versions and invocations of *Ulysses* replay the novel's legacy, recycling properties of its reputation such as its stature and smuttiness. The obvious places *Ulysses* turns up are literary. The novel provides fertile hunting ground for an array of scholarly agendas; meanwhile, writers of fiction and poetry reckon with *Ulysses* as a monument of stylistic innovation. Unexpected allusions to the work proliferate as well, such as the epigram above, lyrics from a popular novelty song in which a neurotically masculinized camp counselor reads *Ulysses* to baffled children. The less predictable appearances can be the more fascinating, since they reveal much about the book's position within larger cultural spheres, its relationship to Joyce's renown, and its circulation among readers and audiences.

A few years ago my father returned from vacation in Ireland wearing a T-shirt emblazoned with the novel's opening sentence: "Stately, plump, Buck Mulligan ...." A well-educated person with advanced degrees, my father has never read *Ulysses*. Something, though – something beyond paternal inclination to identify with his son's profession – spurred this purchase. What was it? The issues that accompany this question shape the afterlives of the novel. To announce affiliation with *Ulysses* – whether through expertise, adaptation, allusion, or attire – is to partake of its value as a signifier of high culture, a status derived from the novel's notorious difficulty and expansiveness.

However, while academic mastery promises membership within a supposedly select order, wearing the T-shirt does not, because *Ulysses* is "the
book everyone claims to have read but no one actually has," in the words
of Jennifer Wicke.[2] Part of the novel's fame, that is, for *not* being read. The
typical owners of *Ulysses*, Gerry Flaherty has said, are individuals who start
reading, get stuck, put the book back on the shelf, try again, get stuck,
and put it back on the shelf again, until by dint of seeing it there so often,
they feel like they have read it.[3] The novel, which was hard to find for
years because of state suppression, is now known as a commodity easily
purchased but not easily consumed.

Considered alongside the novel's reputation for remaining unread, the
T-shirt might presuppose only passing familiarity with *Ulysses*'s content. It
implies that purchasers know Buck Mulligan inaugurates the novel (and
perhaps knew that before visiting Dublin's gift shops), but not because
they read the book: *Been there. Haven't read that. Bought the T-shirt.* The
T-shirt wearers, however, actively recirculate the reputation of the novel.
Placing its value on display, they demonstrate that reading *Ulysses* is but
one association with its cultural stature, strangely unnecessary for partaking of that stature. The book's audience, we might say, extends beyond its
readers; we might even say that the act of reading *Ulysses* does not mean
what it does for other texts, since we can read and even share in the repute
of the novel without opening the book.

The T-shirt works most dynamically when its words are instantly recognized. *Ulysses*'s opening sentence is meant to be identified at a glance
by those in the know, like the corporate trademarks or celebrity images
emblazoned on other clothes, other wearers. On the T-shirt, language
becomes logo, trademark, a shorthand that – paradoxically – signals
Ulysses's complexity and exclusivity. The idea that the novel serves as brand
emblem emerges both in *Ulysses*'s content and in its reception, as the novel's myriad afterlives – reckoning with the iconicity of a book qua company
logo – navigate and reprise this function. In this chapter, offering neither
a comprehensive account of *Ulysses*'s resurrections nor a sustained exegesis
of any one, I examine the novel's legacy by first touching down on landmark manifestations where our culture has reforged the book's reputation
and then by wandering through some of its more eccentric incarnations.[4]

The Fame Function

Joyce's international renown and academic canonization are heavily scrutinized in current scholarship, often alongside the early-twentieth-century

marketplace and related cultural forces of Joyce's lifetime. Though modernist literature has frequently been exalted as writing that rejects the taint of the commercial, recent critics find Joyce's promotional practices and publication battles to be rich veins of analysis, and argue that advertising and celebrity, for example, shape his oeuvre.[5] Indeed, *Ulysses* models authorial branding and trademarking through its style, narrative, and processes of composition, publication, and marketing. While it may seem that the kind of instant graspability that undergirds commodity branding would contradict *Ulysses*'s famed multiplicity, the book suggests that commercial codification is an inescapable force – its 1904 setting adding to the sense that there is no turning back from a culture dominated by the marketplace. For example, brands and sound bites saturate the consciousness of protagonist Leopold Bloom, advertising-canvasser. He is haunted by a slogan that repeatedly arises unbidden: "*What is home without/ Plumtree's Potted Meat?/ Incomplete*" (*U* 5.144–46). Eventually he grows exasperated, ejaculating "What a stupid ad!" (*U* 8.743), but the phrase has already made its imprint. Bloom devises a punning advertisement for retailer Alexander Keyes: "Two crossed keys here. A circle. Then here the name. Alexander Keyes" (*U* 7.142–43). In this instance, an image serves as shorthand for the brand. Bloom frequently dwells on several visual icons, including the Bass Ale logo, notable as the first protected trademark under British law. The proliferation of slogans and trademarks implicate *Ulysses* as a participant in the world of branding and visual culture.

The manifestations of market culture in *Ulysses* help make Joyce's fame legible as a product of the early-twentieth-century culture of celebrity. This new form of fame – turning identities into commodities that are simultaneously distinct and reproducible – retains the idea of the individual for a mass-technological society. During the composition of *Ulysses* (1914–1921) and in the ensuing decade, celebrity was spurred by the mass reproduction and dissemination of images, especially the moving pictures of cinema. Recognition of Hollywood actors and familiarity with their material existence (presented in promotional literature and the press) became an intrinsic aspect of cinematic reception. The stardom of Rudolph Valentino, Clara Bow, and Charlie Chaplin inflects their films, which generate textual meaning by signaling beyond plot toward the performers' so-called real lives. Analogously, *Ulysses*'s textual methods – including its stylistic variety, obscurity, play with autobiographical detail, and Joyce's extra-textual guides – announce the author's renown and connote his genius, rationalizing the book's idiosyncrasies as experiments.

Joyce's celebrity thus parallels the form and function of early-twentieth-century popular fame.[6]

The celebrity system fueled Joyce's authorial brand after *Ulysses* was published and does so to this day – a durability signaled by *Time* magazine's ongoing engagement with the book, to take one manifestation that has attracted critics.[7] In the 1930s, *Time* reviewed Stuart Gilbert's study *James Joyce's "Ulysses"* and eventually the novel itself, while featuring Joyce on two covers. Over sixty years later, the magazine's "All Time 100 Novels" omits *Ulysses*, but only because it restricts itself to works published since the magazine's March 1923 birth. It is a list, Aaron Jaffe says, not of the "All-Time 100" but of the "All-*Time* 100" ("Afterlives" 209). The chronological limit, judge Richard Lacayo notes, "means that *Ulysses* (1922) doesn't make the cut.... [P]lease, no emails about *Ulysses*."[8] Spotlighting *Ulysses* in absentia, he implies that the work that defines high value would render moot any sense of competition. *Time*'s approach may be in response to Modern Library's 1999 tally of the 100 best novels of the 1900s, which predictably puts *Ulysses* on top. Both best-of lists – a device that lies somewhere between canonization and guilt trip (*Have you read all these? You should have*) – use *Ulysses* to define value. Joyce looms over the lists as the novel circulates his stature.

The book's emblematic status also shines through Eve Arnold's 1954 photograph of Marilyn Monroe reading *Ulysses* during her downtime (see Figure 3.1). This anti-pinup implies that the actress's choice of leisure activity is a surprise: that either *Ulysses* is not the impenetrable object people expect or that Monroe is not the dumb blond people expect. The photo contrasts the celebrity's Hollywood image with this supposedly authentic Monroe – Joyce enthusiast and thoughtful consumer of high art. Novelist Jeannette Winterson writes, "[W]e're not being asked to look at Marilyn, we're being given a chance to look inside her."[9] In other words, the picture suggests that consuming *Ulysses* exposes Monroe's private life, which in turn transforms her public identity. The photograph's candidness enhances this: It proposes itself as a private, un-staged moment that acknowledges its public role through its circulation. This interplay of the false oppositions that saturate twentieth-century celebrity – private and public, real and performed, inner and outer – underscores that the discourse of fame inflects *Ulysses*'s afterlives. And of course, the photograph prompts us to ask whether Monroe is truly reading the novel, thus recirculating *Ulysses*'s legacy of unread-ness.[10]

Figure 3.1: Marilyn Monroe, Actress and Singer (photograph by Eve Arnold, Long Island, NY: Magnum Photos, 1955).

Ulysses Arises

Joyce's rising repute during his lifetime prompted references to *Ulysses* by other authors, allusions that confirm and recirculate the novel's legacy and stature. In Michael Arlen's *The Green Hat* (1924), femme fatale Iris scandalously disregards *Ulysses*'s various forms of value: "[S]he picked up Joyce's *Ulysses*, looked at it vaguely, dropped it absently on the floor amongst the others."[11] The narrator mentally responds with a "financial brief" for the book, contemplating the monetary worth of a rare edition while leaving un-editorialized the blithe treatment of high literature. The 1940 detective novel *Hugger-Mugger in the Louvre* by Joyce's friend Elliot Paul depicts an American in Paris who buys *Ulysses* for his daughter only to learn that it is "not the book for a high school girl to read."[12] *Ulysses* becomes a tourist's scandalous souvenir of a country where obscenity in English goes unsuppressed. Such moments rehearse a popular understanding of *Ulysses* as an object rare to possess and rarer to read; scarcity intertwines with the novel's risqué repute. Both texts cast *Ulysses* as resistant to popular readership and contrast its inaccessibility with the more generic narratives where the novel is mentioned.

These cameos presage the central role *Ulysses* plays in literature after Joyce's death, as subsequent generations have navigated its legacy. In verse, Patrick Kavanagh's "Who Killed James Joyce" (1951) addresses the pedantry of expertism, specifically railing against the United States's academic treatment of Joyce. It ironically rhymes "*Ulysses*" with "Harvard thesis" (a murder weapon); one "Yale-man" also participates in this figurative assassination.[13] American scholars, Kavanagh complains, are colonizing *Ulysses*, ruining the book for everyone else. The poem does not go so far as to suggest that Joyce should have a more populist readership. It prefers to keep Joyce for the Irish, but in proposing to take him out of the hands of academics, it swaps one form of restriction for another. Kavanagh's possessiveness points to the giant shadow that Joyce casts over Irish writers, the impulse to address his mythos. For example, novelist Flann O'Brien, whom Joyce admired, rewrites the compositional history of *Ulysses* to make it not Irish, not even by Joyce. His *The Dalkey Archive* (1964) depicts an elderly but quite living Joyce whose 1941 death was a ruse. This Joyce claims to have had no hand in creating *Ulysses*, which is a hoax perpetrated by publisher Sylvia Beach and her confederates.[14] He thinks of the writings attributed to him as blasphemy and hopes they will not upend his application to the Jesuits. O'Brien reckons with a national literary monument by denying its Irishness and puncturing the author's brand.

O'Brien's satire depends on reader awareness of Joyce's repute. Mining a similar vein is playwright Tom Stoppard's *Travesties* (1977), a counterfactual comedy that stages a 1917 encounter between Joyce, V. I. Lenin, and Tristan Tzara – all of whom indeed lived in Zurich during *Ulysses*'s composition.[15] Hijinks ensue. The play borrows heavily from Joyce's biography; its protagonist is Henry Carr, the British government functionary who in 1917 had the misfortune of rubbing Joyce the wrong way over the bill for a pair of pants. In turn, Joyce used the name Private Carr for *Ulysses*'s most cartoonish character: revenge mixed with a pun on railway travel. In *Travesties*, Carr's uncertain memories offer up both a caricatured, stage-Irish version of Joyce (who speaks in limericks and borrows money) and a soberer Joyce (who discusses literary method and borrows money). The one is a joke, the other a lightly mocked narcissist embodying artistic genius. When Carr questions Joyce's sense of patriotic responsibility, asking the famous question, "[W]hat did you do in the Great War?" Joyce retorts, "I wrote *Ulysses* .... What did you do?" (*Travesties* 44). Aesthetic labor has value, and *Ulysses* is its apex, the indisputable excuse for sitting out the world's problems.

While these examples evoke *Ulysses*'s composition and reception, many works allude to the book by redeploying elements of its content. Enumerating the texts that evince stylistic influence from the novel would be a lengthy chore, one perhaps devalued by the fact that, to many, *Ulysses*'s major stylistic trait is its mimicry of other voices. Likewise, a comprehensive list of post–1922 works set on a single day would probably outgrow the interest it would raise. One more intriguing way that writers invoke *Ulysses* is by recalling its language. For example, two modernist novels end with echoes of *Ulysses*'s ending, alluding to the moment when Molly Bloom draws Leopold atop her and thinks, "yes I said yes I will Yes" (*U* 18.1608–09). In Jean Rhys's *Good Morning Midnight* (1938), Sasha Jensen, embracing a previously repellent partner, mimics Molly's physical actions while thinking, "Yes–yes–yes."[16] Ernest Hemingway's *The Sun Also Rises* (1926) ends with Jake Barnes's bleak response to romantic possibility: "'Yes,' I said. 'Isn't it pretty to think so?'"[17] At their conclusions, these novels claim a relation (however ironized) to *Ulysses*, self-consciously partaking of its capital.

We might ask: Do allusions to Joyce make readers appreciate these texts more? Should they? Answers to these questions will vary according to readers' approaches to literature and culture – will, indeed, illuminate their approaches. Similarly, the activity of searching for textual allusions to *Ulysses* raises theoretical complications, because the results will depend on how deep one feels like digging. In *The U.S.A. Trilogy* (1931–36) John Dos

Passos writes, "when the telegram came that she was dying the bellglass cracked in a screech of slate pencils."[18] This passage evokes multiple elements of Stephen Dedalus's morning in *Ulysses* (a telegram, a dying woman, a cracked glass): allusion or coincidence? Further afield, Elvis Costello's song "Battered Old Bird" (1986) mentions burgundy, breakfast, a typewriter, and "the MacIntosh man" – four signature details of Bloom's day.[19] Are such resonances intentional, and if so, how do they affect our understanding of these works? For some, intentionality is irrelevant; any echo of Joyce inflects the text's meaning, regardless of the author's aims. With this in mind, we can consider the impulse to find such references, and see that this approach imposes Joyce as a reading filter over other cultural products. *Ulysses* is known as a hunting ground for literary allusions; in turn, the world has become a hunting ground for *Ulysses* allusions. While gauging Joyce's influence on writers has helped create a version of literary history, assessing Joyce's influence on readers can help us understand how products of high culture determine our reading practices.

Retailing

Of course *Ulysses* is frequently, simply, the source material for other narrative works. Prose revisions of the novel appear from time to time, while the story is often pried from the printed page and adapted for song, stage, and other audio and video productions. The cinema world has long viewed *Ulysses* as compelling material: Film adaptations seemed on the horizon as early as the 1930s, when Sergei Eisenstein and Louis Zukofsky separately expressed interest.[20] However, it was not until 1967 that a motion picture version of *Ulysses* arrived in the form of director Joseph Strick's adaptation. The film ambitiously translates narrative experiment into cinematic technique. For example, its "Aeolus" episode shows extras traversing the scene carrying large printed signs, analogs for the boldface inter-titles of the novel. One quirk of the film is its 1960s Dublin setting, a choice made from financial necessity. Strick's *Ulysses* thus contrasts with the 2002 adaption *Bloom*, which relies on the charm and manufactured nostalgia of a recreated 1904 Dublin. *Bloom* puts its highly sexualized and scandalously blond Molly Bloom at the center of its story, interspersing Leopold's and Stephen's actions between segments of her monologue and montages of her sexual activities. Unlike Strick's version, *Bloom* registers as an attempt to bring a wider audience to *Ulysses*, but both smack of self-fulfilling exercises, as if to prove by their existence that *Ulysses* can be translated to film.

Figure 3.2: Robert Berry, *Ulysses Seen*, "Calypso," page 11.

Cinema struggles to adapt *Ulysses* because, while full of motion and pictures, the novel teems with interior monologue. A more intuitive medium for adaptation is thus the comic book, a genre that incorporates thought bubbles into images, its format suggesting motion and time. The best-known comic book version is Robert Berry's *Ulysses Seen*, in progress since 2009 and available mostly online. Like Strick's film, it manipulates its medium to revisit the novel's narrative methods, though it does so to focus on character thought; Berry explores visually the way the novel's interior monologues seep into descriptions of the setting. For example, the "Calypso" episode depicts Bloom imagining himself in a Middle Eastern metropolis. In *Ulysses Seen*, Bloom's thoughts cause the Dublin buildings to fade under bright sunlight. (*Ulysses Seen* 11; see Figure 3.2).[21] The subsequent panel transforms Dublin and its passersby into clichéd signifiers of foreignness, and shows Bloom wearing a turban and earring (12; see Figure 3.3). When Bloom mentally returns to Dublin, deciding that his fantasy is "probably not a bit like" the Middle Eastern world, his attire and surroundings change back (*Ulysses Seen* 14). The comic book conventions mirror the

Figure 3.3: Robert Berry, *Ulysses Seen*, "Calypso," page 12.

technique of *Ulysses*, evoking the interior monologue that governs stretches of the novel's narrative. Befitting a visual medium, *Ulysses Seen* renders visible the thoughts that carry the plot. Befitting a digital medium, furthermore, the work is available as an application for touch-screen tablets, using the interface to provide explanatory notes. *Ulysses Seen* thus uses both of its technologies to simultaneously address *Ulysses* enthusiasts and introduce the novel to new audiences, serving as an interactive teaching text.

Predating *Ulysses Seen*, David Lasky's succinct 1991 comic book *Ulysses* takes a canny tack, representing each episode in two panels. Its use of shorthand distills *Ulysses* into thirty-six images of uniform size, mostly devoid of speech or thought bubbles. For example, one panel of the "Nausicaa" episode manages to evoke Gertie MacDowell's exhibitionism, Bloom's arousal, the Star of the Sea Church, and the fireworks display that becomes a metaphor for sexual climax (see Figure 3.4).[22] It depicts the chapter's primary plot in key details – such as a bead of sweat on Bloom's face – that signify beyond their immediate text to the voluminous novel. In other words, Lasky reduces Joyce's book to visual emblems that depend on familiarity with the novel. Unlike *Ulysess Seen*, it is a work designed not

Figure 3.4: David Lasky, *Ulysses*, the second of two "Nausicaa" panels.

to introduce *Ulysses*, but to represent its inside jokes and reprise its thematizing of codification.

Ulysses in Space

Ulysses Seen is interactive. Its Web-based social apparatus – including a discussion board – creates a virtual community that combines openness with a whiff of intellectual exclusivity. *Ulysses Seen* thus illuminates a dominant aspect of *Ulysses*'s afterlives: that the novel is recirculated by people in public space. The most formalized such population is the scholarly community devoted to Joyce, sometimes called Joyceans, who frequently convene; since 1968, the International James Joyce Foundation has held biennial symposia, which merit their own histories.[23] Other Joyce conferences have met regularly over the years, and other manifestations of this academic community exist geographically, including intensive Joyce summer schools in Dublin and Trieste, and such as, listservs and websites.

The academic conferences find a somewhat populist reflection in the widespread Bloomsday celebrations, held every June 16, the day the novel takes place. These date at least to 1954, when the Dublin gathering counted Kavanagh and O'Brien among its participants. Bloomsday festivities feature reenactments, meals, lectures, and above all, readings by experts and novices alike. They are as varied in their rationales as they are in their locales. While Hungarian Joyceans gather in Szombathely, hometown of Bloom's (fictional) father, Parisian readers head to Shakespeare & Company, a reincarnation (not on the original site) of Sylvia Beach's bookstore that published the 1922 *Ulysses*. Dubliners breakfast outdoors on O'Connell Street before tracing Bloom's peregrinations, and New Yorkers meet at the Ulysses Pub, one of the world's countless bars named for Joyce, to reap the benefits of corporate beer sponsorship (free libations, baseball caps, and naturally, T-shirts). Around the globe, Irish government officials throw parties intended to promote tourism, and Irish-based organizations host events intended to promote national identity.

Bloomsdays bridge attitudinal divisions among expertise, fandom, obsessiveness, ambivalence, and dilettantism. Thorough scrutiny of the novel, however, only rarely arises to interfere with audience pleasure. For New York's "Bloomsday on Broadway" event actors and writers (including, recently, Stephen Colbert) read selections while intermittent commentary celebrates *Ulysses*, mostly without explication. The point is clear: you are there to fête the stature of a book without necessarily understanding it. A 2011 Bloomsday breakfast signaled the same message. It was held alongside the New York Public Library's stately main branch, on a terrace presided over by a statue of Gertrude Stein, who disdained Joyce. Performers danced, sang turn-of-the-century numbers, and mingled with the crowd in 1904 costume. The Irish finance minister, visiting New York for a summit, had been corralled into attending. Asked by the press about Ireland's economic agenda, he responded that his administration would emulate *Ulysses* for the balanced budget that appears in its pages. However, Bloom balances his budget (in "Ithaca") only by ignoring the money spent at Bella Cohen's brothel. The minister's mistake, if noticed at all, was allowed to slide. As one wag has put it, "Bloomsday has as much to do with Joyce as Christmas has to do with Jesus."[24] Though lamenting the situation, this comment shows that bringing *Ulysses* into public space allows for novices and eccentrics to stand alongside the institutionally accredited. Such events – whether gaudy, anarchic, sanitized, or stately – mix elements of expertise with unequivocal celebration of the novel's reputation.

Such inclusiveness is reflected in the Bloomsday activities of the expanding online Joyce community. The *Ulysses* Project, for example, incorporates wide-ranging content such as surprising adaptations (e.g., images of a series of jewelry pieces inspired by *Ulysses*'s chapters) and videos of scholars answering queries. The site links to social media to allow, for instance, Twitter users to narrate *Ulysses* in real time throughout Bloomsday, in 140 characters or fewer. The novel's Internet afterlife also spawns events such as the Modernist Versions Project's Bloomsday 2012 revisiting of Arnold's photograph of Monroe, for which participants contributed images of themselves (or their friends, babies, cats, etc.) reading *Ulysses*. The submissions, to be sure, do not prove that their subjects are actually reading the book any more than does the Monroe image.

Owning *Ulysses*

The Modernist Versions Project's photograph collection puts on display contributors' personal copies of *Ulysses*. It thus mirrors the non-Internet Bloomsday celebrations, which feature crowds of readers brandishing their books, some copies inviolate but many ragged, dog-eared, extensively tagged by pen, pencil, or Post-It – branded, one might say, by their owners, for whom the book has talismanic properties. This fetishizing evokes, among other things, a specious association of copies of the book with the rare editions, a phenomenon that helps explain why reprints and facsimiles of the 1922 publication remain profitable despite their overwhelming amount of errata. Meanwhile, the various corrected versions, with disputable passages and conflicting editorial approaches, contribute to the sense that *Ulysses* is a book to be multiply collected. It is not just a material thing, but material things: multiple editions, translations, and adaptations (read or otherwise) for the bookshelf. Their reproducibility and individuality pleasurably coexist.

While any copy of *Ulysses* may be treated as mystical and subject to ritual, the rarest receive the most veneration. A 2011 essay by novelist Colum McCann suggests the power that *Ulysses*, the object, exerts over its audience. McCann recounts an opportunity to view the New York Public Library's first edition, a Shakespeare & Company 1922. In an obscure room, away from the library crowds, he gazes and breathes; touching is not permitted. Eventually the librarians move to put away the volume, accidentally causing one small corner of a page to break off and flutter aside unnoticed. McCann does, he explains, what any "joycesick fool would do": he picks up the joyceflake, places it in his mouth, and swallows, performing *Ulysses* communion and mimicking the ingestion of certain psychotropic drugs.[25] What McCann does not mention – curiously, for a lover of the scatalogically inclined Joyce – is that *Ulysses* will traverse his alimentary canal, its journey transforming it from sacrament to excrement, then recirculating it to the world. It turns out *Ulysses* is easily consumed. Digesting it is another matter, but in the end everyone passes it on.

Notes

* The title nods to Aaron Jaffe's "Joyce's Afterlives: Why He Didn't Win the Nobel Prize," in *James Joyce: Visions and Revisions,* ed. Sean Latham (Dublin: Irish Academic Press, 2009), pp. 189–214. Further references to this essay will be cited parenthetically as "Afterlives."

1 Allan Sherman, "Hello Muddah, Hello Fadduh," on *My Son, the Nut,* 1965, compact disc, Warner Brothers, 2003. Coincidentally, the song's melody derives from Amilcare Ponchieri's "Dance of the Hours," a ballet that Bloom recalls in *Ulysses* (*U* 4.526).

2 Jennifer Wicke, "Joyce and Consumer Culture," in *The Cambridge Companion to James Joyce,* ed. Derek Attridge (Cambridge: Cambridge University Press, 2004), p. 234.

3 My paraphrase of his remarks at "Joyce's Reception by the Irish," roundtable at the 2012 International James Joyce Symposium, Dublin, June 15, 2012.

4 This essay bypasses critical analyses, but for a survey of Joyce's critical reception see Chapters 2 and 12. In the interest of managing expectations, here are other *Ulysses* sites that go unexamined in my essay: press, publicity, recorded reactions by notable names, memoirs, legal documents, translations, recorded books, and the published guides, handbooks, and reductions that help people fake having read the book. Also: visual renderings and invocations of Joyce unaccompanied by *Ulysses* references.

5 Examples include Jennifer Wicke, *Advertising Fictions: Literature, Advertisement, and Social Reading* (New York: Columbia University Press, 1989); Mark Osteen, *The Economy of Ulysses: Making Both Ends Meet* (Syracuse, NY: Syracuse University Press, 1994); Joseph Kelly, *Our Joyce:*

From Outcast to Icon (Austin: University of Texas Press, 1999); Lawrence Rainey, *Institutions of Modernism: Literary Elites and Public Culture* (New Haven, CT: Yale University Press, 1999); and the collection *Joyce and Popular Culture*, ed. R. Brandon Kershner (Gainesville: University of Florida Press, 1996).

6 I address Joyce's relation to celebrity culture more extensively in *Modernism Is the Literature of Celebrity* (Austin: University of Texas Press, 2011), esp. pp. 8–14 and 55–80.

7 Maurizia Boscagli and Enda Duffy analyze the *Time* appearances in "Joyce's Face," in *Marketing Modernisms*, eds. Kevin Dettmar and Stephen J. Watt (Ann Arbor: University of Michigan Press, 1996), pp. 133–61.

8 Richard Lacayo, "How We Picked the List," *Time*, October 16, 2005, entertainment.time.com/2005/10/16/all-time-100-novels. Accessed July 31, 2011.

9 Jeannette Winterson, "Solitary Pleasures," *The Guardian*, April 28, 2006, http://www.guardian.co.uk/artanddesign/2006/apr/29/art?INTCMP=SRCH. Accessed July 31, 2011.

10 According to Arnold, Monroe had been reading the novel in parts. I owe this fact and some of my sense of the photograph to Joseph Kelly's "Saving Joyce from the Professors," a review of *Ulysses and Us: The Art of Everyday Living*, by Declan Kiberd, *South Carolina Review* **43** (Fall 2010): 263–67.

11 Michael Arlen, *The Green Hat* (New York: George H. Doran Company, 1924), p. 35.

12 Elliott Paul, *Hugger-Mugger in the Louvre,* 1940 (New York: Dover Publications, 1986), p. 97.

13 Patrick Kavanagh, "Who Killed James Joyce," 1951, *Irish Writing in the Twentieth Century: A Reader*, ed. David Pierce (Cork: Cork University Press, 2001), p. 650.

14 Flann O'Brien, *The Dalkey Archive,* 1964 (Normal, IL: The Dalkey Archive Press, 1993), 175–78.

15 Tom Stoppard, *Travesties* (New York: Grove Press, 1975). Further references to the text will be cited parenthetically as *Travesties*.

16 Jean Rhys, *Good Morning, Midnight,* 1937 (New York: W.W. Norton and Company, 2000), p. 190.

17 Ernest Hemingway, *The Sun Also Rises,* 1926 (New York: Charles Scribner and Sons, 1954), p. 251.

18 John Dos Passos, *1919,* 1932 (Boston: Mariner Books, 2000), p. 6.

19 Elvis Costello, "Battered Old Bird," on *Blood and Chocolate,* 1986, Warner Brothers, LP. I once asked on the musician's website whether he had been thinking of Joyce while composing the song, to no response.

20 See Maria Di Battista, "Cinema," in *James Joyce In Context,* ed. John McCourt (Cambridge: Cambridge University Press, 2009), p. 360.

21 Robert Berry, *Ulysses Seen,* http://ulyssesseen.com. Accessed July 31, 2011. Further references to this text will be cited parenthetically as *Ulysses Seen*.

22 David Lasky, *Ulysses* (Seattle, WA: Minit Classics, 1991).

23 See, for example, Kelly, *Our Joyce*, pp. 187–208; and Morris Beja, "Synjoysium: An Informal History of the International James Joyce Symposia," *JJQ* 22 (Winter 1985): 113–29.

24 This was Robert Nicholson, speaking at the same symposium panel where Flaherty flashed his witticism.

25 Colum McCann, "Ineluctable Modality of the Visible," in *Know the Past, Know the Future: The New York Public Library at 100*, ed. Caro Llewellyn (New York: Penguin Classics, 2011), pp. 219–20.

PART II

The Story of Ulysses

CHAPTER 4

Beginnings

Scarlett Baron

For writers and readers, novelistic beginnings are thresholds, portals of discovery, starting points from which a text unfolds and builds speed and intensity, travelling towards the potential climaxes of middle and ending. "A *beginning*," Aristotle writes in the *Poetics*, "is that which itself does not follow necessarily from anything else, but some second thing naturally exists or occurs after it."[1] Today – as in 1918 when the book's serialization began in *The Little Review*, and as in 1922 when it was first published by Shakespeare & Company – *Ulysses* is recognized as a revolution in culture, an irruption of newness: a beginning satisfying Aristotle's first tenet.[2] Radically breaking with literary traditions and conventions, by far exceeding the sum of the preceding artistic experiments upon which it drew, *Ulysses* was experienced by contemporary readers as rupture, difference, singularity.

Yet for all its widely acknowledged position at the apogee of prose modernism and at the beginning of countless literary movements and artistic practices, *Ulysses* itself seems to lack the kind of beginning evoked in Aristotle's second clause: the kind of beginning from which other things – a novelistic middle and a novelistic ending, for instance – "naturally" follow. *Ulysses* emphatically does not go on as it begins. In going against the grain of classical conceptions of aesthetic wholeness – "A *whole*," according to Aristotle, "is that which has a beginning, a middle and an end" (*Poetics* 5.1) – it resists readerly expectations of unity and order. It does this first and foremost by disrupting assumptions of normal novelistic sequence. Karen Lawrence observes that "[t]he concept of development in most novels insures that the early parts of the work in some way prepare the reader for what is to come," but that the reader of *Ulysses* is denied such a grounding.[3] For Lawrence it is "a book that changes its mind as it progresses and forces a corresponding change in the mind of the reader" (*Odyssey of Style* 6). In *"Ulysses" in Progress*, Michael

Groden shows that Joyce himself repeatedly changed his mind during the labour of composition, and that the marked and regular discontinuities in the book we read emerged from the stages of a complex, prolonged, and tortuous genesis.[4]

Joyce's earlier works bear intimations of his interest in flouting classical precepts of formal unity and stylistic uniformity. The three opening stories of *Dubliners*, for instance, are narrated in the first person while all subsequent stories in the collection are told through the medium of impersonal third-person narration. In an analogous if reversed pattern, *A Portrait of the Artist as a Young Man* unfolds in the third person until its final pages, when the intimately focalized narration gives way to Stephen Dedalus's diary entries. In *Finnegans Wake* (1939) Joyce would go further, eliding beginning and ending into a single sentence to turn the whole book into "a commodius vicus of recirculation" (*FW* 1.2). As he revealed to Harriet Shaw Weaver in 1926: "The book really has no beginning or end. ... It ends in the middle of a sentence and begins in the middle of the same sentence" (*Letters I* 246).

Ulysses evinces the same interest in overhauling the traditional novelistic architecture of beginnings and endings. Joyce's letters show that he also thought about *Ulysses* in these broad, relatively nebulous terms. In October 1916 he announced: "I have almost finished the first part and have written out part of the middle and end" (*Letters II* 387). In a notebook he was using in the early months of 1918, Joyce jotted down a maxim encountered in a French-language copy of Aristotle's *Rhetoric*:

> – qui de soi a un commencement et une fin est de grandeur à être vue [sic] tout d'un coup sans donner de peine.
>
> [– that which in itself has a beginning and an ending is of such a size as to be wholly visible without difficulty.][5]

Interpretation of the note can only be speculative, but in the light of Joyce's structural innovations the extracted axiom reads as an emblem of his preoccupation with beginnings and endings and their relationship to aesthetic wholeness.

Three years later, as work on the book entered its final months, Joyce used the Aristotelian terms again to highlight his own subversions: "The *Ithaca* episode ... is in reality the end as *Penelope* has no beginning, middle or end" (*Letters I* 172). To upset the conventional novelistic sequence of beginning, middle and ending formed part of Joyce's plan for *Ulysses*.

Different Beginnings

How does *Ulysses* begin?

The question, straightforward though it may seem, is unmanageably vast, inviting a plethora of answers springing from different (if interrelated) types of investigation. The privileged field of enquiry might, for instance, be biographical: When did Joyce first conceive of *Ulysses* and how did events in his life impinge on the book's composition? It might be intratextual: How does *Ulysses* emerge from and reprise Joyce's own prior writings? Or intertextual: How did Joyce's reading inflect the writing of *Ulysses*, and how does the book insert itself into the matrix of existing texts? Such a listing, incomplete though it is, adumbrates a useful distinction between two kinds of beginning: the beginning of the compositional process that led to *Ulysses* on the one hand, and the beginning of the published text the reader experiences on the other.

In 1917 Joyce told Ezra Pound that he was writing *Ulysses* "as Aristotle would say, by different means in different parts."[6] It is from this choice to begin again in every episode that much of the novel's extreme originality derives. In September 1920 Joyce explained to Carlo Linati that:

> each adventure (that is, every hour, every organ, every art being interconnected and interrelated in the structural scheme of the whole) should not only condition but even create its own technique. Each adventure is so to say one person although it is composed of persons – as Aquinas relates of the angelic hosts. (*Letters I* 147)

Joyce's schemas offer intriguing representations of *Ulysses*'s eighteen-part structure.[7] Valery Larbaud referred to the book's episodes as "eighteen sub-divided panels" or "compartments" forming "a genuine example of the art of mosaic."[8] The headings in Joyce's tables, like his letter to Linati, emphasize both the individuality of the episodes and their intriguing multiplicity. By giving the episodes names and numbers that featured nowhere in *The Little Review* or in the published book ("chapters have no apparent relation to one another, and neither numbers nor titles," complained one early reviewer[9]), the schemas also make visible *Ulysses*'s substructures, entrenching the reader's sense of the book's segmentation. The Linati schema comprises temporal subheadings – "Dawn" (episodes 1–3), "Morning" (4–6), "Midday" (7–9), "Day" (10–15), "Midnight" (16–18), "Deep Night – Dawn" (after episode 18) – while the Gilbert schema features those Homeric headings – the "Telemachia" (episodes 1–3), the "Odyssey" (4–15), and the "Nostos" (16–18) – which present the book as a tripartite structure. These contending extra-diegetic articulations are fascinating because of their ambiguous status (why did Joyce, having written the Homeric chapter headings on the manuscript, remove them from the published text but provide them in these supplementary documents?), but also because they leave the text open to so many differing configurations.

Joyce's tables reflect and formalize the experience of *Ulysses* as a sequence of stops and starts. As such, they would seem to caution against over-investment in any one beginning at the expense of any other. These ceaseless deviations from the fictional norm and from its own pre-established norms pit *Ulysses* against "the (traditional) Book," which according to Barthes, "*connects, develops, runs,* and *flows.*"[10] But immersion in the text makes clear what cannot be inferred from the schematic grids: that the episodes – as Joyce intimated when he wrote of "every art being interconnected and interrelated in the structural scheme of the whole"– are as intricately woven together as they are different from each other. *Ulysses* is thus more accurately described as an organic continuum of beginnings than as a concatenation of discrete, end-stopped sections.[11]

Second Things First

But how – for the first-time reader approaching the text without knowledge of the schema – does *Ulysses* begin?

One answer is that it begins with its title, "Ulysses," the Roman, Latinate (and by association, colonial) form of a Homeric, Greek (and by association, colonized) name. In the first edition, this name was printed, at Joyce's insistence, on a carefully chosen, Hellenic shade of blue.[12] The word thus stands as a hint, on the very cover of the book, of the fraught relationship between colonial England and colonized Ireland which is one of the book's themes.

"Ulysses" signals a return as much as a beginning: a return, more specifically, to the *Odyssey*, one of the foundational texts of Western culture and a text which itself chronicles its hero's long-postponed return to his point of origin. In foregrounding its intertextual relationship to Homer's epic, and in doing so in translation (translation being a process whereby an original text produces a second text), Joyce's title is not merely the novel's first word, but also a second word. And to complicate things further, "Ulysses" is also, in another sense, the last word: the word that gives meaning to the book as a whole. *Ulysses*, as Kenner states, "come[s] equipped with a metal plate ... to tell us where to stand if we desire certain simplifications":

> He permitted himself one extraneous element only, attached to the book itself: one word of seven letters: the title: *Ulysses*. That title we may describe as an auctorial comment, the sole *remark* the author (otherwise invisible, paring his fingernails) permits himself amid a quarter-million words. ...
> We find Ulysses in *Ulysses* because the author told us to.[13]

The book, in other words, begins with an emphatic infringement of the authorial impersonality by which it otherwise so studiously abides.

How else does *Ulysses* begin?

With other second things. With Stephen Dedalus, son and heir to Simon Dedalus – a second Dedalus corresponding, as both schemas indicate, to Telemachus, son and heir to Odysseus. And this second Dedalus, corresponding to a second Ulysses, appears in a book whose opening reads like a sequel (or second book) to *A Portrait*. *Ulysses*, in other words, begins with a second-hand character wearing second-hand clothes[14] in a second-hand epic which begins like a second *Portrait*. This second Stephen is older, sadder, and more disillusioned, which perhaps explains the air of postlapsarian languor that hangs over the "Telemachiad." "Telemachus" begins with "Warm sunshine merrying over the sea" (*U* 1.306) at the dawn of a new day, but as Richard Ellmann remarks: "there is a curious air of corruption about the opening of *Ulysses*. It is not exactly the morning of creation, it is the morning after."[15] *Ulysses* begins, then, in an atmosphere of belatedness, of secondariness.

"Stately, Plump Buck Mulligan"

How else does *Ulysses* begin?

It begins with a first sentence: "Stately, plump Buck Mulligan came from the stairhead, bearing a bowl of lather on which a mirror and a razor lay crossed." (*U* 1.1–2) This gently springing, lightly alliterative opening – the first nine words, as Kenner notes, "mimick[ing] a Homeric hexameter"[16] – is often taken to be the first sentence of the book's "initial style," to use a phrase Joyce himself coined. In a letter sent to Harriet Shaw Weaver in August 1919, partly in defence of the stylistic kaleidoscope *Ulysses* was by then becoming, Joyce expressed sympathy for readers looking back nostalgically to the calmer waters with which *Ulysses* had begun: "I understand that you may begin to regard the various styles of the episodes with dismay and prefer the initial style much as the wanderer did who longed for the rock of Ithaca" (*SL* 242). The phrase's cryptic simplicity has become talismanic in Joyce criticism. In fact, *Ulysses's* stylistic beginnings are far more complex (and less initial) than Joyce's casual description would suggest.

Take the opening word. Is "stately" an adjective or adverb? The question, in a book which plays with syntax at every turn, is not as trivial as it may seem. Is Buck Mulligan "stately" in the same way as he is "plump" – as an apposition of adjectives would suggest – or does the word denote the manner of his comportment at this particular point – as an adverbial reading of "stately" would suggest? Richard Ellmann reads the word as an adjective denoting Mulligan's sturdy physicality, thereby setting the tone for a triad of episodes in which "the external world has to be posited before it can be countered and undermined" (*Liffey* 19). By contrast, John Porter Houston parses "stately" as an adverb, partly on the grounds of the word's likely allusion to the beginning of *Hamlet*, one of *Ulysses's* most prominent intertexts.[17] In Act I, scene 2, Horatio tells Hamlet about the apparitions of his father's ghost: "a figure like your father, /... / Appears before them, and with solemn march, / Goes slow and stately by them."[18] *Ulysses* begins, then, with a word that conjures another usurped and grieving son.

It also begins with a foretaste of the "pervasive strangeness" of Joyce's syntax (*Joyce and Prose* 20). "Stately" may seem anodyne, but the ambiguity of the term's syntactical role has consequences: It bifurcates meaning, and thereby alerts the reader, however subliminally, to the high degree of polysemy and allusiveness which characterizes Joyce's prose in all its various styles. "Stately" encodes an ambiguity as to whether Buck's stateliness is an essence or a manner. As such it is a forerunner to dozens of other adverbs and adverbial phrases which swarm the text in the opening pages: Mulligan "called out coarsely," "blessed gravely thrice the tower," "covered the bowl smartly," "said sternly," "cried briskly," "looked gravely," "said gaily," "said frankly," "shaved warily," "cried thickly," "wiped the razorblade neatly," "said quietly," "turned abruptly," and "shaved evenly and with care, in silence, seriously" – to quote only from the first three pages (*U* 1.6–7, 10, 17–18, 19, 28, 30, 34, 51, 56, 66, 71, 77, 86, 99). In "Telemachus" especially, the marked attention paid to manner and to mannerism itself amounts to an idiosyncratic stylistic mannerism. Kenner interprets this style's peculiarities as an indication that the characters are play-acting (Mulligan the 'stage-Irishman', Stephen the 'stage-poet'), exaggerating their own mannerisms and affectations on the stage-like platform of the Tower's gun rest (*Voices* 68, 69). Like the allusion to *Hamlet's* beginning, the effect is to augment the self-consciousness that suffuses *Ulysses's* textual threshold: "Joyce sensed," Kenner writes, "that the book should begin with someone who is deliberately, theatrically, beginning his day, and beginning it with an act of mockery" (*"Ulysses"* 34).

Adverbs are not the only part of speech to be accorded unusual prominence. Adjectival present participles also abound, generating an impression of ceaseless activity. Motion is imparted to habitually static scenes and objects: We read of "the surrounding land and the awaking mountains," "the shaking gurgling face," "the scrotumtightening sea," "the fraying edge of his shiny black coatsleeve," "his dangling watchchain," and "his talking hands" (*U* 1.10–11, 14, 78, 101, 514, 518). John Porter Houston provides a striking listing:

> In *Telemachus* Buck is involved in peeping, skipping, frowning, thrusting, swinging, flinging, tramping, howling, tossing, jumping, hacking, slapping, hewing, wheedling, lunging, blinking, growling, rasping, cramming, munching, droning, sighing, twisting, chiding, plunging, rummaging, clubbing, shouting, slinging, tugging, fluttering, capering, leaping, struggling, gurgling, and shaking

further noting that a number of these "indicate both a general kind of activity and the manner in which it is done" (*Joyce and Prose* 41). Throughout the episode, the narrative, in other words, continues to manifest the concern with manner evinced by the book's opening word.

Lawrence detects yet another pattern in the prose – a throng of introductory speech markers: "The proliferation of the following phrases in the early pages of the novel suggests that something strange is taking place in the narrative: 'he said sternly,' 'he cried briskly,' 'he said gaily'" (*Odyssey of Style* 45). For Lawrence, these "formulaic narrative constructions" are the stuff of "the unsophisticated prose of fourth-rate fiction" (*Odyssey of Style* 45). To account for this strand of bad writing, Kenner posits an Edwardian narrator, "moving characters about, and reporting their doings, in fluent unemphatic novelese, barely to be distinguished from a neutral idiom" (*Voices* 70). The novelese may be unemphatic, but it is not discreet enough to escape notice. And to notice its excesses – to be alert to the "adverbial mania," the hum of present participles, the litany of "he saids" – is to recognize the subtle parody which is already afoot in the opening pages: "[A] novel that begins this way parodies its own ability to tell a story. Even in the first chapter of the novel, Joyce begins to turn novelistic convention into novelistic cliché" (*Odyssey of Style* 45). Lawrence's account short-circuits Kenner's description of the trajectory of the book; whereas Kenner claims that "Joyce began *Ulysses* in naturalism and ended it in parody," naturalism and parody, as she shows, are in tension from the start (*Voices* ix). The initial style, whilst seeming to be merely naïve and

derivative – the Gilbert schema names "narrative (young)" as the technic
for "Telemachus" – is in fact already knowing, sophisticated, parodic. It is
like Stephen's "cold steel pen" with its split nib: at least double (*U* 1.153).

The initial style evinces several other dualities. The "bad" writing in
"Telemachus," for instance, cohabits with writing of arresting brilliance.
Mulligan has "smokeblue mobile eyes" and feels his shaven face "with
stroking palps of fingers" (*U* 1.126, 123). The diction is rare, crisply evocative. "Smokeblue" is one of hundreds of compounds coined by Joyce in
the book. The apposition of adjectives, "smokeblue mobile eyes," omit-
ting punctuation and disrupting conventional word order (without breaking any rules), is also typical of the liberties Joyce takes with syntax. In
a densely alliterative and allusive passage which loiters on the borderline
between Stephen-inflected free indirect discourse and interior monologue,
we read that "Woodshadows floated silently by through the morning
peace from the stairhead seaward where he gazed" (*U* 1.242–43). Kenner
deals with such sudden departures from "unemphatic novelese" by posit-
ing a second narrator: Where the first "attends to the chapter's housekeeping" in the manner of an Edwardian novelist, the second performs "many
little triumphs of linguistic virtuosity" (*Voices* 30). In the living room of
the Tower, for instance, "Two shafts of soft daylight fell across the flagged
floor from the high barbicans: and at the meeting of their rays a cloud of
coalsmoke and fumes of fried grease floated, turning" (*U* 1.315–17). While
for Kenner Joyce's "registration of so-many-things-almost-in-an-equal-
number-of-words" produces "miracles of one-word *naming*" (*Voices* 71,
73), for Ellmann, the hyperrealist precision of the prose brings to mind
the perfection of Adamic language: "Every object is defined as if Adam
has just given it a name, or as if Aristotle had just enmattered its essence"
(*Liffey* 9). In almost all such cases the exactitude, unconventionality and
lyrical swell of the prose is attributable to Stephen: It is he who looks
into Mulligan's "smokeblue mobile eyes" and sees his "stroking palps of
fingers." Likewise, it is Stephen who observes the progress of a ship at
the close of "Proteus," and whose words and rhythms sculpt each expertly
moulded phrase: "Moving through the air high spars of a threemaster, her
sails brailed up on the crosstrees, homing, upstream, silently moving, a
silent ship" (*U* 3.503–05).

As in *Dubliners* and *A Portrait*, *Ulysses*'s third-person narration is a very
finely graduated linguistic milieu, occasionally neutral but more often
shaped by syntactical and idiomatic elements appropriated from the
"gravitational field of the nearest person" (*Voices* 16). This is the Uncle

Charles Principle – an individuating technique identified and defined by Hugh Kenner. The procedure is named after the character of Uncle Charles in *A Portrait*, who, as we are told, "Every morning ... *repaired* to his outhouse" (*P* 60; my italics). Kenner remarks that in using this verb, the narration privileges the term Uncle Charles himself would use were he to mention his outhouse: "The Uncle Charles Principle entails writing about someone much as that someone would choose to be written about" (*Voices* 17, 21). Thanks to this technique, "the narrative point of view," from *Dubliners* to *A Portrait* to *Ulysses*, "unobtrusively fluctuates" (*Voices* 16). It is an extension of the Uncle Charles Principle that explains the arresting beauty of the woodshadows Stephen visualizes in "Telemachus" (a typically erudite and poetic response to Mulligan's recitation of Yeats's "Who Goes with Fergus," which evokes "the deep wood's woven shade").[19] Indeed, the reader of *A Portrait* may recognize the alliterative otherworldliness of the language as one of the defining characteristics of Stephen's thought processes in later chapters. Kenner's imagined second narrator is one who "has served an apprenticeship on *A Portrait of the Artist as a Young Man* and become a virtuoso of the Uncle Charles Principle" (*Voices* 71). The technique also extends to other characters. In "Lotus-Eaters," we see Bloom think in his own idiosyncratic way, despite the framing third-person narration: "He tore the flower gravely from its pinhold smelt its almost no smell and placed it in his heart pocket" (*U* 5.260–61). These minutely sensitive oscillations in the texture of the novel's free indirect discourse do not exhaust the variety of the initial style. Yet another phenomenon, distinct from dialogue and third-person narration, must be accounted for: interior monologue.

Interior Monologue

Amid the diverse continuities connecting the initial style of *Ulysses* to *Dubliners* and *A Portrait*, interior monologue is the great technical innovation, the vehicle of unrivalled effects of intimacy and immediacy.[20] Interior monologue makes characterization internal rather than external; it renders a character's thoughts in his or her own words, in the first person, and in the present tense. The technique makes a discreet début on the book's first page. "Chrysostomos," thinks Stephen to himself (*U* 1.26). Or so we later infer, once we have learnt to recognize short nominal sentences as one of interior monologue's staple forms. "Chrysostomos" – the name summoned to Stephen's mind by the sight of Mulligan's "even white

teeth glistening here and there with gold points" (*U* 1.25–26) – might be
a reference to Dion Chrysostomos (c. 50–117), the "golden-mouthed"
Greek rhetorician; St John Chrysostomos (c. 345–407), patriarch of
Constantinople and Father of the Early Church; Pope Gregory I (c. 540–
604), who sent an English mission to Ireland and was known there as
"Gregory Goldenmouth," or to all three (*"Ulysses" Annotated* 14). A dense
mesh of possible allusions, the snippet is representative of the laconic
erudition of Stephen's musings. As is typical of interior monologue, the
one-word sentence bears no accompanying sign of its plunge into the
character's stream of consciousness. Bloom's thoughts are sometimes as
economical ("Charnelhouses. Dreadful" – *U* 6.777), but are generally
more periphrastic, often (endearingly) speculative or ill-informed: "Black
conducts, reflects, (refracts is it?), the heat," "Broken heart. A pump after
all, pumping thousands of gallons of blood every day. One fine day it
gets bunged up: and there you are" (*U* 4.79–80, 6.673–75). What is lost
in arcane knowledge and linguistic sophistication, however, is gained in
frequently humorous down-to-earth simplicity: "Heavenly weather really.
If life was always like that. Cricket weather. Sit around under sunshades.
Over after over" (*U* 5.558–59).

Joyce excels at individuating his characters' thoughts: Stephen, Bloom,
and Molly (as well as the various characters to whom the technique is
extended in "Wandering Rocks") all think in their own characteristic
idiom and syntax. As Pound noted in 1921, "Joyce's characters not only
speak their own language, but they think their own language" (*Pound/Joyce*
195). The contrast is stark between Stephen's abstruse associative meta-
physical reflections in "Proteus" ("Ineluctable modality of the visible"),
Bloom's sparks of half-knowledge ("Chinese cemeteries with giant pop-
pies growing produce the best opium") and Molly's frank musings about
Bloom and other men ("I cant help it if Im young still can I its a wonder
Im not an old shrivelled hag before my time living with him so cold never
embracing me") (*U* 3.1, 6.769–70, 18.1398–1400).

Contemporary readers responded to this new kind of narrative with a
mixture of awe and disgust. To some, the intimacy the interior monologue
fostered was indecent: "from his pages," noted one aghast reviewer, "there
leap out at us all our most secret and most unsavoury private thoughts."[21]
Others commented on the heteroclite jumble wrought by Joyce's incomplete sentences – "the mixture of styles, of languages"[22] – and what seemed
like typographical and syntactical chaos: "Quotation marks for conversational passages are omitted; punctuation follows new and unknown rules;
sentences begin and forget to end."[23]

Virginia Woolf, however, was swift to recognize that Joyce, in *A Portrait* but especially in *Ulysses*, was writing the psychologically realistic fiction she advocated:

> Let us record the atoms as they fall upon the mind in the order in which they fall, let us trace the pattern, however disconnected and incoherent in appearance, which each sight or incident scores upon the consciousness. ... Any one who has read *The Portrait of the Artist as a Young Man* or what promises to be a far more interesting work, *Ulysses*, now appearing in the *Little Review*, will have hazarded some theory of this nature as to Mr. Joyce's intention.[24]

Woolf could tell, from the beginning alone, that what Joyce was achieving in *Ulysses* was revolutionary. Through the initial style's fluctuating precipitations of neutral narration, free indirect discourse, and interior monologue, he combined the unstinting realism of *Dubliners* and *A Portrait* with a radically new depiction of consciousness.

"A Mirror and a Razor Lay Crossed"

With these two aspects of Joyce's realism in mind, let us turn back to the book's opening sentence. On Mulligan's shaving bowl, "a mirror and a razor lay crossed." What are these objects doing here? On one level, they are to be taken literally as the implements of a morning shave. On another they are – partly by virtue of the "stately" ring of the opening words – symbolic, their significance extending beyond the momentary blasphemies of Mulligan's improvised black mass: Foregrounded as they are, they seem to have bearing on the text that is just beginning. The mirror, arch symbol of realist art, soon appears again, "cleft by a crooked crack," so that Stephen, his own image cleft in twain, grandiloquently declares it "a symbol of Irish art. The cracked lookingglass of a servant" (*U* 1.135–36, 146). The words recall Joyce's description of *Dubliners* – a more straightforwardly realistic text than *Ulysses* – as a "nicely polished looking-glass" held up to the people of Dublin (*SL* 90). If the realistic mirror is cracked in *Ulysses*, its fiendish, crooked cleft may be a sign, on the threshold of the text, of the many infringements to realist convention that lie in waiting, encoded in the text's beginning. *Ulysses*, it is already intimated here, may not be a mirror so much as a hall of broken mirrors – rather like that which Bloom encounters at the entrance to Nighttown (*U* 15.141–49) – each reflecting and distorting reality in its own distinctive way.

The razor also stands in a potentially illuminating relationship to earlier Joycean statements. In *Stephen Hero*, the highly autobiographical protagonist explains to his brother Maurice that "The modern spirit is vivisective".[25] Stephen Daedalus, like Flaubert and Zola before him, calls for modern literature to be scientific and impersonal – to slice through surfaces to reveal the truths that lie within.[26] In "Telemachus," Stephen wants his "cold steel pen" to be as surgical as a "lancet": not for nothing has Mulligan renamed him "Kinch, the knifeblade" (*U* 1.153, 152, 55).[27]

The mirror and the razor thus represent two strands of the initial style. On the one hand, Joyce's meticulous attention to the physical, social, and geographical realities of Dublin inscribes *Ulysses* within the realistic tradition represented by the mirror. On the other, his exploration of the inner mind through an array of stream-of-consciousness techniques extends the scope of realism to the realm of psychology symbolized by the vivisective razor.

The mirror and the razor, finally, lie *crossed*, indicating that in *Ulysses* the realisms these objects represent constantly blend and intersect. But neither mirror nor razor, whether considered singly or in combination, are sufficient to figure the stylistic elaborations of the book's later chapters: they may be crossed because, like all the styles of *Ulysses*, the realisms they stand for are ultimately outdone. "Any "style," writes Kenner, "is a system of limits" (*Voices* 81). This is why styles – including realisms – proliferate in *Ulysses*, each showing up the limitations of the others.

The initial style endures through the move into the "Odyssey" section, past the shock of the "Aeolian" headlines, the increasingly obtrusive stylistic games played in "Scylla and Charybdis" ("Piper! Mr Best piped" – *U* 9.275), the symphonic range of "Wandering Rocks" (with its orchestration of the simultaneous thoughts and actions of a vast cast of characters), and the musical extravaganza of "Sirens." It drops away in "Cyclops," only to return in the second half of "Nausicaa" before receding again before the pageant of styles staged in "Oxen of the Sun." The initial style is not confined to the initial stages of *Ulysses*. As such, it exemplifies the complexity of *Ulysses*'s beginnings – their refractoriness to definition and classification.

"Calypso"

Ulysses begins again, however, even while the initial style still holds sway. In the fourth episode, "Calypso," a new character, "Mr Leopold Bloom", takes centre-stage, and the book that opened as a sequel to *A Portrait* begins to slip its moorings (*U* 4.1). Pound – who would, when faced with "Sirens," come to wish Stephen had retained his privileged place in the narrative ("Where in hell is Stephen Tellemachus[sic]?" – *Pound/Joyce*

158) – greeted Joyce's new creation as an important breakthrough: "*Bloom* answers the query that people made after *The Portrait*. Joyce has created his second character; he has moved from autobiography to the creation of the complementary figure" (*Pound/Joyce* 139–140).

Readerly impressions of a new beginning in "Calypso" have to do with the temporal context as much as with the arrival of a new character. As the schemas confirm, the episode takes us back in time to 8:00 AM: We watch Leopold Bloom prepare breakfast just as we watched Mulligan prepare breakfast – the first of many correspondences between the second and first triad of episodes.[28] This rent in the tapestry of linear progression prompted one reviewer to describe Joyce's style as being "in the new fashionable kinematographic vein, very jerky and elliptical."[29] Another, more disgruntled reader complained that

> since he introduces several characters and seeks to show the sort of instinctive reaction they severally experience on the same event, he has to present the simultaneous consecutively. But neither paint nor words can thus convey, by means of a series, the simultaneous. We do not even float equably down the dim disgusting sewer, but continually find ourselves hitched back, with a jerk, to where we started from. Hence a new impression of a desperate nightmare.[30]

Pound, whose reception of the early episodes had at first been extremely positive, later dismissed Joyce's rewinding of the clock in "Calypso" as an irksome contrivance: "[T]he abrupt break after the *Telemachiad* (Stephen's chapters) is not particularly felicitous ... to the reader who is really reading *Ulysses* as a book and not as a design or a demonstration or a bit of archaeological research, this chop-off gives no pleasure and has no particular intrinsic merit" (*Pound/Joyce* 250).

The fissure effected in "Calypso" functions as a relatively gentle intimation of the more drastically defamiliarizing breaks to come. Even as we are "hitched back, with a jerk" to where we began, the endurance of the technical blend of the initial style and carefully planted "linking devices" (*Progress* 30) – which foster "[t]he symmetry of this second triad with the 'Telemachiad'" (*Odyssey of Style* 49) – smooth over this first major crack in the book's structure.

"Aeolus"

A second major break – a third beginning – comes in "Aeolus," the seventh episode. For Karen Lawrence, "Aeolus" marks "the beginning of the middle" of *Ulysses* because Stephen and Bloom's paths finally meet (*Odyssey of*

Style 56). But the greater development is stylistic. There are continuities: adverbs and present participles ("Slipping his words deftly into the pauses of the clanking he drew swiftly on the scarred woodwork" – *U* 7.139–40), for instance, make a noticeable return in this rhetorically minded episode ("rhetoric" is named as the "art" of the episode in both schemas). Yet the dominant impression – effected by the headlines which fragment the text of this episode – is one of stark and unexplained departure.

More than other episodes, "Aeolus" demands that *Ulysses*'s compositional history be taken into account since the magazine version of the text and the version published in book form differ markedly. "Aeolus" appeared in *The Little Review* in October 1918, but it was only during the final stages of his work, in 1921, that Joyce introduced the headlines that now constitute the episode's most striking feature.[31] Combined with the addition of dozens of rhetorical figures, the headlines substantially altered the role of "Aeolus" in the book: "As it appears in *The Little Review*, the chapter seems like a direct sequel to the first six; as it appears in the 1922 version of the book, it offers a departure from the 'novel' of the first six chapters and an adumbration of the experimentation of subsequent chapters" (*Odyssey of Style* 57). Like the book's title, but without so clearly suggesting a meaning, the centred and capitalized headlines of "Aeolus" derive from no identifiable source and bear no clear or consistent relationship to the sections of text that follow. As such, they entrench our sense of the novel's difficulty and impersonality while raising the kinds of questions – as to meaning and authorial intention – that the more flashily experimental later chapters also raise. Like "Calypso," "Aeolus" thus functions as a stepping-stone to later developments as well as a rupture with foregoing episodes.

As if to alert his readers to this combination of continuity and upheaval, Joyce makes this latest beginning hark back to his first. Under the fourth of the "Aeolian" headlines ("WILLIAM BRAYDEN, ESQUIRE, OF OAKLANDS, SANDYMOUNT" – *U* 7.38–39), "stately" – deployed in conjunction with its adverbial cognate, "statelily" – makes a comeback: "a stately figure entered between the newsboards of the *Weekly Freeman and National Press* and the *Freeman's Journal and National Press*. ... It passed statelily up the staircase, steered by an umbrella, a solemn beardframed face" (*U* 7.42–46). Stately/statelily: a cleft in the mirror. Is it an editorial mistake, in an episode set in a newsroom? Is it a deliberate declension, masterminded by a playfully omniscient if impeccably impersonal author? At all events, the beginning of "Aeolus" repeats the beginning of *Ulysses* with a difference. The book, at the moment of its first really ostentatious bifurcation – and in a pattern which will become increasingly pronounced as we progress through its segmented but organic body – begins to revisit and recycle its own elements, drawing attention to the bifurcation with which it began.

If *Ulysses* begins on its Greek-blue cover, on its first page, with its first word, with its first style(s), where does that beginning end? Is it over by the end of "Telemachus"? Does it end with the "Telemachiad"? Does it end with "Hades," the last chapter of the opening sextet? Or with "Aeolus," forerunner to the book's later stylistic extravagances? Does it end with "Scylla and Charybdis," *Ulysses*'s mid-way point? Or with "Wandering Rocks," an episode without analogue in the *Odyssey*? Does it end with "Sirens," in which the book appears to declare itself "Done" and enjoin itself to "Begin!" (*U* 11.62–63). Joyce's text both invites and resists these contending divisions. The book's structure offers itself up to analysis into sections on the one hand, and to synthesis into a single organic unit on the other. The observation also holds true of the initial style. Even before the range of its manifold configurations is scrutinized, the elements and "technics" of Joyce's schema bring into question the uniformity implied in his vague phrase. Lawrence calls Joyce's initial style his "signature style," a counterpoint to the "rhetorical masks" deployed in the later episodes of *Ulysses* (*Odyssey of Style* 8, 112). But the initial style does not precede Joyce's rhetorical masks: The initial style *is* a rhetorical mask. Nor does it recede before its successors, re-emerging as it does at numerous points along the way to Molly Bloom's final "Yes." The initial style is not a norm from which the book deviates: Joyce's "book of many turns" has no norm if not of its own ceaseless gyrations and reinventions, its own serial upheavals and beginnings (*Dislocutions* 121).

Notes

1 Aristotle, *Poetics*, trans. Malcolm Heath (London: Penguin Books, 1996), 5.1. Further references will be cited parenthetically in the text as *Poetics*.
2 Episodes of *Ulysses* ("Telemachus" to "Oxen of the Sun") appeared in *The Little Review* between March 1918 and September–December 1920. Shakespeare & Company published *Ulysses* in Paris on February 2, 1922 (*JJ* 442, 523).
3 Karen Lawrence, *The Odyssey of Style in "Ulysses"* (Princeton, NJ: Princeton University Press, 1981), p. 53. Further references will be cited parenthetically in the text as *Odyssey of Style*.
4 See Michael Groden, *"Ulysses" in Progress* (Princeton, NJ: Princeton University Press, 1977). Further references will be cited parenthetically in the text as *Progress*.

5 My translation. See notebook VIII.A.5 in *Joyce's Notes and Early Drafts for "Ulysses": Selections from the Buffalo Collection*, ed. Philip Herring (Charlottesville: University of Virginia Press, 1977), pp. 10, 25. The book Joyce was using (in a 1733 Amsterdam edition at the Zentralbibliothek in Zürich) is identified by Philip Herring as *La Rhétorique d'Aristote en françois*, trans. François Cassandre (Paris: 1654; 2nd edn, Amsterdam: J. Covens & C. Mortier, 1733). The extracted maxim is from III.ix. The final 'e' in "vue" is a spelling mistake on Joyce's part. Groden discusses the jotting in *"Ulysses" in Progress*, p. 80.

6 Joyce to Ezra Pound, 9 April 1917 in *Pound/Joyce: The Letters of Ezra Pound to James Joyce with Pound's Essays on James Joyce*, ed. Forrest Read (London: Faber & Faber, 1968), p. 105. Further references will be cited parenthetically in the text as *Pound/Joyce*.

7 Gifford and Seidman give the following account of the schemas: "The first schema was sent to Carlo Linati in September 1920; the second was loaned to Valery Larbaud late in 1921 and circulated (somewhat secretly) by Sylvia Beach during the 1920s. The second schema was first published in part in Stuart Gilbert's *James Joyce's 'Ulysses'* (New York, 1930; revised, 1952) and finally published in full, edited by H. K. Croessman, in *James Joyce Miscellany*, 2d ser., ed. Marvin Magalaner (Carbondale, IL, 1959)." See Don Gifford with Robert J. Seidman, *"Ulysses" Annotated: Notes for James Joyce's "Ulysses"* (London: University of California Press, 1998), p. 12n2. Both schemas are reproduced in James Joyce, *Ulysses*, ed. Jeri Johnson (Oxford: Oxford University Press, 1993), pp. 734–35 and 736–39 respectively. Further references will be cited parenthetically in the text as *"Ulysses" Annotated*.

8 Valery Larbaud, "James Joyce," *Nouvelle Revue Française* xviii (April 1922), pp. 385–405, repr. in *James Joyce: The Critical Heritage*, Vol. I, 1902–1927, ed. Robert H. Deming (London: Routledge & Kegan Paul, 1970), p. 261.

9 Holbrook Jackson, "*Ulysses* à la Joyce," in *To-Day* ix (June 1922), pp. 47–49, repr. in Deming, *The Critical Heritage*, p. 199.

10 Roland Barthes, "Littérature et discontinu," in *Essais critiques* (Paris: Seuil, 1964), pp. 175–87, quoted in the original French and in translation in *Odyssey of Style*, pp. 60–61.

11 This agrees with Fritz Senn's sense of Joyce's entire corpus: "Joyce's works can be seen, with equal validity, either as one great whole or as a series of self-contained units." See *Joyce's Dislocutions: Essays on Reading as Translation*, ed. John Paul Riquelme (Baltimore, MD: Johns Hopkins University Press, 1984), p. 121. Further references will be cited parenthetically in the text as *Dislocutions*.

12 As Ellmann recounts, "It was bound in the Greek colors – white letters on a blue field – that he considered lucky for him, and suggested the myth of Greece and of Homer, the white island rising from the sea" (*JJ* 524).

13 Hugh Kenner, *Joyce's Voices* (Rochester, NY; McLean, IL; London: Dalkey Archive Press, 2007), pp. 59–60. Further references will be cited parenthetically in the text as *Voices*.

14 "Mother is putting my new secondhand clothes in order," notes Stephen at the end of *A Portrait* (p. 252); "How are the secondhand breeks?" asks Mulligan in "Telemachus" (*U* 1.113).

15 Richard Ellmann, *"Ulysses" on the Liffey* (London: Faber and Faber, 1972), pp. 8–9. Further references will be cited parenthetically in the text as *Liffey*.

16 Hugh Kenner, *Ulysses*, rev. edn (Baltimore, MD: Johns Hopkins University Press, 1987), p. 34. Further references will be cited parenthetically in the text as *"Ulysses."*

17 John Porter Houston, *Joyce and Prose: An Exploration of the Language of "Ulysses"* (Cranbury, NJ: Associated University Presses, 1989), p. 19. By the end of the episode, Mulligan will have teased Stephen about his outlandish Shakespearean theory, later the centrepiece of "Scylla and Charybdis" ("He proves by algebra that Hamlet's grandson is Shakespeare's grandfather and that he himself is the ghost of his own father"), and Haines likened the Martello Tower to Elsinore ("this tower and the cliffs here remind me somehow of Elsinore) (*U* 1.555–57, 566–67). *Hamlet* was also on Stephen's mind at the end of *A Portrait* ("A moment before the ghost of the ancient kingdom of the Danes had looked forth through the vesture of the hazewrapped city" – *P* 168–69) and as such functions as an intertextual bridge between Joyce's two texts. Further references will be cited parenthetically in the text as *Joyce and Prose*.

18 Shakespeare, *Hamlet*, ed. Harold Jenkins (London: Methuen & Co., 1982), Act 1, sc. 2, lines 199–202, pp. 192–93.

19 See *U* 1.239–41. Also see W. B. Yeats, "Who Goes with Fergus?" in *The Collected Poems of W. B. Yeats*, ed. Richard J. Finneran (New York: Scribner Paperback Poetry, 1996), p. 43.

20 Although Joyce famously credited the discovery and first use of the technique to Édouard Dujardin, author of *Les Lauriers sont coupés* (see *JJ* 126), it is difficult, reading that book, to believe that its author really contributed anything beyond the spark of an initial idea. There are worlds between the crisp economy of Joyce's interior monologue and Dujardin's turgid, affected prose.

21 S. P. B. Mais, "An Irish Revel: And Some Flappers," *Daily Express* (25 March 1922), n. p., repr. in *Critical Heritage*, p. 191.

22 C. C. Martindale, *"Ulysses,"* *Dublin Review* clxxi (1922): repr. in *Critical Heritage*, p. 205.

23 Holbrook Jackson, *"Ulysses* à la Joyce," in *To-Day* ix (June 1922): pp. 47–49, repr. in Deming, *The Critical Heritage*, p. 199.

24 Virginia Woolf, "Modern Novels," *Times Literary Supplement* (10 April 1919), repr. as "Modern Fiction" in *The Common Reader* [1925] (London: Hogarth Press, 1948), p. 189.

25 James Joyce, *Stephen Hero*, ed. Theodore Spencer (1944), revised edition incorporating additional manuscript pages from Yale and Cornell University libraries, ed. John J. Slocum and Herbert Cahoon (New York: New Directions Publishing Corporation, 1969), p. 186.

26 Flaubert called for the application to art of "all the precision of the physical sciences." See Gustave Flaubert, *Selected Letters*, trans. Geoffrey Wall

(Harmondsworth: Penguin, 1997), p. 248. Zola called for the application to literature of the "experimental method." See Émile Zola, *Le Roman expérimental* [1880] (Paris: Flammarion, 2006), p. 79 (my translation).

27 "Circe" – that expressionistic alternative to the vivisection of interior monologue – appears to recall and to fulfil Stephen's aspirations when Mrs Bellingham orders Mrs Mervyn Talboys to "Vivisect" Bloom (*U* 15.1105).

28 For "A Timetable of Corresponding Events and Implied Action in *Ulysses*," see Ian Gunn and Clive Hart with Harald Beck, *James Joyce's Dublin: A Topographical Guide to the Dublin of "Ulysses"* (London: Thames and Hudson, 2004), pp. 81–86.

29 Unsigned review, "A New *Ulysses*," part of the column "Diary of a Man about Town" (8 April 1922): p. 4, repr. in *Critical Heritage*, p. 194.

30 C. C. Martindale, "*Ulysses*," *Dublin Review* clxxi (1922): repr. in *Critical Heritage*, p. 205.

31 See *Progress*, pp. 60 and 64–66.

CHAPTER 5

Character, Plot, and Myth

Margot Norris

What would it have been like to buy a copy of James Joyce's *Ulysses* hot off the press in 1922 and try to read it? Hugh Kenner suggests that in those early days "*Ulysses* seemed, to most readers able to pick up a copy, not a mirror of Homer, not a story at all, but something as featureless as a telephone directory."[1] The work's extravagant stylistic experiments undoubtedly daunted readers trying to figure out its characters and plot, as they still baffle many first-time readers in the twenty-first century. Over time, scholarship came to the rescue to offer explanation and illumination. Kenner credits two early works with ushering this process along: Stuart Gilbert's 1931 *James Joyce's "Ulysses"*[2] and Frank Budgen's 1934 *James Joyce and the Making of "Ulysses."*[3] Gilbert offered a particularly helpful device in his book by including a version of the schema that Joyce had sent to Carlo Linati for his personal use in 1920 and which had been circulated largely in secrecy until then, according to Richard Ellmann (*JJ* 521). The schema shows that each of the eighteen chapters of Joyce's novel correspond to an adventure, character, or figure in Homer's classical epic, the *Odyssey*, and this reference does indeed provide an important "key," as it were, to the work. This recognition also speaks to the broader context of Joyce's enterprise in modernism, the period of literary history in the early twentieth century often characterized by the stunning marriage between an unprecedented realism in poetry and fiction infused by both the myths and structural principles of classical literature.

Set in Dublin on June 16, 1904, *Ulysses* preserves the unities of time, place, and action that structure classical drama even as it presents a modern world of bustling commercialism, colonial politics, and popular culture. We are introduced to three major figures – Stephen Dedalus, Leopold Bloom, and his wife Molly Bloom – and to a huge cast of minor characters. Do we discuss them in the light of the Homeric framework or not? The question reflects the complex relationship between *Ulysses* and the *Odyssey*, beginning with the fact that their connection is implicit rather than explicit. Only the work's title points directly to Homer's work, and it is important to remember that even though Joyce's Odyssean references have become the conventional names for its eighteen chapters, such titles as "Telemachus" or "Calypso" appear nowhere in the book. Also, even though *Ulysses* is cited as the exemplar of a work with an intertext in Gerald Prince's *Dictionary of Narratology*, it is by no means clear that the relationship between the classical epic and the modern novel is parallel rather than ironic – or even counterfactual.[4] Does *Ulysses* revisit the *Odyssey* to show us their similarities, or does it ask how Homer's text might appear if its events had turned out differently? We now have sophisticated scholarship by Keri Ames to provide a complex evaluation of the classical connection, but Hugh Kenner's admonition remains valid: "We need to observe what the characters are up to before we can ask what to make of the Homeric presence."[5]

So what are Stephen Dedalus, Leopold Bloom, and Molly Bloom up to? The best way to approach this question may be in reverse, by asking how a novelistic plot operates and what features constitute characters in fiction. The new fields of narratology and Possible Worlds Theory also complicate these questions, but we can simplify them by restricting the initial focus to conflict and action. Plot requires action, and the three main figures in *Ulysses* are introduced as suffering from a variety of conflicts that prompt them to take actions – which they may or may not pursue, and which may or may not be successful in resolving their conflicts. These conflicts are often intermeshed and related. Stephen Dedalus is shown in the first episode ("Telemachus") as the victim in an abusive relationship with a friend and roommate who teases, mocks, and humiliates him, at times in front of an English visitor. This inequity reflects a difference in class, since both the friend, Buck Mulligan, and the Oxford student, Haines, enjoy greater affluence and social standing than the nearly destitute Stephen, whose family has fallen apart since the death of his mother a year before. The painful topic of his mother's dying represents another conflict for Stephen, who refused to pray at her deathbed following his difficult break with his Catholic religion and who is consequently troubled by guilt. Mulligan and Haines appear to appreciate Stephen's intellect and talent but are also poised to exploit him, as when Haines asks to publish Stephen's sayings without offering recompense. Each of these conflicts have larger political resonances since they reflect differences in class, the oppressive role of the church, and the effects of colonialism that have given an Englishman access to the Gaelic language that many Irish people (including both Stephen and Joyce) no longer possess. This last issue relates to Stephen's most pressing conflict: how to ignite a career as an Irish artist and writer while working within the dominant English literary tradition.

How does Stephen deal with these conflicts in the chapters that follow "Telemachus"? The response to this question not only sketches out the plot of Stephen's story in the novel, but also illuminates the complex ways that plot itself can operate in a work of fiction. Stephen's first act follows soon after "Telemachus": When walking along Sandymount strand in "Proteus," he decides not to return to the Martello tower where he had been living with Mulligan. He also works on his art in this episode, composing a vampire poem that alludes to Irish writers (Bram Stoker) and translators (Douglas Hyde) – a sign that he may be trying to refigure himself as a specifically Irish artist (*U* 3.397–98, 7.522–26). This creative moment is followed by another in the newspaper office, when Stephen offers the men there a parable he has constructed about two elderly Dublin spinsters whose outing to the top of Nelson's pillar echoes another parable of Moses overlooking the promised land, which he has just heard. Stephen here demonstrates a further advance in his Irish art by displaying a unique form of realism as a mode of illuminating what Joyce himself called the "paralysis" of Irish life (*Letters II* 134). Stephen next stands up Mulligan and Haines, whom he was to meet at a pub, by going to the National Library of Ireland instead and there presenting his novel theory of Shakespeare to a group of Irish literati. This becomes his boldest bid yet for acceptance into and recognition by the Irish literary establishment. Up to this point, we might consider the plot of Stephen's story euphoric – a story line with the promise that things will change for the better. But by the end of this episode ("Scylla and Charybdis"), the plot turns dysphoric, with matters changing for the worse rather than becoming better. The literary figures George Russell and John Eglinton are not impressed with Stephen's brilliant analysis of Shakespeare's life and work, and Stephen learns that he is invited neither to the distinguished writer George Moore's soirée, nor to contribute his poetry to a collection of young Irish poets' verses.

If we turn now to Stephen's mythic counterpart in the *Odyssey*, how does he compare? While Odysseus is delayed on his journey back to his kingdom and family in Ithaca, his son Telemachus has had to watch his mother's suitors despoil the palace and usurp his prerogatives. His response to this crisis is to search for his father with the questionable support of surrogates along the way. Stephen tackles his own usurpers both more and less directly. Like Telemachus, he does confront them, making

Mulligan defensive about his offense to Stephen, and reminding Haines that independence is not easy for a country under considerable Catholic and British control. But he takes additional actions without a father's or a surrogate's support by forging ahead with the production of his art and his efforts to engage patrons on his behalf. Stephen's plot thereby takes on a tragic dimension. His recent history as a wastrel, failing to repay loans to his creditors, suggests that Stephen is to blame for his own failures. After his failure at the library, Mulligan has him once again in tow. We see little more of Stephen until later in the evening when he is already quite drunk, disporting with Mulligan and other medical students at the Holles Street maternity hospital, where Leopold Bloom becomes concerned about him. Hugh Kenner suggests that Stephen may take a swing at Mulligan before going off with his friend Lynch to Dublin's red light district.[6] If so, he again tries to disentangle himself from his usurper. At the house of prostitution to which Bloom has followed him, Stephen may finally experience a moment of catharsis as he relives in fantasy his encounter with the literati and meets his dead mother's challenge to repent with a resounding "*Non serviam*" (*U* 15.4228). His conflicts may not be resolved, but they have been confronted.

Stephen differs more significantly from Telemachus in his relationship to his parents. Telemachus is devoted to and protective of his mother and dependent on his father to restore the family's rights in Ithaca. Stephen Dedalus, however, is in conflict with his mother and avoids rather than seeks a father on whom he has learned not to rely for protection or support. We might construe this to mean that he is a stronger figure than his mythic counterpart, with a complex inner life that requires him to meet his challenges on moral, cultural, and social levels – and to meet them alone. Yet his most complicated relationship on this particular day in Dublin will play out in relation to a surrogate father he never sought or pursued, but who nonetheless takes it upon himself to protect and care for a now homeless Stephen Dedalus. And it is here that the novel will confound the reader with respect to plot and character by providing an uncertain outcome to Stephen's adventure in *Ulysses*. The climax of the interaction between surrogate father and son – Leopold Bloom and Stephen Dedalus, safely back in the Bloom home on 7 Eccles Street after a long, eventful night – occurs when Stephen disrupts the growing friendship between the two men by responding to Bloom's singing of the anthem of Zion with his own singing of an anti-Semitic ballad. This act is difficult to decipher partly because the style of the "Ithaca" episode makes his motive and his response to seeing Bloom's surprise and discomfort unclear. Also, the action is out of character for Stephen, who offered his own trenchant critique of Shakespeare's anti-Semitism earlier that day at the library. Is this offense inadvertent on Stephen's part, or perhaps an unconscious effort to repel Bloom's kindly patronage in the interest of maintaining his independence and freedom of action? The question remains both controversial and irresolvable.

So what about Bloom? What is Bloom up to on this day, and how does he compare with his Homeric prototype, Odysseus? Like Stephen, Bloom suffers a series of conflicts, some of which have an uncanny resemblance to Stephen's own. He also suffered devastating familial losses in his past – not only a father who committed suicide in the despair of widowerhood, but also an infant son who died within days of his birth eleven years prior to the events of the novel. And just as Stephen feels guilt in relation to his mother's death, Bloom feels guilt and anguish over the death of the baby boy, although its source is totally different. Both men feel shadowed by usurpers on this day, although again, in different arenas of their lives. Stephen sees Mulligan and Haines enjoy insider status among Dublin's Irish literati and intellectuals, while he himself is in danger of becoming increasingly sidelined. Bloom feels himself in danger of being replaced in Molly's affection by a lover, Hugh Boylan, who threatens the comfortable home life he enjoys with his wife. For both men, nationality and race is another potential source of conflict, as Stephen struggles with positioning himself as a specifically Irish artist, while Bloom's Jewish background may be responsible for the increasing social marginalization he suffers over the course of the day. Stephen could do beneficial work as an Irish artist, he feels (and as his "Parable of the Plums" demonstrates), while Bloom could contribute to Irish political welfare with his pacifism and utopian socialism. But the men receive neither credit for their talents nor encouragement for their quiet ambitions in these areas. These related conflicts set the conditions for potential sympathy and friendship between Stephen and Bloom, although their encounters in the different venues of their nighttime sojourns do not yet constitute a bond of communion.

How then is Bloom an Odyssean counterpart? He is certainly no Odysseus when it comes to steering a ship. Molly swore she would never get into a boat with him again after he nearly capsized a rowboat when the water became rough during an outing in Bray (*U* 18.954–60). According to Frank Budgen, Joyce admired Odysseus less as a warrior than as a figure of wisdom and courage in the face of trials (*The Making of "Ulysses"* 16). Keri Ames also construes Odysseus less as a heroic figure than as a skilled survivor.[7] In the case of Bloom, this may be reflected in a day of relatively little positive action in favor of what critic Marie-Laure Ryan calls "habitual doings" or "repetitive gestures pursuing maintenance goals such as surviving in the world of everyday life."[8] Bloom's challenges are often psychological, and his coping mechanism is one of a deliberate passivity that accounts for at least some of the plotless effect of the novel. At the same time, Bloom, like Odysseus, encounters a number of what Ryan calls "happenings" or accidental occurrences that, unlike actions, are not produced by the characters but can nonetheless have important effects on the plot (*Possible Worlds* 129). In the case of Bloom, the chief example of this is the problematic *Throwaway* misunderstanding: Bantam Lyons's mistaken assumption that Bloom has given him a tip on a long-shot in the Gold Cup horse race, followed by Lenehan's error in concluding that Bloom has hit the jackpot when the dark horse wins. Although Bloom never learns of this error, the men in Barney Kiernan's assume that he keeps his winnings secret to avoid standing drinks; this misunderstanding inspires much of the animus that explodes in the citizen's anti-Semitic attack on him. But even without understanding its cause, Bloom will be obliged to react and cope with this in the course of the day.

The passivity Bloom cultivates to deal with his psychological Homeric trials at times appears to border on repression. This is most notable in his social relations with other Dubliners. Bloom is introduced to us as a self-confident individual, comfortable in his own skin and in his judgments of the world around him, with no signs of social insecurity. His first contacts with men outside his home show him deciding not to consort with figures who do not impress him: He defers becoming friendly with Dlugacz, is a bit contemptuous of M'Coy, and recoils from the unclean Bantam Lyons. But as the day proceeds, Bloom is the last to enter the carriage in "Hades," is treated rudely by Miles Crawford, and is disparaged behind his back by Nosey Flynn and a succession of other characters. Yet Bloom rarely registers these slights and has apparently internalized none of their potentially anti-Semitic implications. He spends little time feeling injured or mistreated, and even when he is aware of an animus, as in the case of John Henry Menton, his suspicion of "bias" as a cause appears to refer more to the angle of the ball in a game of bowls than to a racial response (*U* 6.1012). But when mention of race becomes too overt to be ignored in Barney Kiernan's pub, Bloom counters it directly and vigorously. "And I belong to a race too ... that is hated and persecuted," he retorts to insidious questions about his nationality in "Cyclops" (*U* 12.1467). In his own estimation, his response to the citizen's attack is both measured and effective: "He called me a jew and in a heated fashion offensively. So I without deviating from plain facts in the least told him his God, I mean Christ, was a jew too" (*U* 16.1082–84). Bloom's courage is exemplified in the strength to resist feeling slighted, injured, bitter, or resentful by trusting his own worthiness and thereby refusing to internalize the judgments of men less worthy than himself.

Bloom's strategy of passivity is far more problematic as a way of dealing with his most painful conflict on this day: his suspicion that Molly's 4:00 PM appointment with her impresario, Boylan, will lead to an affair. This event has significance for the plot of *Ulysses* on two levels: the deepening of the characters produced by the complexity of its causes, and the creation of suspense with respect to its actual outcome. Understanding why an impending adultery clouds this particular day requires the reader to reconstruct a complex family dynamic set in motion by little Rudy's death eleven years earlier. Bloom is devastated by this loss, but instead of interpreting it as a cruel twist of fate, he attributes it to the baby's conception as the product of Molly's indecent arousal by two copulating dogs outside her window. Bloom appears to blame himself, but also blames Molly, as we learn from her monologue late in the novel ("it wasnt my fault we came together when I was watching the two dogs" – *U* 18.1446). This guilt and blame produce a partial sexual dysfunction that keeps him from internal sex with Molly, in turn frustrating her and stoking her need to feel desirable and satisfied once again. The larger context of this particular plot element is to place *Ulysses* into the generic category of the adultery novel, whose chief nineteenth-century exemplars include *Madame Bovary* by Gustave Flaubert and *Anna Karenina* by Leo Tolstoy, two writers Joyce particularly admired. *Ulysses* makes several important contributions to the genre. Joyce offers a much greater elaboration of the husband's perspective and responsibility for the problem even as the novel refrains from punishing the adulterous wife with remorse and suicide as Flaubert and Tolstoy do. As a result, *Ulysses* functions more specifically as a *marriage novel* than as an adultery novel, with a much more concentrated focus on the marital dynamic than on the emotional vectors of the affair. Suspense is produced because whether or not the affair occurs remains unverified until the very last chapter. The reader is thereby suspended between the foreshadowing implicit in Bloom's anxious suspicion and the implicit promise of the Homeric analogue that the novel's Penelope will ward off suitors and remain faithful to her husband.

Given Bloom's initial despair in "Calypso," he struggles to process his marital crisis in the course of his day: "Will happen, yes. Prevent. Useless:

can't move," he thinks (*U* 4.447–48). He acknowledges at times that he could intervene in the upcoming event – by returning home at the appointed hour, for example. He could, of course, also confront Molly in the morning, or even Boylan in the afternoon, when he sees him enter the Ormond Bar just before four. Instead, Bloom sidesteps conflict resolution. He satisfies his own sexual needs by turning a paid typist and correspondent into an (arguably ineffective) dominatrix, and by masturbating at Gerty MacDowell's minor provocation of lifted skirt and raised leg. Only much later, at Bella Cohen's brothel in Nighttown, does Bloom confront his needs and fears in much more dramatic form, albeit strictly in fantasies that may never rise to the level of his consciousness or leave residual memories when the evening is over. Yet the fantasy confrontations in "Circe" nonetheless address all levels of conflict that Bloom has experienced on this day. His social disregard is met with a wish-fulfillment scenario giving him a role as an Irish savior and martyr, similar to the politician Charles Stewart Parnell whom Joyce admired. Bloom's grief over the loss of Rudy lets him imagine himself as the mother of eight wonderful sons, "*respectably dressed and wellconducted, speaking five modern languages fluently and interested in various arts and sciences*" (*U* 15.1824–26). His masochistic desires allow him to turn the mercenary brothel madam into the dominatrix eluded by the morning letter writer who dislikes "that other world" of erotic fantasy (*U* 5.245). And his reading of Sacher-Masoch's fiction prompts him to imagine himself as a liveried servant and antlered cuckold ushering Boylan into his wife's bedroom – a scenario that lets Bloom's masochistic proclivities mix his anguish over the feared adultery with at least some pleasure. "Circe" does not resolve Bloom's conflicts, but it obliges him to confront them in forms that are manageable and that therefore offer at least the possibility of catharsis.

This may account for the surprising "equanimity" Bloom feels in "Ithaca" – following envy, jealousy, and abnegation – after perceiving (if only in imagination) traces of Boylan's presence in his bed at the end of the night. There is still no confrontation with Molly in the bedroom, and she actually interrogates him about his whereabouts when they speak briefly before Bloom goes to sleep. That interrogation returns us to the Homeric homecoming of Odysseus to Ithaca, which requires a series of tests before Penelope is convinced that the returned figure is indeed her husband and before they are reunited in their fabled marriage bed. The bed cannot be moved because it is partly constructed from a living olive tree, as only Odysseus would know. In *Ulysses*, the secret of the marriage bed may take the form of Bloom's notice that the furniture has been moved (a detail Hugh Kenner has discussed[9]) which functions as a veiled warning to Bloom that Boylan is making inroads not only with his wife but also into his home. How Bloom will react to all this remains unknown; further answers to the resolution of the marital conflict shift finally to the last chapter of *Ulysses* with Molly Bloom's detailed and unvarnished monologue. Here we will learn that adultery has indeed occurred, that Molly has taken Boylan as a lover, that the sex was exhilarating, and that she looks forward to traveling to her Belfast concert with Boylan alone, since Bloom will be visiting Ennis on the anniversary of his father's death and will not accompany them. Does this mean the end of the marriage, in total opposition to the outcome of the Homeric epic? We will never know, but we do learn that Molly Bloom's own way of dealing with the marital conflict is more active and direct than Bloom's, if still surprisingly complex. She may not resist her suitors, as Penelope does, but she nonetheless keeps a sharp eye on her marriage and on the stakes of her maneuver.

Keri Ames has argued that shifts in the cultural and historical context between the writing of the *Odyssey* and the time of *Ulysses* make the counterfactual situation of the Blooms plausible, even though they entail a "full inversion of sex roles" between husband and wife. "In some sense, Odysseus has become Molly, and Penelope has become Leopold," Ames writes ("The Oxymoron of Fidelity" 163). Molly's keen intelligence lets her see through people and situations that fail to make perfect sense, including her husband's innocent demeanor and protestations. She is sure he came somewhere and speculates that he was either with a prostitute or has some woman on the sly, having seen him cover up a letter he was writing (*U* 18.49). Without the full context, her interpretation is not quite right – Bloom was in Nighttown for paternalistic rather than erotic reasons, after all – but her sense that Bloom is also out there seeking sexual satisfaction is correct. Her speculation that he may be rekindling an old romance with Josie Breen is also off the mark, but she makes it clear that she would handle the matter forcefully if it emerged that something was going on between them: "Id just go to her and ask her do you love him and look her square in the eyes she couldnt fool me" (*U* 18.193–94). Bloom could take a lesson from his wife about how to handle a rival, we may feel. What are her feelings about Boylan, given her repeated bouts of jealousy over her husband's possible interest in other women? Boylan has certainly given her pleasure on this day, and she clearly enjoys the sex, likes the fact that he has money, and in general appreciates his ability to satisfy present needs that her marital and economic situation at this time fail to fulfill. But she displays little admiration for his character, and before long offers a relatively scathing assessment of him as an "ignoramus" with "no manners nor no refinement" who "doesnt know poetry from a cabbage" (*U* 18.1370, 1368, 1370–71). In contrast, she counters her criticism of Bloom's assorted flaws with equally generous concessions to his many virtues. There are hints throughout that Boylan is less a grand passion than a device for giving her leverage to negotiate her marital dilemma. He could serve as a trigger for arousing Bloom's jealousy ("Ive a mind to tell him every scrap" – *U* 18.1515) and as a warning to her husband that he cannot take her fidelity and loyalty for granted indefinitely.

There is, of course, more to Molly Bloom than just her marital problem and her need to find a tactical resolution. Her background, it turns out, is arguably more complicated than even Bloom's Hungarian-Jewish heritage. Molly grew up in Gibraltar, we learn, with an Irish father who was a drum major with the British forces there – presumably raising her alone because marriage to her Jewish mother was culturally impossible. This experience gives her a broader horizon than many other Dubliners, and endows her with a more complex colonial status. The peculiarities of their backgrounds and their atypical appearances as Irish persons give Molly and Bloom a common bond from the very beginning. Gibraltar was also the scene of Molly's first romance with a young man named Mulvey, whose courtship of her prefigured features of her subsequent courtship by Bloom: occurring in May, on a picnic out of doors, with allusions to flowers both literal and figurative. Molly's powerful memories of Gibraltar on this night arouse her vivid romantic memories of Bloom's proposal on Howth Head at the end of her monologue. But even before this, Molly makes some plans that augur well for her marriage in the days to come – her planned trip to Belfast with Boylan notwithstanding. She decides she will serve Bloom the breakfast of eggs in bed he requests, and given that Stephen may return, she will go to the market, order some flowers, and clean the ivory keys of the piano in case there is an occasion for music and cigarettes that evening. She also plans to offer Bloom sexual satisfaction, not on her terms but on his, by accommodating his fetishes, playing his question and answer games, talking dirty, and generally working to excite him. Finally, as she is beginning to drift off to sleep, her memories of the first time she made love with Bloom powerfully evoke his own memories earlier in the day. Husband and wife are on the same wavelength in this respect, and there remains hope for this marriage yet.

Unlike the *Odyssey*, which appears to offer a general and satisfactory resolution to all the conflicts of its protagonists, *Ulysses* remains open-ended and suspenseful even at the novel's close. The most worrisome issue concerns Bloom's future if the false rumors about his secrecy and stinginess are spread around Dublin by the bill collector who narrates the "Cyclops" episode, thereby fueling further anti-Semitic sentiments against him. Will Stephen Dedalus, the recipient of Bloom's great kindness on this day, counteract this danger by telling people how Bloom looked after him, protected his money, saved him from possible arrest, fed him cocoa, and offered him a room to spend the night and possibly stay on if he wished? Or will he continue to be preoccupied with his own discouraging situation as a talented artist who cannot get a career off the ground in Dublin, who has no reliable friends at this point in his life, and whose family continues on a downward spiral into poverty. Margaret McBride offers the optimistic assessment that Stephen may go on to write *Ulysses* after this day, thereby redeeming both Bloom and himself – but the text offers no specific hints with respect to this possibility.[10] And the upcoming concert tour of Belfast with Boylan leaves Molly Bloom's strategies in dealing with her marital dilemmas as risky as before. Myth provides Joyce with illuminating parallels, ironies, and alternatives for structuring his story of early twentieth-century life in Ireland's capital, and he daringly crafts a far more complex set of characters with more intractable conflicts and uncertain resolutions than those imagined by Homer.

Notes

1 Hugh Kenner, *"Ulysses,"* rev. ed. (Baltimore, MD: Johns Hopkins University Press, 1987), p. 2.

2 Stuart Gilbert, *James Joyce's "Ulysses": A Study by Stuart Gilbert* (New York: Vintage Books, 1952).

3 Frank Budgen, *James Joyce and the Making of "Ulysses"* (Bloomington: Indiana University Press, 1973). Further references to this text will be cited parenthetically in the text as *The Making of "Ulysses."*

4 See Gerald Prince, *A Dictionary of Narratology*, rev. ed. (Lincoln: University of Nebraska Press, 2003), p. 46.

5 Kenner, *"Ulysses,"* p. 19.

6 Ibid., p. 116.

7 Keri Elizabeth Ames, "The Oxymoron of Fidelity in Homer's *Odyssey* and Joyce's *Ulysses*," *Joyce Studies Annual* 14 (Summer 2003): 163. Further references will be cited parenthetically in the text as "The Oxymoron of Fidelity." Also see Ames, "The Rebirth of Heroism from Homer's *Odyssey* to Joyce's *Ulysses*,"

in *Twenty-First Joyce*, eds. Ellen Carol Jones and Morris Beja (Gainesville: University Press of Florida, 2004), pp. 157–78.

8 Marie-Laure Ryan, *Possible Worlds, Artificial Intelligence, and Narrative Theory* (Bloomington: Indiana University Press 1991), p. 130. Further references to this text will be cited parenthetically in the text as *Possible Worlds*.

9 Hugh Kenner, "Molly's Masterstroke," *JJQ* 10 (Fall 1972): 19–28.

10 See Margaret McBride, *"Ulysses" and the Metamorphosis of Stephen Dedalus*, (Cranbury, NJ: Associated University Presses, Inc., 2001).

CHAPTER 6

Setting: Dublin 1904/1922

Enda Duffy

Ulysses has both a date and a duration. The date is the day on which the book is set: June 16, 1904. The duration is the seven years the novel took to write, noted exactly by Joyce, as if he were signing off a letter, at the very end of his text: "Trieste-Zurich-Paris, 1914–1921" (*U* 18.1610–11). In *Ulysses*, this single day and these seven years it took to describe it face each other in magnificent tension, throwing open questions of time, of dating, and of history itself in the text. On the one hand, to concentrate the whole book in a single day might be seen as an attempt to ignore history – as a record of changes over a long period of time – altogether. On the other, this strategy accords each day, even the most apparently mundane ones, the enormous respect of its historical representativeness. The seven carefully noted years of composition, along with the invocation of the biblical seven days of creation, might be read as the artist's attempt to stand in some ideal creative – rather than historical – time. Or it might be seen as a reminder that the book was written in exactly some of the most tumultuous years of Irish, and indeed of world history. By setting his book in a relatively uneventful earlier year, while writing it amid violent, revolutionary and transformative times, *Ulysses* can know the future without admitting to such knowledge. It can secrete within its account of a day in 1904 a palimpsest or secret history of the revolutionary occurrences of 1914–21, when the book was being written. *Ulysses*, then, double-times its readers, encoding a post–1904 future which the author of 1914–21 has seen unfold into a book which appears to be only able to look back.

Yet it behooves every reader of the novel to understand the Irish political, economic, social and cultural situation in 1904, as it is upon this context that any hints about the future are inscribed.[1] *Ulysses* itself limits such understanding, in that its initial modernist tactic is to leave unsaid any information on background whatsoever. Hints are dropped, but this book puts us in the middle of a conversation already in progress, and we must research the context for ourselves. Note first that 1904 was a relatively quiet year in Irish politics. It falls almost midway between the death of Irish Nationalist parliamentary leader Charles Stewart Parnell in 1891 and the 1916 Easter Rebellion. Thus the novel is set in the heart of what would turn out to be the final phase of British colonial rule in Ireland. The years between 1870 and 1891 had witnessed the last great push for a limited form of independence for Ireland attempted by peaceful means, spearheaded by the Irish Party in the British Parliament. The first phase of this struggle culminated with the defeat of the First Home Rule Bill in the British House of Commons in 1886, and ended in the downfall of Parnell after the exposure of his affair with Katharine O'Shea in 1890. The charismatic leader's downfall had a traumatic effect, as Joyce makes clear in continuous elegiac reminders: the talk in "Ivy Day in the Committee Room" in *Dubliners*, Stephen's dream of Parnell's coffin at Kingstown in *A Portrait*, the discussion of the leader's grave and the myth that he might still be alive in the "Hades" and "Eumaeus" episodes of *Ulysses* (*U* 6.919–27, 16.1297–98). It cast a lingering shadow of betrayal and bitter division between Parnellites and anti-Parnellites across the Irish political landscape. Nevertheless, the Second Irish Home Rule Bill of 1893 passed the Commons, only to be defeated in the House of Lords, while in 1914 the Third Home Rule Bill finally received royal assent, only to be suspended because of the coming Great War.

Parnell's downfall nevertheless left a vacuum that was filled first by the exciting and unprecedented developments which would become known as the "Celtic Revival," through which nothing less than a whole new sense of Irish cultural identity was developed and popularized. At the same time, the physical force movement – attracting those who believed that the British would never surrender their Irish dominion peacefully and would only be compelled to do so with violence – began a slow revival. Finally, there emerged in the early years of the twentieth century an impassioned trade union movement, especially in Dublin.

In fact, each of these strands of revived cultural and political history appear in *Ulysses*, intricately interwoven in a web of reference to pre–1904 events and possible predictions about later ones. Arthur Griffith, whom Molly in "Penelope" thinks of as "the coming man," has in 1904 published *The Resurrection of Hungary* in which he advocated that Irish members of parliament, following the Hungarian example, should unilaterally withdraw from the British Parliament and set up their own government in Dublin (*U* 18.385–86). This was exactly the course followed by the members of his party, Sinn Fein ("Ourselves Alone") in January 1919, after they swept most of the country in the postwar general election. Published in

1904, this seminal document in modern Irish history had appeared just in time for the denizens of Barney Kiernan's pub in the "Cyclops" episode to claim that it was known in Dublin Castle (*U* 12.1574), seat of British rule in Ireland, and that Griffith had gotten his revolutionary idea from none other than Leopold Bloom, whose father had emigrated from Hungary to Ireland. Is this a Joycean joke? By the time he wrote "Cyclops," the proposal's revolutionary impact had been made clear. Is Joyce here granting us a glimpse of Bloom – who, when asked by the Sinn Feiner and sectarian citizen in the same episode, "What is your nation if I may ask?", replies "Ireland.... I was born here. Ireland." (*U* 12.1430–31) – as inadvertent architect of the country's path to national independence? Arguably, yes. After 1904, Sinn Fein gained supporters; it was organized as a political movement in 1908, and in 1913 many of its members joined the Irish Volunteers – from whose membership, in turn, came most of those who fought in the 1916 Easter Rebellion. In sum, set in 1904, when the anti-Parnellite bitterness was ebbing and the Sinn Fein-centered physical force movement that would eventually be successful was only gathering strength, *Ulysses* both reflects the years prior to its setting and somewhat coyly points to the future in which it was composed.

On the surface, the Dublin of 1904 was an Edwardian provincial city, a world of straw hats (like that worn by Blazes Boylan), "seaside girls" (like Gerty McDowell and her friends on Sandymount Strand), proprietary biscuits sold in tins (like the one the citizen throws in "Cyclops"), shop-window displays behind plate-glass (like the display of silk underwear, which arouses Bloom to an erotic reverie in "Lestrygonians"), advertising hoardings (such as the one for a concert by Eugene Stratton that Fr. Conmee passes), Gaiety Theatre variety shows (one of which Bloom falsely tells Molly he has attended), and, crossing the city in the afternoon, the viceregal cavalcade.

The Dublin of these years could claim a meager prosperity. Since the 1860s, a building boom meant the construction of a ring of prosperous new suburbs in the places for which the trams leave at the opening of "Aeolus": "Blackrock, Kingstown and Dalkey, Clonskea, Rathgar and Terenure, Palmerston Park and upper Rathmines, Sandymount Green, Rathmines, Ringsend and Sandymount Tower, Harold's Cross" (*U* 7.4–6). In the city center, in the great oval encircled by the Grand and Royal Canals, some of the eighteenth-century mansions the aristocracy vacated after the Act of Union in 1800 were still occupied by the professional class; David Sheehy MP – whose wife Fr. Conmee encounters at the opening of "Wandering Rocks" (*U* 10.26) – owned one such in real life near the corner of Mountjoy Square, while not far away, in the Dublin of the novel, a less grand but still roomy house was occupied by Leopold and Molly Bloom. Even such precariously middle-class families as the Blooms employed a servant. South of the Liffey River, such benevolent employers as the Guinnesses were spearheading slum clearance and the provision of workers' housing. Dublin had an electric tram system and even some electric lighting; Bloom and Stephen, walking up Gardiner Street in "Ithaca," discuss "The influence of gaslight or electric light on the growth of adjoining paraheliotropic trees" (*U* 17.44–45).[2] Here, in short, was an emerging bourgeois city on the European model.

Yet this version of bourgeois prosperity in 1904 Dublin was tenuous at best. The Dublin of *Ulysses* is largely a city of lower-middle-class men who are only precariously employed. It was as if there was a new Catholic middle class with little or no actual work available for its members in the late-colonial city. Slum conditions receive only sidelong glances, as when, early in "Lotus Eaters," Bloom sees a boy carrying a bucket of offal by Brady's cottages (*U* 5.5). One of the bitterest moments of the whole novel comes in "Wandering Rocks" when Stephen encounters his own hungry sisters on the quays, and, even though he has just been paid for his work in the private school in Dalkey, declines to offer them any of the money he may well spend in pubs or in a brothel later in the day. This moment of refusal to help the desperately poor even when they belong to your own family vividly points up the dilemma of the new and thoroughly precarious Catholic middle class in the late-colonial moment. Its members realize that they have at last the opportunity not to be victims, but, under the current administration, only by differentiating themselves from the masses of their desperately poor fellow countrymen and women. At the same time, their hope for advancement within the colonial system was always more or less doomed – rife, at best, with possibilities for alienation. Hence Stephen's attitude – when he listens to the Englishman Haines' condescension at the novel's opening, or his near despair as he tries to teach "Lycidas" to the complacent Protestant (and therefore, likely Anglo-Irish) boys – amplifies the dilemmas evident to every member of this nascent class.

Colonial Dublin offered the prospect of conventional bourgeois prosperity, then withheld it. The alienation, the boozy afternoons in the public house, the gossip and the backbiting, the half-hearted keeping up of appearances (like Tom Kiernan in his new secondhand coat – *U* 10.738–47), the dreams of betting on "Throwaway" in a British horse race, the endless search for work (as when Stephen, drunkenly staggering along with Bloom after midnight, is asked by Corley, who is loitering under the Loop Line railway bridge, if he might help find him a job – *U* 16.100–203), all bespeak a world of middle-class desperation and unending battles with poverty. Those who do labor are often women with the grimmest service occupations: the servant girl who has been "surprised" by Bloom "in the rere of the premises" (*U* 15.885), the barmaids at the Ormond Hotel, and the prostitutes in Nighttown. Late-colonial Dublin had nurtured a small, thoroughly insecure middle class with little or no work for its members to perform. Hence their aimless quality, their drunkenness, their endless time for talk, and – perhaps – their desperate raucous quality, their some-times profligacy.

It may be this comedic laughter in the face of incredible uncertainty that is the hallmark of *Ulysses* and of the Dublin of 1904 it describes. Modernist art offers us no shortage of alienated, under-employed fig-ures streaming through the night-streets, but *Ulysses* stands out because it alone treats this predicament with a carnival of laughter. More, not only the book but the characters themselves take this approach, and it is this aspect that keeps us interested in their fates. It makes us laugh on hearing of J. J. O'Molloy's belch as he reaches the peroration of a famous speech he repeats from memory – and we laugh again when we are told without a halt: "He lifted his voice above it boldly" (*U* 7.860–61). This bravado in defeat is evident in every character: Even Mulligan, despicable toady to the Englishman Haines and all the more deplorable because he is well aware of his toadying, can make us howl with laughter at his plans for Lambay Island and the Hellenization of Ireland; the hopeless, bullying Simon Dedalus can tell us that the weather is as changeable as a baby's bottom; even Stephen's gall is leavened by his undoubted wit: "We can't change the country. Let us change the subject" (*U* 16.1171). Molly is the novel's most vital character because she carries this bravado the furthest – in her life, in her sensations and in her thoughts. Bloom's pathos comes from his timidity in the face of this profligate comedic laughter everyone else seems to possess.

Ulysses, like virtually every great novel, is a document from a specifically bourgeois viewpoint; the novel as a genre may be said to be an inven-tion of the middle class and a vehicle for its point of view. Yet *Ulysses*'s middle-class characters come from the lowest rung of that class. To grasp the nature of their bravura in the face of desperation (rather than attrib-uting it, as Haines might, to some stereotypical "Irishness"), we must consider the cultural forces as well as the political and economic realities which fomented it. Here we will briefly survey three: the influence of the

Catholic Church, the attraction of the new Celtic Revival, and the power of the new, international (but, for the Irish middle classes, usually British) popular culture.

The Roman Catholic Church was *the* bastion of respectability for the new native middle class, and thus the very antithesis of the raucousness at the prospect of dropping out of the middle class which characterizes *Ulysses*. As the prestige of the Anglo-Irish aristocracy waned, that of the Catholic Church grew. Diocesan colleges for boys and convent schools for girls were founded everywhere, and the Church assumed responsibility for hospitals, orphanages, Magdalene laundries, and the missionary societies that sent Irish Catholic missionaries to every outpost of the British empire. This vast apparatus was staffed by priests and nuns recruited by and large from the new Irish middle class, and indeed was a considerable source of employment for that class. In families such as Joyce's own, it would have been considered an honor for a son to become a priest and a daughter a nun (in the Joyces' case, only the second of these occurred). Thus, in *A Portrait*, the offering to Stephen's father of a scholarship for his two eldest sons to attend Belvedere College – and the subsequent invitation to Stephen to become a priest – has a social as well as, or more than, a spiritual dimension. At the same time, the Irish Catholic Church's version of respectability and rectitude as presumed middle-class virtues had a certain impoverished and even abashed quality. The Catholic Church in late-Victorian Ireland operated in part as a vanguard of the middle class, leading a formerly peasant and largely impoverished population into bourgeois modernity. Yet, given the reactionary attitude of the broader European Catholic Church toward modernity, the Church's message was not geared to the mentality of entrepreneurship. Thus the Church's stance both goaded its flock toward middle-classness and held its members back. At the same time, its version of charity – as in the hospitals, schools and missions – worked as a mechanism of class gatekeeping, and so could appear hypocritical.

The particular version of unctuousness bred by this contradiction is brilliantly reflected in *Ulysses'* pen-portrait of Fr. Conmee in "Wandering Rocks" (*U* 10.1–205). Conmee's unnerving oscillation between overweening pride and nervous parsimoniousness, between self-satisfaction and servility, between a sense of history and a string of clichés – all as he sets off on an errand of mercy that will see a boy committed to an orphanage whose name has more recently become a byword for vicious institutional cruelty – records with perfect pitch the ambivalent pomposity and underconfident respectability of turn-of-the-century Irish Catholicism. Conmee, it turns out, is the well-fed, thoroughly comfortable version of the novel's apparent ne'er-do-wells, such as Simon Dedalus or even Ben Dollard. The Church's timidity in the face of anti-colonial violence – Bishop Moriarty of Kerry had famously declared of the Fenians that "Hell is not hot enough nor eternity long enough to punish such miscreants," and clerical disapproval had aided Parnell's fall – enraged Simon and others. Yet their thirst for middle-class status meant that the new Irish bourgeoisie mostly approved of the church's increasing power.[3] Joyce's own anti-clericalism was rare among members of his class (or any class) in 1904 Ireland, and feels like a French or Italian import.

If the message to the new and highly precarious native Irish Catholic bourgeoisie from their church, therefore, was ambivalent, the message from another emerging strand of Irish middle-class culture – the various artistic movements which became known as the Celtic Revival – was even more convoluted and challenging. For literary critics now, the Revival can all too easily be conceived of as the successful project of a coterie of geniuses, who built an imaginative body of literature and art upon the foundations set in place by an honorable tradition of antiquarians from Charles O'Conor to William Wilde, and who had kept the knowledge of native Gaelic culture alive. This group, the story goes, invented a new mythology of Irishness, a cultural formation that fired the revolutionary nationalists and in which the new postcolonial nation would eventually anchor its sense of self. In this vein, therefore, when Yeats in 1922 wrote, "Did that play of mine send out / Certain men the English shot?" he was not only displaying a commendable sense of contrition, but also drawing attention to his self-professed powers of modernizing and publicizing archaic mythology to the point where it inspired self-sacrifice.[4] This account is persuasive partly because even if the stories told in modern adaptations of ancient myth cycles and folktales were often ones of failure, the story of the Revival itself was one of a purpose achieved, and therefore a success.

Yet this account begs a host of questions. First, where exactly did the Revival come from? That is, what persuaded a band of marginal members of the Anglo-Irish ascendancy to imagine that Ireland might provide the material for their creative endeavors and, however dimly, to intuit the possible political utility for Irish revolutionary politics of this work? Second, how did they achieve such immense popular success? Regarding the movement's origins, it might be theorized that its members, as the more rebellious and liberal elements of the Anglo-Irish upper classes, were engaged in a rear-guard act of expiation for the cultural genocide their ancestors

had visited upon the Irish (and even for the economic hardships that the
land agents who worked for the landlords were visiting on Irish peasants
still). In this charmed logic, it was the British planter class who, as a final
(possibly poisoned) gift to the native Irish, invented the most passionate
forms of modern Irish nationalism before they finally surrendered power.
One merit of this account is that it highlights the Anglo-Irish origins of
most Revival authors – and thus suggests the unlikelihood that it would
be taken seriously by the mass of the "native" population. But how might
we otherwise account for the Revival? Europe in these years witnessed
the revivals of a host of minor, marginal nationalisms: the experiences of
Norway, Finland, Hungary, Armenia, Portugal, Catalonia, Brittany and
Wales offer numerous parallels to those of Ireland. Like Ireland's, these
national revivals get written about almost solely in national histories.
However, to compare them is to discern that at the century's end, there
was a second wave of the grand nationalist fervor that had swept Europe
at mid-century and which, in that earlier phase, had led to the formation
of the modern nation-states of Germany and Italy. What then was the
impetus and role of this second wave of regional and marginal nationalist
fervor? These local nationalisms seemed to fly in the face of the first wave,
since that initial movement had brought marginal statelets into union with
larger units, as when Sicily became part of the new Italian state. The fin-
de-siècle provincial nationalisms in Ireland or Norway, however, dreamed
of the independence of such possibly economically unviable territories
and their peoples.

One explanation is that the central power – in London, Vienna or
wherever, especially through modern education systems – had fostered the
emergence of local elites but had not fostered economic opportunities of
which the members of these new elites could take advantage, so that they
found themselves frustrated and dissatisfied. This is the class, in the Irish
case, that was Joyce's prime subject. It was, paradoxically, also the class in
which the marginal Anglo-Irish intellectuals and artists now found themselves, for with the eminent withdrawal of the British and the dismantling
of their legal, administrative, judicial and military apparatus in Ireland,
the prospects for this class had dimmed. Thus for a moment, some members of the Anglo-Irish class from which sprung Yeats, Synge, A. E., Hyde
and even George Moore, found that they could treat with the better-off
members of the new Catholic middle class. (In *Ulysses*, Mulligan is the preeminent example of this group.) For the Anglo-Irish, an interest in matters Celtic worked as a standard imperialist primitivism transmuted into
local antiquarianism. For the emergent native middle class, their betters'

interest in what they themselves had left behind was possibly gratifying, although they were suspicious of its motives.

This ambivalence about the Revival among the native Irish middle class is laid out unequivocally in *Ulysses*, where Stephen's and Mulligan's derisive references to the Cuala Press[5] and the Irish language contrast with the attitude of the Englishman Haines, who has tried to learn the language. Only gullible Britishers, the implication is, would be taken in by the latest version of "Oirishry." Still, Stephen remembers playing Yeats's "Fergus' Song" to his mother as she lay dying, and when he sees her "crying in her wretched bed," she tells him that it is because she understands "those words, Stephen: love's bitter mystery" (*U* 1.249, 252–53). Yeats's Revivalist phrases, then, can bring tears to the eyes of a Catholic Dublin grocer's daughter as she lays dying; despite the new middle class's suspicion of Revivalist Irishness, *Ulysses* implies, the members of this class still found its versions of Irish heroic feeling and gesture poignant – because it was indeed their heritage.

The very mixed message that we saw being promulgated by the Irish Catholic Church to its emergent middle class constituency, therefore, was also evident in that class's reception of the cultural productions and implicit messages of the Revival. The movement spoke to the members of this class, but it came out of the mouths of the cadre which had always despised them – and which, as Yeats showed in such poems as "September 1913," continued to do so. Joyce pointedly has Stephen express an up-to-the-minute British taste for Renaissance poets from Shakespeare to Dowland. Likewise, the fact that he framed his account of Dublin with a classical rather than an Irish myth – with the *Odyssey* rather than *An Tain* – implies his quite correct impression that the class about which he writes will always – despite affectations of local identity – primarily see itself as cosmopolitan, and hence deracinated and international. In this sense, Bloom's somewhat soi-disant Jewishness – embraced while he rejects Jewish religious teaching – makes him an ideal member of this middle class, well practiced in adjusting quotients of identity and disdain. Note that *Ulysses* reserves the full resources of its satire for the citizen in "Cyclops," for not only does he appear to bear the marks of what Marx called "the idiocy of rural life," but he is said to be modeled on Michael Cusack, the founder of the Gaelic Athletic Association (GAA), which very successfully revived native sports throughout Ireland.[6] The GAA was one plank of the Revival that had mass popular appeal, and possibly the strongest claim to building on existing popular traditions; *Ulysses*'s attack on its founder suggests its author's sense that for the middle class which concerns him, such continuity and such mass appeal cannot be countenanced.

Ulysses anticipates Benedict Anderson's observation that modern nationalisms are uncannily similar everywhere, even if they appear to be about local differences.[7] In every case, local singularity is a fiction provided by the new middle class that will form the new nation. In the Irish case, it was perhaps an unfortunate freak of history that members of the class itself did not provide it. This meant that the emergent Irish Catholic middle class knew all too well that their revived Celtic culture was a fabrication. Joyce's suspicion of Celticism in *Ulysses*, like his suspicion of Catholicism, was an amplification of the basic instincts of the middle-class Irish, rather than a lone-voice rejection of the middle-class's conventional wisdom. This is why Bloom is the ultimate modern Irish hero, and why middle-class readers today – in Ireland and throughout the world – can find much to sympathize with in the book's rejection of local national identity as an eccentric atavism.

Thus to grasp the full context of *Ulysses*, we need to look beyond Parnell and 1916, beyond the wane of British rule in Ireland, beyond the power of the Catholic Church and the influence of the Celtic Revival, to consider the rise of a transnational – in the first instance Western – middle class, and the culture to which this gave rise. This was a class that possibly for the first time in history might have disposable income, so that its members were practitioners of a new economic literacy. Hence the savings-box mentality of Mr. Deasy, butt of many a joke in the "Nestor" episode, comes home to roost by the end of the novel when Bloom's double-entry bookkeeping tells us more about the truth of his day – the exact monetary measure of his kindness to the widow Dignam, for example – than can be discerned by even the most alert readers. *Ulysses*, from Stephen's "Would I make any money by it?" in "Telemachus," to Molly's thoughts of entertaining Stephen with "fairy cakes in Liptons I love the smell of a rich big shop at 7 1/2d a lb" is an epic poem about money (*U* 1.490, 18.1554–55). It is also a book about consumption. As June 16, 1904 begins, the young men first meet the world when they buy the milk from the old milk woman, while Bloom has his first meaningful human eye contact of the day with Duglacz as he buys the kidneys for his breakfast.

The mode of textual persuasion the novel considers most explicitly is advertising, which is Bloom's own special interest and profession. *Ulysses'* vast and unprecedented mobilization of all and every aspect of the new mass popular culture – from Irish rebel songs of the 1898 centenary of the Croppy rebellion to mentions of proto-cinematic viewing machines such as the Capel Street mutoscope and the myorama (*U* 10.793) – has been amply documented by Cheryl Herr, Brandon Kreshner, Garry Leonard and others.[8] It is a novel immersed in modern media – the medium of the day being the newspaper, which takes over the very style of the "Aeolus" episode, where it is powerful enough to kick-start the book's full-frontal modernist experimentation. It is also a book about the modern subject's interaction with the newly efficient urban world with its scheduled systems of rapid transit by tram, train and horse-drawn car and communications by letter, telegraph and telephone; its class- and gender-coded sites of refreshment and repose, from the Lincoln Place baths to Bella Cohen's Monto brothel; its alert policemen, obsequious waiters, tourists and tradesmen such as the piano tuner, ever-ready to monitor even the city's vibrations. Much of this modern urbanism, to the nationalist Irish eye, would have borne the unmistakable stamp of Britishness, yet it is striking how much of it – from Molly's remembered dress "from the B Marche paris" to the preachings of the American evangelist Alexander J. Dowie – are not British but rather part of a new transnational and therefore apparently deracinated culture (*U* 18.612–13). Far from decrying such deracination, *Ulysses* delineates it lovingly, celebrates it, and lets its raw attractions show.

Joyce wrote *Ulysses*, then, not only about a single country, Ireland, and a single city, Dublin, but also about a single class in that city: its new Catholic middle class. It is the contexts in which that class emerged that provide the true historical, social, economic and cultural contexts for understanding *Ulysses*. In every country, the mercantile middle class has been the subject of the novel since it emerged as a literary genre. Similarly, modernism concerned itself with the members of that class at the moment of its great turn-of-the-century expansion – at the time of the huge movement of people to urban centers, the extension of the franchise, the rise in literacy – with the arrival of armies of office workers who commuted to work from the new suburbs, and the advent of their consumer habits, their new forms of leisure such as the cinema, and above all, their new protocols of human interaction, sexual conduct, intimacy, and community. This new subject of the expanded middle class recurs in modernist texts in a whole series of western urban settings, but the characters and the city Joyce portrays are in fact poorer, more trapped, more desperate and more abject than Eliot's characters in London or Barnes's in Paris or Kafka's in Prague. They desperately cling to the low-hanging tatters of their middle-class status with a humorous determination and a comic bravura that seems lacking in the work of the more cosmopolitan modernists.

And this raucous comedy becomes the base note of the book. It is what makes *Ulysses* exceptional, and it is its key pleasure. To grasp how the contexts of *Ulysses* effect it, the question we must grapple with is this: From where does this raucous comedy that characterizes the characters and is shot through the whole novel as its chief achievement come?

To answer this, we may return to where we began: the fact that *Ulysses* is a novel of two dates – June 16, 1904, and the years 1914–21. The novel shows the new Irish middle class in all its pathetic and precarious desperation at the tail end of the British colonial regime in Ireland in 1904. But it was written in 1914–21, the years when this class fought for and won independence. The 1916 rebellion and the subsequent War of Independence – despite the involvement of James Connolly's working-class Irish Citizen Army – was very much a middle-class struggle. Even Yeats, in the first stanza of "Easter, 1916" admits as much, noting that he never would have thought that the clerks he had met leaving their offices "at close of day" would have such determination in them.[9] Similarly, the arrival of independence with the Anglo-Irish Treaty of 1921 benefited the new Catholic middle class, particularly of Dublin, above all others. If their frustration under the colonial administration was such that they were willing to use armed rebellion to escape it, then the achievement of national independence was clearly the political change that would and did bring the members of this class to power. How much of their exultation at this victory managed to get into *Ulysses* is an open question. Yet the book did grow wild in its modernism the further onward it went, and the later (after 1916, and then during the years 1919–21 when the War of Independence burst upon Dublin and Ireland) it was written. A good case can be made that the bolder the modernist form, the more fully in key with the raucous comedy of the novel's characters Joyce became. This reaches a crescendo in the crazed phantasmagoria of "Circe," written during the height of the War of Independence, which features the cry "Dublin's burning! Dublin's burning! On fire, on fire!" at its heart (*U* 15.4660).

Ulysses, in other words, is the exception to the drear modernism of the metropoles because of its historical context. The middle class it portrays was a new one, only allowed on sufferance by the colonial British administration in Ireland and kept largely unemployed, on standby. Thus its members were not merely bored, anomie-haunted clerks; they were without work, wondering what they could borrow or pawn. Or so it seemed in 1904. Yet, between 1914 and 1921, they made a huge leap forward. They had gained a whole new nation to run and manage and in which to do business. The members of this class, before 1916, were despised by their self-anointed betters, who included the Anglo-Irish Revivalists, as "shoneens," as "west-Britons," and as "gombeen men." Yet in James Joyce, paradoxically, they have found their champion, and their great literary voice. His attacks on the forces of late-colonial Irish culture to which they might have turned for reinforcement – the Catholic Church, the cultural movement known as the Celtic Revival, the post-Parnellite Irish political establishment – should not be mistaken for a blanket condemnation of the class itself. Rather, his critiques were amplifications of the suspicions harbored by most members of the class about a religious establishment that cloaked its own insecurities in unctuous respectability, and a cultural turn that impractically told them to be as heroic as Cuchulain and as passionate as Diarmuid and Grainne. "Kuskykorked himself up tight in his inkbattle house," as Joyce notes ruefully in *Finnegans Wake*, while his class, which is his sole literary subject, seized Ireland from British rule and gained national power, prestige and responsibility for themselves, Joyce amped up his modernist experimentation episode by episode as his class was victorious beyond imagining (*FW* 176.30–31). The coming to power of the previously abject middle class in an independent Ireland, which happened as *Ulysses* was being written, is one major reason for the book's wild and raucous comedy. It is why the keynote of *Ulysses* is not angst-ridden anomie, but defiance. It is also why *Ulysses*, much more even that Yeats's brilliant but shock-riven "Easter, 1916," is *the* work that commemorates and celebrates a newly independent Ireland. Modern nations are middle-class formations. And *Ulysses* is the nation-text of a new, postcolonial, middle-class Ireland.

Notes

1 Some of the best histories of modern Ireland include F. S. L. Lyons, *Ireland Since the Famine* (London: Fontana Press, 1985); R. F. Foster, *Modern Ireland, 1600–1972* (London: Penguin, 1990); and Joseph J. Lee, *Ireland, 1912–1985: Politics and Society* (Cambridge: Cambridge University Press, 1990).

2 Dublin also had a good water delivery system in the Vartry Waterworks Scheme, developed after 1861. See Michael Rubenstein, "Aquacity: Plumbing Consciousness in Joyce's Dublin," in *Public Works: Infrastructure, Irish Modernism, and the Postcolonial* (Notre Dame, IN: University of Notre Dame Press, 2010), pp. 43–92.

3 See Mark Tierney, *Modern Ireland 1850–1950* (Dublin: Gill and Macmillan, 1972), p. 13.

4 William Butler Yeats, "Man and the Echo," in *The Collected Poems of W. B. Yeats*, ed. Richard J. Finneran, 2nd rev. ed. (New York: Scribner, 1996), p. 345.

5 A press established by Yeats's sister Elizabeth in 1908 that published over seventy works by Irish Revivalists.

6 Karl Marx and Friedrich Engels, *The Communist Manifesto* (New York: Verso, 1998), p. 40.

7 Benedict Anderson, *Imagined Communities: Reflections on the Origin and Spread of Nationalisms* (London: Verso Books, 1983).

8 See Cheryl Herr, *Joyce's Anatomy of Culture* (Urbana: University of Illinois Press, 1986); R. Brandon Kershner, *Joyce, Bakhtin, and Popular Literature: Chronicles of Disorder* (Chapel Hill: University of North Carolina Press, 1989); and Garry Leonard, *Advertising and Commodity Culture in Joyce* (Gainsville: University Press of Florida, 1998).

9 Yeats, "Easter, 1916," in Finneran, *Collected Poems*, p. 180.

CHAPTER 7

Endings

Maud Ellmann

In *The Sense of an Ending*, Frank Kermode makes the famous observation that "*tick* is our word for a physical beginning, *tock* our word for an end."[1] When tick-tock seems "too easily fictional," writers "produce plots containing a good deal of *tock-tick*; such a plot is that of *Ulysses*" (*Ending* 44–5). There is much tock-tick in *Ulysses*, much digression from the teleological impetus. But there is also a strong sense of tick-tock, especially in the last three episodes, which are modeled on the *Nostos*, or homecoming, of the *Odyssey*. It is hard to imagine a more satisfying ending than a homecoming, in which the narrative turns full circle, restoring the hero to his origins. Joyce adopts this Homeric model by restoring Bloom to 7 Eccles Street, but it is unclear if Bloom returns to the same home that he left in "Lotus Eaters." In the intervening hours somebody has rearranged the furniture, causing Bloom to bash his head against an unexpected sideboard, and Blazes Boylan has left his imprint on the conjugal bed, along with telltale flakes of Plumtree's Potted Meat.

These details, however, scarcely interfere with the tick-tock of the archetypal plot. It is in the style, rather than the represented action of Joyce's *Nostos* that the most startling examples of tock-tick can be found. Where style is concerned, there is no homecoming in *Ulysses*, no return to Bloom's or Stephen's stream of consciousness. On the contrary, each of the last triad of episodes introduces a strange new voice, which cannot be attributed to either of the male protagonists. The blundering clichés of "Eumaeus," followed by the catechistic drill of "Ithaca," seem designed to distance Bloom and Stephen from the reader, exorcising these characters' distinctive idioms to make way for the unprecedented eloquence of Molly Bloom.

A homecoming bespeaks a balanced narrative economy in which the outlay of the journey is rewarded by return: indeed, the word "economy" derives from the Greek word for home (*oikos*).[2] The rhetorical excesses of Joyce's *Nostos*, however, defy good housekeeping. Instead of making both ends meet, as in the circular narrative of Homer's *Odyssey*, the concluding chapters of *Ulysses* abound with images and acts of waste.[3] These include the wasted lives of the drunkards of "Eumaeus," the wasted information rattled off in "Ithaca," and the wasted fertility of Molly's menses in "Penelope." Above all, Joyce wastes words: Much of the comedy of these episodes lies in the incongruity between the paucity of action and the extravagance – or "squandermania" – of style (*U* 16.87).

The traditional novel concludes in redemption, in both the moral and the financial sense, whereby characters receive their just deserts, and the reader's "great expectations" are fulfilled. For this reason, Henry James mocks the typical ending of the popular nineteenth-century novel as "a distribution at the last of prizes, pensions, husbands, wives, babies, millions, appended paragraphs, and cheerful remarks."[4] In contrast to this final reckoning, Joyce concludes *Ulysses* with the triumph of the dark horse Throwaway, whose name evokes the adventitious and gratuitous, as well as the idea of waste. This horse won the Gold Cup on June 16, 1904, at odds of 20:1, a historical fact reported in the *Evening Telegraph* in "Eumaeus" (*U* 16.1242). In place of the traditional economy of plot, where the supply of words is budgeted to the demands of action, Joyce introduces a throwaway aesthetic in which words outnumber deeds by at least 20:1.

This chapter considers how this throwaway aesthetic transforms the sense of an ending of *Ulysses*. Whereas the traditional novel ends in marriage, *Ulysses* ends with the throwaway encounter of Bloom and Stephen, which is broken off before it has a chance to blossom, followed by the celibate encounter of Bloom and Molly in the conjugal bed. Both encounters have no issue, whether in the form of friendship or fecundity; the Blooms achieve no sexual union, and Stephen walks off into the night, abandoning Bloom to "[t]he cold of interstellar space" (*U* 17.1246). In the traditional marriage plot, the ending represents a new beginning because it promises perpetuation of the family. In French, the equivalent formula for "they lived happily ever after" is "*ils eurent beaucoup d'enfants*" (they had lots of children), which indicates that the sense of an ending depends on the promise of posterity (*Strangers* 8). *Ulysses*, by contrast, challenges the family values embedded in traditional narrative form by reveling in throwaway forms of textuality and sexuality. Rather than reaffirming marriage, or looking forward to *beaucoup d'enfants*, *Ulysses* concludes with images of unproductive eroticism: hallucinatory perversions in "Circe," homosexual innuendoes in "Eumaeus," masturbation in "Penelope." These images are accompanied by a perverse enjoyment of language for its own sake, not for its semantic "issue."

In each of the final chapters, consummation is avoided or postponed indefinitely; the closest Bloom comes to sexual congress is peeing with Stephen *en plein air*. These chapters substitute images of waste for those of procreation: "Ithaca" culminates in "the micturition in the garden," "Eumaeus" in a trinity of turds excreted by a cabman's horse, and "Penelope" in menstruation (*Letters I* 159–60; *SL* 278).[5] Such scatological images lend a carnivalesque humor to Joyce's finale, yet they also belong to a revaluation of waste that looks forward to *Finnegans Wake* and its celebration of "litter" – a pun on waste, fecundity, and literature (*FW* 93.24). Indeed, the dissemination of puns corresponds to that of litter, insofar as both evade the sense of an ending, spreading sideways rather than progressing teleologically toward the aim of reproduction or logical consequence.

The *Oxford English Dictionary* (*OED*) provides several definitions of the noun "waste," most of them calamitous – destruction, devastation, sterile land, useless expenditure.[6] But waste can also mean profusion or lavish abundance, as in the *OED*'s citation from Pope's translation of the *Odyssey*: "And there the garden yields a waste of flow'rs."[7] Molly Bloom's soliloquy concludes with such a waste of flowers: "I love flowers Id love to have the whole place swimming in roses" (*U* 18.1557–58). As we shall see, these flowers also yield a waste of puns, whose rhizomatic proliferation lays waste to the economy of representation established in the first half of the novel.

In a compelling study of Joyce, Joseph Valente argues that *Ulysses* contains two odysseys, the first wedded to representation, whereas the second involves the "radical disfiguration" of representational norms.[8] The first is an "odyssey of character," the second an "odyssey of style" – a term borrowed from Karen Lawrence (*Justice* 190–91).[9] The odyssey of character comprises the narrative dimension of the text, the story of the inner lives of Stephen and Bloom as they progress toward their putative union in "Ithaca." This story is dominated by the stream-of-consciousness technique, which is "perhaps the most profoundly representational of literary devices" because it represents the mind reflecting on its own representations of the world (*Justice* 190). Dominating the first half of the novel, the odyssey of character retells the "archetypal romance of masculinity: the oedipal coming together of father and son," from which the mother is pointedly excluded (*Justice* 190). The odyssey of style, on the other hand, "unfolds under the sign of the feminine," and corresponds to what I have described as waste (*Justice* 191). Beginning with "Sirens," each episode introduces an extravagant new style that upstages the masculine protagonists. Although these styles no longer emanate from an identifiable point of view, whether masculine or feminine, they attach themselves to female archetypes such as the Virgin ("Nausicaa"), the Witch ("Circe"), and the Wife ("Penelope"). In the final episode, "the last great stylistic disfiguration of the novel," Valente argues that Joyce strives to overcome representation by "becoming-woman" (*Justice* 191, 237). According to Gilles Deleuze and Félix Guattari, who coined this term, "becoming-woman" is not a matter of representing, ventriloquizing, or appropriating a ready-made sexual identity, but of dismantling the dualism between masculine and feminine into "a thousand tiny sexes."[10]

In the odyssey of character, women are relegated to the margins of representation. Largely absent from the early chapters of the novel, Molly Bloom appears only in bits: a disembodied murmur in "Calypso," or a plump white arm that drops a charitable coin out of an upper-story window in "Wandering Rocks." Her invisibility implies that the order of representation depends on "a figure of feminine otherness that it excludes" (*Justice* 191). It is only when representation breaks down during the phantasmagoria of "Circe" that Molly bursts into the limelight. Before she performs her star turn in "Penelope," however, "Eumaeus" and "Ithaca" stage a showdown between the odyssey of character and the odyssey of style, in which the story of Bloom and Stephen's putative "at-onement" explodes in a waste of verbal fireworks. The remainder of this chapter tracks these developments through the last three chapters of *Ulysses*, showing how the resurgence of waste confounds the duality of gender.

"Eumaeus"

After the vertiginous hallucinations of "Circe," "Eumaeus" comes as a crashing anticlimax. "[A]lmost disappointingly intelligible," "Eumaeus" is written in a slack and enervated style ridden with blunders, clichés, and commonplaces, as if the narrator were too tired to grope for fresh expressions.[11] In the Linati schema, Joyce designated the technic of this episode as "[n]arrative (old)," and described its style as "prosa rilassata" (relaxed prose).[12] Relaxed is an understatement: This prose is "sinewless and wobbly," like Bloom's "strange ... flesh," which presses against Stephen when Bloom escorts him to the cabman's shelter in one of the rare instances of bodily contact in the episode (*U* 16.1724, 1723–24).

Another instance of wobbly prose is the opening sentence: "Preparatory to anything else Mr Bloom brushed off the greater bulk of the shavings and handed Stephen the hat and ashplant and bucked him up generally in orthodox Samaritan fashion which he very badly needed" (*U* 16.1–3). This sentence provides a foretaste of the style of "Eumaeus," with its oxymorons ("orthodox Samaritan"), mismatched clichés, labored ironies, and pompous formalities – it is a long time since Poldy has been formally announced as "Mr Bloom." Flaccid in construction, the sentence seems afflicted by the narcolepsy that pervades this episode, as if the narrator were stringing words together, too exhausted to attend to syntax or grammar. Throughout the episode, sentences peter out before they reach a grammatical conclusion: "he took out his pocketbook and, turning over the various contents it contained rapidly finally he" (*U* 16.1422–24). Collapsing before they reach their goal, such sentences encapsulate the theme of premature decline, which is embodied in the "waifs and strays" assembled in the cabman's shelter, "nipped in the bud of premature decay and nobody to blame but themselves" (*U* 16.327–28,1184–85). It is this fate that awaits Stephen, Bloom fears, if the young man persists in his "squandermania," frittering away his genius in a haze of alcohol. "Eumaeus" opens up the possibility that Stephen's masterpiece will remain unwritten – just as the chapter's sentences remain unfinished – while the promising young writer degenerates into a Dublin drunk.

Clichés are shop-soiled expressions that have lost their sparkle through excessive circulation. The waste products of culture, they present themselves as authorless, drawn from the junkyard of common speech. For this reason, clichés serve as agents of social interpolation; to resort to a cliché is to relinquish singularity in favor of conformity. This is why many readers recoil from the language of "Eumaeus" as an affront to the male protagonists, who up to now have stood out for their difference from the hoi polloi – being smarter, deeper, odder, funnier, or kinder than the common run, and possessing an interiority denied to other Dubliners. While Stephen's distinctive voice continues to break through the doddering prose of "Eumaeus," Bloom's idiolect is drowned in the barrage of clichés.

These clichés preclude intimacy – distancing the reader from the amiable hero – and therefore correspond to the physical standoffishness that marks this episode. As Jennifer Levine has pointed out, "the act of touching is nervously kept to a minimum" in "Eumaeus" (*Homosocial Desire* 281). For instance, Bloom urges Stephen to take nourishment, but instead of handing him the bun and coffee, he pushes them across the table; later, when Bloom wants Stephen to admire Molly's photograph, he places it between them on the table, where Stephen declines to pick it up. In an episode bristling with homosexual innuendoes, particularly with regard to the self-styled "sailor" Murphy, this embargo against touching suggests homophobic panic, perhaps as a defense against the risk of carnal union between Bloom and Stephen. This embargo also reflects the estrangement imposed by the narrator: At the moment we expect to be drawing closer to the male protagonists, while they are also drawing closer to each other, the hackneyed style denies their individuality.

By presenting Bloom as a petit-bourgeois windbag, the narrator is exposed as a liar and impostor who suppresses the hero's endearing quirks, as well as his inventive wit. Furthermore, the narrator's sloppy use of pronouns means that every "he" could be mistaken for another, thus invoking a potential battalion of impostors. An atmosphere of "dubiosity" pervades the episode, extending even to the refreshments that Bloom presses on Stephen: the "socalled roll" and "the cup of what was temporarily supposed to be called coffee" (*U* 16.574, 366, 360). Most dubious of all is the "redbearded bibulous individual" who calls himself D. B. Murphy and claims to be a sailor, although he is probably a convict fresh from prison (*U* 16.337, 833). Joyce described this fishy character as "Ulysses Pseudangelos," which means Ulysses the false messenger (*Liffey* 154–55, 187).

While Bloom is a mock-heroic version of Odysseus, Murphy is an arrant fraud. Nonetheless this "*soi-disant* sailor" bears many resemblances to his Homeric antecedent, not least in spinning a seaman's yarns about his improbable adventures (*U* 16.620). He has traveled across two hemispheres, contending with pirates, icebergs, crocodiles, and cannibals; he also boasts a faithful Penelope: "my own true wife I haven't seen for seven years now, sailing about" (*U* 16.421). His equivalent to Odysseus's scar is his tattoos, supposedly executed by a Greek with the unlikely name Antonio. A portrait of this artist, who was "[a]te by sharks," is engraved on Murphy's chest, and the "old tarpaulin" entertains his audience by squeezing Antonio's face into a smile or a frown (*U* 16.691, 1021).

Also tattooed on this hairy chest is the number "16," which provokes much curiosity in Murphy's onlookers and Joyce's critics (*U* 16.675). The number could refer to "Eumaeus" itself as the sixteenth episode of *Ulysses*; it may also refer to Bloomsday, June 16, 1904. Furthermore, Don Gifford has identified the number sixteen as a code for homosexuality, an interpretation supported by other innuendos in the episode.[13] Even the term "sailor," which is frequently (mis)applied to Murphy, is a byword for homosexuality. When a "loafer" asks if "16" means "[e]aten alive," the supposed fate of the unfortunate Antonio, Murphy replies, "Ate. A Greek he was" (*U* 16.695, 696, 699). The term "Greek" has previously been used by Mulligan to insinuate that Bloom is gay (*U* 9.614–15); the word "Ate" refers back to "Ate by sharks," but it is also the name of the Greek goddess of delusion, infatuation, reckless impulse, and rash action who leads men to ruin.

Although women are excluded from this episode, a goddess of destruction seems to hover at the margins of this derelict fraternity. She takes the form, for instance, of the haggard streetwalker who beckons from the doorway of the cabman's shelter before the keeper hustles her away. Bloom is "flusterfied" by her intrusion, having recognized her as the "partially idiotic female" who once "begged the chance of his washing" (*U* 16.708, 713, 714–15). But he conceals his discomfort by launching into a Poloniad about the dangers of venereal disease, warning Stephen to avoid such Ates.

Equally dangerous was Katharine O'Shea, another absent goddess denounced in the cabman's shelter, where her adulterous liaison with Parnell is blamed for having brought about the leader's fall: "That bitch, that English whore, did for him, the shebeen proprietor commented. She put the first nail in his coffin" (*U* 16.1352–53). Invoking a well-worn ethnic stereotype, Bloom attributes this ill-fated love affair to Katharine's hot-blooded Spanish ancestry. However it is Molly Bloom, not Katharine O'Shea, who is half-Spanish and has recently succumbed to the "passionate abandon of the south" (*U* 16.1409–10). In this chapter of disguises, Parnell's supposedly horny mistress serves as a decoy for Bloom's own adulterous wife.

Other absent Ates materialize in the form of photographs. The first is Murphy's picture postcard of "maneaters in Peru," which depicts a group of "savage women" surrounded by a swarm of infants (*U* 16.470, 475–76). Murphy shares this postcard with the riff-raff in the shelter, thereby confirming Claude Lévi-Strauss's theory that the exchange of women serves to reinforce alliances between men.[14] Later, Bloom shows Stephen a "slightly soiled" photo of Molly, a gesture that mirrors Murphy's previous display of ethnographic porn, thus aligning Molly with the "maneaters" (*U* 16.1465). Furthermore, by sharing Molly's photograph with Stephen, Bloom seems to be inviting him to share her "heaving *embonpoint*" (*U* 16.1468). Indeed, it has been evident throughout the day that Bloom is colluding in his own betrayal, almost to the point of pimping for his wife. Whereas Homer's Odysseus routs the suitors from the palace, Bloom seems to encourage their invasion.

In Greek mythology, Ate was expelled from heaven for deceiving her father Zeus. Although the fleeting appearance of her name may be nothing but an accident of punctuation, the male discourse of "Eumaeus" is besieged by "maneaters" who threaten to devour, cuckold, syphilize, or ruin men. The bookended scenes in which men stare at female photographs demonstrate how male bonds are established by objectifying women, who are seen but not heard throughout this episode. Yet the exclusion of women seems only to intensify their power. It is intriguing to conjecture that Ate the deceiver is the speaker of this episode, who disguises Bloom in worn-out words, just as Odysseus is disguised in worn-out clothes. This is a goddess of waste, in the double sense of ruin and abundance, who brings forth a squandermania of style, in which the representational paradigm of the first half of the novel is "nipped in the bud of premature decay." In "Ithaca" Joyce continues to lay waste to the odyssey of character with a waste of scientific information, the excess of which defeats its own didactic pretext.

"Ithaca"

After their mock marriage by *"Father Maher"* at the end of "Eumaeus," Bloom and Stephen make their way to 7 Eccles Street (*U* 16.1887–88). Since Bloom has forgotten his key, his homecoming requires Odyssean ingenuity. In Homer, Odysseus reenters his palace as a beggar; similarly, Bloom breaks into his house as a thief, jumping into the area to penetrate the bastion from below. Here he enters through the scullery door, which has been left unlocked, providing as little security against invasion as Molly's orifices. If the house and its mistress are incontinent, so is the language of this episode. Organized as a "mathematical catechism," each question unleashes a waste of supererogatory information (*Letters I* 159; *SL* 278). The most celebrated example of this verbal profligacy occurs at the beginning of the episode, where a question about Bloom's faucet – "Did it flow?" – opens the floodgates to a deluge of particulars about the Dublin waterworks, followed by the famous "water hymn" that praises all the transformations of "aquacity" across the globe, including "seaquakes, waterspouts, artesian wells, eruptions, torrents, eddies, freshets, spates, groundswells, watersheds, waterpartings, geysers, cataracts, whirlpools, maelstroms, inundations, deluges, cloudbursts" – just to name a few (*U* 17.163, 247, 205–208).

Joyce told his patron Harriet Shaw Weaver that "Ithaca" was the true ending of *Ulysses* because "Penelope" had "no beginning, middle or end" (*Letters I* 172). He also confessed that "Ithaca" was his favorite episode, perhaps because its persnickety attention to facts and figures – along with lists, budgets, catalogues, and inventories – demonstrates what Joyce described as his "grocer's assistant's mind" (*JJ* 28, *Letters III* 304). In fact, the geeky narrator of "Ithaca" seems afflicted with a severe case of obsessive compulsive disorder. In accordance with Freud's principle that psychic mechanisms of defense ultimately coincide with that which they repress, this narrator creates waste by attempting to control it.[15]

"Ithaca" is the chapter where the odyssey of character comes to fruition with the symbolic union of Bloom and Stephen; yet their potential intimacy is subverted by what Joyce called the process of "mathematico-astronomico-physico-mechanico-geometrico-chemico sublimation" (*Letters I* 164). Instead of establishing a meaningful connection between these characters, "Ithaca" offers a parody of fusion, or as Marilyn French puts it, "a series of irrelevant parallels, contrasts, quantitative relations and intermeshings of wholly inane crossing points."[16] Any union Bloom and Stephen achieve in "Ithaca" is based on symbolic identification as opposed to blood ties. Earlier in the day, Stephen had insisted that fatherhood was a "mystical estate," founded on speculation rather than biology, and that this "legal fiction" of paternity undergirds the symbolic order of civilization (*U* 9:838, 844). Motherhood, by contrast, is associated with the facts of life rather than the fictions of the intellect.

It is therefore logical that Molly Bloom should be excluded from the symbolic union of father and son, dozing upstairs while the men enjoy their sacramental cocoa. Yet although she remains invisible in "Ithaca," she exercises a magnetic force on the conversation between Bloom and Stephen, which orbits around the female members of Bloom's household, Molly and Milly. In "Hades," Bloom contemplates these homophonous names: "Molly. Milly. Same thing watered down" (*U* 6.87). "Same thing," in that both his wife and daughter are betraying him for other men, Molly for Boylan and Milly for Bannon; "watered down," in that women are associated with the changeability of water. "How can you own water really?" Bloom wonders in "Lestrygonians" (*U* 8.93–94). If women are water – "same thing watered down" – this implies that they are equally resistant to ownership. In "Ithaca," the obsessive inventories of Bloom's possessions, both real and imaginary, could be interpreted as a defense against the loss of that which cannot be possessed – a woman's love.

Water is governed by the moon, which is traditionally associated with the feminine stereotype of "variability" (*U* 17.189). Bloom endorses this cliché: When the questioner asks, "What special affinities appeared to him to exist between the moon and woman," the lengthy answer includes "her potency over effluent and refluent waters" (*U* 17:1157–59, 1163–64). Another such affinity is "her splendour, when visible: her attraction,

when invisible," which alludes to Molly's covert influence over this scene
(*U* 17:1169–70). Invisible herself, she is "denoted by a visible splendid
sign," the light emitted by a paraffin lamp in the upper story of the house
(*U* 17.1177). This light triangulates the men below with the woman above,
whose absence serves to clinch the symbolic identification of father and
son: "each contemplating the other in both mirrors of the reciprocal flesh
of theirhisnothis fellowfaces" (*U* 17:1183–84). In "Ithaca" as in "Eumaeus,"
the excluded woman features only as a sign – a photograph, a lamp in the
darkness – to bring about the union between men.

Yet at the same time, "Ithaca" mocks this much-anticipated Oedipal
conclusion to the odyssey of character. By heaping up ridiculous equations and correspondences between the heroes and merging their names
into the spoonerism Stoom and Blephen, the narrative makes fun of their
supposed at-onement (*U* 17.549–51). Regardless of the bloated full stop
that brings the chapter to a close, the frequent references to infinity – of
the stars, of Molly's suitors, or even of the possibilities of advertisement –
belie the sense of an ending. Instead of moving forward toward closure, "Ithaca" turns backward to investigate what Stephen has previously
described as the "room of ... infinite possibilities" ousted by the irrevers-
ible events of history (*U* 2.50–51). To this purpose, every cupboard and
drawer of the house at 7 Eccles Street is ransacked for traces of the past. As
Barry McCrea has pointed out, "this process, the retrospective expansion
of the past, replaces the genealogical promise of reproduction – instead of
promising to generate new realities in the future, it accommodates more
and more of those that are excluded from any one version of the past"
(*Strangers* 138–39). In this way, "Ithaca" prepares us for Molly's monologue, "the indispensable countersign to Bloom's passport to eternity," in
which she talks back to her own creator, rewriting the novel by providing
a feisty new version of the past (*Letters I* 160, *SL* 278).

"Penelope"

"O Jamesy let me up out of this pooh!" (*U* 18.1128–29). Rarely has a fictional character accosted her creator in such terms. Since the beginnings
of Western philosophy, femaleness has been conflated with the "pooh"
that masculine reason has striven to transcend – pooh associated with the
wasting, waste-producing body. This waste has been relegated to the margins of the symbolic order, just as women are restricted to the sidelines of
male discourse in *Ulysses*, where they figure as objects of exchange – like
the soiled photographs in "Eumaeus" – rather than participants. In this

economy of gender, the transcendence of the masculine depends on the poohing (expulsion) and pooh-poohing (denigration) of the feminine.

In her extraordinary outburst, Molly demands to be released from this economy, rising up against her author. She also rose up against him in a dream that Joyce wrote down for Herbert Gorman. In this dream Molly Bloom flung a black child's coffin at Bloom's retreating figure with the words, "I've done with you." Joyce then launched into an eloquent explanation of the last episode of *Ulysses*, but when he reached "an astronomical climax," Molly smiled, "and then, bending, picked up a tiny snuffbox, in the form of a little black coffin, and tossed it towards me, saying, 'And I have done with you, too, Mr. Joyce'" (*JJ* 549).

In the seventeen episodes leading up to "Penelope," Molly has been virtually silenced, apart from a few charming sound bites such as "met him pike hoses," which haunt Bloom's reveries throughout the day (*U* 8.112). But Joyce told Frank Budgen that "The last word (human, all too human) is left to Penelope" (*Letters I* 160; *SL* 278). By giving Molly "[t]he last word" – that is, the latest innovation as well as the final say – Joyce redresses the omission of woman from the story of masculine transcendence that concludes in "Ithaca." He described "Penelope" as the "clou," meaning the star turn of the novel, but this episode also provides the "clue" to the subversion of representational norms (*Letters I* 170; *SL* 285). Instead of representing Molly, Joyce experiments in "becoming-woman" by weaving and unweaving sexual personae. Thus, Molly is the grieving mother and the raunchy whore, the wide-eyed virgin and the nagging housewife. She also experiments in becoming-man: "God I wouldnt mind being a man and get up on a lovely woman" (*U* 18.1146–47).

Her metempsychoses continue to unfold in the prolific critical literature on "Penelope," in which Molly has been reinvented with every generation. As Kathleen McCormack observes, Molly has been "seen as obscene by many reviewers in the twenties, an earth goddess in the thirties and forties, a whore in the fifties and sixties, and most recently a symbol of *écriture féminine*."[17] Molly invites critical controversy because she constantly contradicts herself, slipping out of every role that she performs. Her embrace of contradiction defies the logical structures of identity so heavy-handedly established in "Ithaca," with its comparisons, equations, roll calls, genealogies, and inventories of personal effects. By setting boundaries between categories, these classification systems serve to defend what Jacques Derrida calls the "propre," a term that combines the idea of cleanliness or purity (propriety) with that of ownership (property).[18] Molly's unpunctuated rhapsody is outrageously improper, insofar as it defies the boundaries of identity as well as those of grammar, taste, and self-control. Instead, her stream of consciousness breaks its banks, overwhelming the temporal and spatial coordinates that distinguish the inner from the outer world. Hence, "Penelope" is the only episode to which Joyce assigned no specific time, replacing the hour with the mathematical symbol of infinity; and although the monologue ostensibly occurs in bed, this physical locality dissolves as Molly drifts among remembered and imagined worlds.

The organ assigned to "Penelope" in the Linati schema is "fat," which is usually disparaged as waste tissue, a dangerous supplement to the lean, efficient, and productive body (*Liffey* 186–7). Fat exceeds the "proper" boundaries of the body, blurring its outlines in billowing folds of useless flesh. In the corpus of the novel, Molly's monologue performs a similar function, spilling out over the ending just as her "heaving embonpoint" spills out over her décolletage. On close inspection, however, Molly's effusion is not as ungirdled as it seems. As Derek Attridge argues, her prose observes the rules of grammar much more faithfully than Bloom or Stephen's fractured sentences, which often lack the mandatory verb.[19] In addition, Molly's frequent use of the exclamation "O," which resembles an enormous hollowed-out full stop, provides an innovative form of punctuation – a loose end rather than a final period. In an episode preoccupied with orifices and "omissions," these O's could be seen as orifices in the prose, portals to unknown zones of pleasure (*U* 18.1170). Exceeding the duality of gender, they interpose "a thousand tiny sexes" into the body of the prose.

Thus Molly unweaves the conventional structure of the sentence to weave a looser tapestry of prose in which omissions are emitted everywhere. Yet she is presented as a weaver of fabrics as well as of words. In the most moving passage of the novel, we are told that she knitted a "little woolly jacket" for her baby son Rudy, who was buried in this garment at the age of eleven days:

> I suppose I oughtnt to have buried him in that little woolly jacket I knitted crying as I was but give it to some poor child but I knew well Id never have another our 1st death too it was we were never the same since O Im not going to think myself into the glooms about that any more. (*U* 18:1448–51)

Although "Ithaca" provides a glut of facts about Bloom's family, including his father's death by suicide, there is only one mention of the death of "Rudolph Bloom, junior," expressed in the most laconic and impersonal of terms (*U* 17.1130). While "Ithaca" resorts to a kind of obsessive-compulsive disorder to circumnavigate the pain of Rudy's death and Molly's infidelity, "Penelope" evades "the glooms" with sexual bravado. The tragedy of Rudy's death has blighted the marriage – "we were never the same since" – and foreclosed the genealogical future: "I knew well Id never have another." This is no fairy tale: *ils n'auront pas beaucoup d'enfants*. Instead, a child's coffin haunts the marriage, reminiscent of the tiny coffins Molly hurls in Joyce's dream, and the anguish of this image may also be associated with the dissolution of the genealogical narrative. Instead of concluding in conception, *Ulysses* ends with Molly masturbating next to the inert body of her sleeping spouse. Their reunion takes place in the past rather than the future, when Molly remembers "the day I got him to propose to me yes ... 16 years ago," the day the lovers lay among the rhododendrons on Howth Heath (*U* 18.1573–55). Thus "Penelope," like "Ithaca," turns away from the future and toward a "retrospective arrangement" of the past (*U* 17.1907).

Molly's recollection of this love scene also sends the reader on a retrospective journey back to "Lestrygonians," where the sight of two flies stuck together on the windowpane, combined with a gorgonzola sandwich and a glass of burgundy, reminds Bloom of the same ecstatic kiss (*U* 8.896–918). Since Bloom is hungry, his memories of love are mixed with images of food, just as the kiss itself was mixed with the seedcake that the lovers exchanged between their tongues. More romantically, Molly's memories abound with flowers:

> the day I got him to propose to me yes first I gave him the bit of seedcake out of my mouth and it was leapyear like now yes 16 years ago my God after that long kiss I near lost my breath yes he said I was a flower of the mountain. (*U* 18:1573–76)

The image of the flower has been applied to both spouses at different times, thus dismantling the opposition of the sexes. The name Bloom is a synonym for "flower," which is the pseudonym that Leopold adopts in his illicit correspondence with Martha Clifford. But Bloom also eulogizes Molly as "a flower of the mountain," thus aligning flowers with the feminine. Furthermore, flowers signify menstruation, as in Rochester's bawdy lines, "It is a thing unfit / That men should fuck in time of flowers."[20] In addition to these meanings, flowers may refer to tropes, the shape-changing "flowers" of rhetoric. Thus the "waste of flowers" that concludes the novel also yields a waste of puns, which overspill the closure of the represented action. In this way, the tick-tock of the *Nostos* is subverted by the tock-tick of the pun, whose wayward meanings never find their way back home to origins.

Notes

1 Frank Kermode, *The Sense of an Ending* (Oxford: Oxford University Press, 2000), pp. 44–45. Hereafter referred to as *Ending*.

2 Steven Connor, "'From the House of Bondage to the Wilderness of Inhabitation': The Domestic Economies of 'Ithaca,'" in *Joyce's "Ithaca,"* ed. Andrew Gibson (Amsterdam: Rodopi, 1996), p. 200.

3 See Mark Osteen, *The Economy of "Ulysses": Making Both Ends Meet* (Syracuse, NY: Syracuse University Press, 1995); and Barry McCrea, *In the Company of Strangers: Family and Narrative in Dickens, Conan Doyle, Joyce, and Proust* (New York: Columbia University Press, 2011), pp. 133–35. McCrea's work is hereafter referred to as *Strangers*.

4 Henry James, "The Art of Fiction," in *The Art of Criticism: Henry James on the Theory and the Practice of Fiction*, eds. William Veeder and Susan M. Griffin (Chicago: University of Chicago Press, 1986), p. 168.

5 See Karen Lawrence, "'Beggaring Description': Politics and Style in Joyce's 'Eumaeus'" *Modern Fiction Studies* 38 (Summer 1992): 355–76.

6 See OED online: http://www.oed.com/view/Entry/226027?rskey=dAINlK&result=1&isAdvanced=false#eid.

7 Alexander Pope, trans., *The Odyssey of Homer* (Edinburgh: John Ross & Co., 1970), book VI, p. 356.

8 Joseph Valente, *James Joyce and the Problem of Justice: Negotiating Sexual and Colonial Difference* (Cambridge: Cambridge University Press, 1995), p. 191. Hereafter referred to as *Justice*.

9 Also see Karen Lawrence, *The Odyssey of Style in "Ulysses"* (Princeton, NJ: Princeton University Press, 1981).

10 Gilles Deleuze and Félix Guattari, *A Thousand Plateaus: Capitalism and Schizophrenia,* trans. Brian Massumi (London: Continuum, 2004), pp. 303–07, 235, and passim.

11 Jennifer Levine, "James Joyce, Tattoo Artist: Tracing the Outlines of Homosocial Desire" *JJQ* 31 (Spring 1994): 277. Hereafter referred to as "Homosocial Desire."

12 See Richard Ellmann, *Ulysses on the Liffey* (New York: Oxford University Press, 1986), pp. 151, 186. Hereafter referred to as *Liffey*.

13 Don Gifford, *"Ulysses" Annotated: Notes for James Joyce's "Ulysses"* (Berkeley: University of California Press, 1988), p. 544.

14 Claude Lévi-Strauss, *The Elementary Structures of Kinship* (1949) trans. James Harle Bell and John Richard von Sturmer, ed. R. Needham (London: Eyre and Spottiswoode, 1969), p. 115.

15 See Freud, "Totem and Taboo" (1913), in *The Complete Psychological Works of Sigmund Freud*, standard ed., trans. James Strachey (London: Hogarth Press, 1953–1974), vol. 13, p. 29.

16 Marilyn French, *The Book as World: James Joyce's "Ulysses"* (London: Abacus, 1982), pp. 221–22.

17 Kathleen McCormick, "Reproducing Molly Bloom: A Revisionist History of the Reception of 'Penelope,' 1922–1970," in *Molly Blooms: A Polylogue on*

"*Penelope*" *and Cultural Studies*, ed. Richard Pearce (Madison: University of Wisconsin Press, 1994), p. 17.

18 For a brief preview of this pervasive theme in Derrida 's writing, see the "Translator's Preface" to Jacques Derrida, *Of Grammatology* (1967), trans. Gayatri Chakravorty Spivak (Baltimore, MD: Johns Hopkins University Press, 1997), pp. lxxxiii–lxxxiv.

19 Derek Attridge, "Molly's Flow: The Writing of 'Penelope' and the Question of Women's Language," *Modern Fiction Studies* 35 (Fall 1989): 545–46.

20 John Wilmot, Second Earl of Rochester, *The Complete Poems of John Wilmot, the Earl of Rochester*, ed. David Veith (New Haven, CT: Yale University Press, 2002), p. 45.

PART III

Reading Ulysses

CHAPTER 8

City Circuits: "Aeolus" and "Wandering Rocks"*

Michael Rubenstein

This chapter addresses the formal experimentation in *Ulysses* that picks up momentum, complexity, and difficulty – along with virtuosity and wonder – in the "Aeolus" and "Wandering Rocks" episodes. If previous episodes of the novel utilized first a fairly standard version of third-person omniscient narration, and then the intense subjectivity of the stream-of-consciousness technique, I will argue here that one of the new formal techniques introduced in "Aeolus" and "Wandering Rocks" models narrative voice on some of the modern technological structures that redefined everyday life both in turn-of-the-century Dublin and in the European metropolis generally. The two technologies central to Joyce's formal experiments in these two episodes are the newspaper in "Aeolus" and Dublin's sewer system in "Wandering Rocks."

The formal experiments of *Ulysses* attempt to give ontological and epistemological teeth to the idea that the city itself can be a character in fiction. Thus the city of Dublin becomes something much more than mere setting. In "Aeolus" and "Wandering Rocks" in particular, *Ulysses* ventriloquizes urban infrastructures for use as plausible points of view from which the action of each episode is perceived and, at a stretch, narrated to us as readers. With this argument, I intend at once to offer an interpretation of the episodes and also to demystify some of their stylistic challenges: to show, that is, that their difficulty is not in the service of a modernist difficulty-for-its-own-sake but rather in the service of an intensified mimeticism that seeks to outdo – not, crucially, undo – narrative realism. *Ulysses* might be an anti-realist novel, but that is true only insofar as it attempts to be more realistic than realism. Joyce's modernism in *Ulysses*, however, is as distinct from nineteenth-century realist fiction as it is from other non- or anti-mimetic texts in the modernist canon. And the distinction from both traditions emerges out of the way that *Ulysses* imagines and then deploys a narrative point of view grounded in Dublin's urban infrastructures.

Such an interpretation draws from two literary-critical strands. The first addresses questions that arise directly from the narrative innovations and difficulties of episodes like "Aeolus" and "Wandering Rocks": who or what speaks in these two chapters of *Ulysses*? How? From what point of view? The other strand comes out of historical thinking about the origins and spread of nationalism, and out of postcolonial theories of narrating the nation: How do the narrative innovations deployed in these episodes work in the service of narrating the Irish nation? To what extent do they forge a sense of national or civic belonging among Dublin's citizens? How do they imagine connections between and among characters as relationships of fellowship and collective endeavor, of belonging to each other, or responsibility toward each other?

I take as my starting assumptions Benedict Anderson's arguments about the construction of national "imagined communities" through print literature like newspapers and novels, and extend them to include aspects of the built environment of modernity, to see in the collective and cooperative technological structures of everyday life – what I call infrastructure here – a model of citizenship that tends to go unnoticed.[1] Of course, not every critic imagines *Ulysses* as a novel that writes the Irish nation. In fact, some argue that *Ulysses* transcends nationality and nationalism, aiming instead for the rarified realm of avant-garde art. I see *Ulysses*, however, as the culmination of Stephen Dedalus's precocious (and pretentious) ambitions as he lays them out at the end of *A Portrait of the Artist as a Young Man*: "to forge in the smithy of my soul the uncreated conscience of my race" (*P* 253). Stephen uses the metaphor of the smithy – and implicitly the sword – as a way to forge national consciousness. But in writing *Ulysses*, Joyce discarded the smithy for the newspaper on the one hand – calling himself a "scissors and paste man" (*Letters I* 297) – and the city's infrastructures on the other – having been likened by his friend Frank Budgen to "an engineer at work with compass and slide-rule."[2]

The metaphorical shift from sword to slide rule is part of the literary-historical shift from the ancient epic to the modern novel; from warrior-king epic heroes like Odysseus to everyday citizen-subject protagonists like Bloom; and, in Joyce's more personal history, the artistic shift from the immaturity of Stephen Dedalus in *A Portrait* to the mature artistic vision of the author of *Ulysses*. In place of Stephen's vision of a poet-warrior, Joyce in *Ulysses* proposes a vision of the artist as an engineer, or a kind of urban planner.

There is evidence that Joyce meant for Stephen's vocation as a writer in *Ulysses* to be a continuation of his naïve statement of purpose in *A Portrait*.

In "Aeolus," Miles Crawford, editor of the *Daily Telegraph*, invites Stephen to write something for the newspaper: "I want you to write something for me ... Something with a bite in it. You can do it. I see it in your face.... Put us all into it, damn its soul.... You can do it ... We'll paralyse Europe as Ignatius Gallaher used to say when he was on the shaughraun" (*U* 7.616–29). Crawford's ambition for Stephen here reflects Stephen's younger ambition for himself: to forge the uncreated conscience of his race or, in Crawford's less flowery terms, to put "us all into it." After exhorting Stephen to write, the older man then celebrates Ignatius Gallaher's ingenious conceit for communicating the logistics of the 1882 Phoenix Park murders over the telephone to *The New York World*. Gallaher, according to Crawford, used an advertisement for Bransome's coffee in the March 17th edition of the *Weekly Freeman* – copies of which were to hand in both the Dublin and New York offices – to imaginatively map out the park and the escape route of the gunmen: "B is parkgate.... T is viceregal lodge. C is where murder took place. K is Knockmaroon gate.... F to P is the route Skin-the-Goat drove the car for an alibi ... X is Davy's publichouse in upper Leeson street" (*U* 7.659–69).

"Gave it to them on a hot plate," Crawford recalls, "the whole bloody history" (*U* 7.676–77). Gallaher's creativity with print here is a model of "scissors and paste" narrative, repurposing a coffee ad to tell a story about a political assassination. His conceit – using the letters on a page of newsprint as a reconstructive map of space and place – indicates something of the narrative innovations Joyce developed in *Ulysses*. If Gallaher can be said to have reconstructed a place from a page of writing, however, Joyce could equally and inversely be said to have constructed pages of writing based on the social geography of place.

Gallaher's move is an act of bricolage, an expedient that exploits the materials at hand to communicate something – the nature of a spatial situation – that would be otherwise difficult or impossible to describe given the technological limitations of the telephone. The inspired innovation of the thing is not in creating something new exactly, but in using old materials to communicate something new. The episode thus serves as metacommentary on what Joyce tries to do with narrative innovation in *Ulysses* more generally, and especially in "Aeolus" and "Wandering Rocks."

This is why it's a good idea to read "Aeolus" and "Wandering Rocks" together. On the one hand, the newspaper in "Aeolus" represents the daily experience of simultaneity and horizontal comradeship that Anderson argues is the newspaper's ideological nation-building effect: the way in which, to quote Hegel, the newspaper enacted a daily "mass ceremony" that served "modern man as a substitute for morning prayers," forging in this way an "imagined community" of the nation (*Imagined* 35). And on the other hand, the sewer in "Wandering Rocks" represents a public works project that is funded by, serves, and defines a polity in a very materialist and geographical way – one that complements the imaginative daily communion of the newspaper with the daily material connections of civic infrastructure. Whereas Anderson's theory of the national imagined community constitutes itself out of language or discourse – for him primarily novels and newspapers – for Joyce the national community is constructed from the combined cultural work of discourse – again, novels and newspapers – and material culture, like the sewer in "Wandering Rocks" or the tramlines that introduce "Aeolus." *Ulysses* synthesizes, in other words, the culture work of the newspaper and the public works of Dublin's civic infrastructure as part of its project of imagining the Irish nation. Ultimately, such a synthesis results in a technique in "Wandering Rocks" that we might call infrastructural narration.

Consider as an example the first lines of "Aeolus": "IN THE HEART OF THE HIBERNIAN METROPOLIS" (*U* 7.1–2). This passage, and the sixty-two others like it, stylistically mimic the form of the newspaper headline, because as it turns out, the episode's main action takes place in the offices of a major nationalist Dublin newspaper in 1904, the *Freeman's Journal*. Thus the formal structure of the episode is dictated, it appears, by its setting in a newspaper printing office. In this particular case, the headline is perfectly apposite to what follows it: a chaotic and noisy scene of tramlines converging and diverging at Nelson's Pillar in the center of the city. The connection between headline and text, or form and content, doesn't last, however, since many of the other "headlines" that pepper "Aeolus" are unrelated and sometimes nonsensical; others sometimes even actively undercut or critique the actions of the characters in the episode. It is hard to imagine a newspaper article titled with the single descriptor "SAD" (*U* 7.291) for example, or "EXIT BLOOM" (*U* 7.429), both of which operate in their contexts more like stage directions than newspaper headlines. The headlines are often confusing and misleading, prompting Declan Kiberd to suggest that "the episode would be more straightforward to read without them."[3] In other words, the headlines operate consistently on the level of form *only*, and not consistently on the level of content. In many ways they do not conform at all to the purpose, method, or content of real newspaper headlines. Instead they tend to ironize the newspaper as a textual form. Joyce imports a formal element of the daily news into his fiction, where it becomes less interested in its regular job of telling a story efficiently, effectively, and eye-catchingly, and more interested in making classical stories (like Odysseus') and non-newsworthy stories (like Bloom's) new through an interplay – and a deformation – of the conventions of news and the conventions of fiction.

The "headlines" in "Aeolus" were added very late to the manuscript; in fact, they did not appear at all in the first published version of the episode, the October 1918 issue of *The Little Review*.[4] We could see them, then, as a surface-level deformation of narrative technique, much like the way that Molly's flowing stream of consciousness in the final episode of *Ulysses*, "Penelope," owes much of its disorienting effect to a fairly simple operation of extracting punctuation from an otherwise standard style of interior monologue. But to say that the insertion of headlines in "Aeolus" or the removal of punctuation in "Penelope" are surface deformations would be to minimize both their profound effects on the experience of reading these episodes and the audacity of Joyce's gestures toward a radical makeover of the novel.

In "Wandering Rocks," on the other hand, Joyce's reconstruction of fictional form is embedded much more deeply in the DNA of the episode. "Wandering Rocks" is exceptional in that it is the only episode in *Ulysses* that does not have a Homeric parallel, since Homer's Odysseus chooses to avoid this hazard altogether. So here we enter a unique zone of invention where Homer's epic is no longer a proper guide.[5] The narrative voice of the episode, which appears to cleave closely to the conventions of a recognizably omniscient narrator so typical of nineteenth-century realist fiction, becomes materially grounded in the structure of the city through the concept-image of Dublin's sewer system. In this way, Joyce's writing makes use of the urban infrastructures of Dublin to structure a narrative set within the city's boundaries.

"Wandering Rocks," more than any other episode of *Ulysses*, stages simultaneity; the nineteen sections of the episode narrate moments in the life of the city collected from a disparate range of geographical locations. Part of the point of the episode is that these moments are unrelated except by coincidence of time and the geographical unit of the city; most of the characters are unaware of the others with whom their story is being synchronously told. No one is doing anything we might call newsworthy here, and many of the sections focus on "minor" characters by traditional fictional standards; indeed, part of the episode's challenge lies in the way it forces questions about the fictional status of minor versus major characters.[6] We gain access to "Wandering Rocks" through a presumably omniscient narrator, though this narrator doesn't appear to be doing the usual work of concentrating on major figures or of sorting between important and unimportant events. Moreover, this narrator has an unusual sense of irony in tone and style. "The mind of this city" in "Wandering Rocks," as Clive Hart puts it, "is both mechanical and maliciously ironic."[7] As characters intersect each other, many of their movements are repeated, interrupted, and re-presented without any of the syntactic cues that would normally allow the reader to switch from one perspective to another. The viceregal cavalcade that gets full treatment in the final section begins its procession at Phoenix Park and, in its path through the city, greets and is greeted by the characters treated earlier in the chapter: "Mr Thomas Kernan … greet[s] [the viceroy] vainly from afar" (*U* 10.1183–84); the cavalcade goes "unsaluted by Mr Dudley White, B. L., M. A." (*U* 10.1185–86); "Mr Simon Dedalus … st[ands] still in midstreet and br[ings] his hat low" (*U* 10.1199–1201). Amid this list of characters, the Poddle River appears where it merges with the Liffey, offering its salute as well: "From its sluice in Wood quay wall under Tom Devan's office Poddle river hung out in fealty a tongue of liquid sewage" (*U* 10.1196–97). That "tongue," I want to suggest, is – barring the improbability of talking sewage – a plausible point of view for the narrating consciousness of "Wandering Rocks" as a whole.

The groundwork for preparing the reader to accept a conscious sewer has in some sense been laid for us as early as "Aeolus," where Bloom musingly anthropomorphizes the printing machines in the *Freemans Journal* office:

> Sllt. The nethermost deck of the first machine jogged forward its flyboard with sllt the first batch of quirefolded papers. Sllt. Almost human the way it sllt to call attention. Doing its level best to speak. That door too sllt creaking, asking to be shut. Everything speaks in its own way. Sllt. (*U* 7.174–77)

"The suggestion," for Declan Kiberd, "is that every single object has its own history and consciousness, albeit mute, and that it will yield a meaning if accorded the sort of loving attention that Bloom gives to things."[8] Here, Bloom imagines the printing machine speaking, but in "Wandering Rocks" the sewer's "tongue" suggests not only a "history and consciousness" but also the possibility of speech.

"The sewer," wrote Victor Hugo in *Les Misérables* in 1862, "is the conscience of the city."[9] The line comes from a chapter in the novel called "The Intestine of Leviathan," which momentarily suspends the plot, pausing to make a lengthy digression into the history of the Parisian sewer system. Digressions like these were a feature of the nineteenth-century epic novel – one thinks, for example, of certain sections of Melville's *Moby*

Dick. In *Ulysses*, however, the sewer as the conscience of the city is not merely asserted but performed through narrative technique. It is one of the signal differences between the nineteenth-century realist novel and Joyce's twentieth-century avant-garde modernism that the former should declare the sewer as the conscience of the city – in French "conscience" serves ambiguously for both the English words conscience and consciousness, and it resonates with Stephen's use of "conscience" at the end of *A Portrait* – while the latter should enact the sewer as the consciousness of the city by ventriloquizing it, personifying it, and endowing it with fictional being. Earlier in the same chapter Hugo writes, "[t]he sewer is a cynic. It tells all,"[10] lines that echo Hart's claim about the "mind of the city" in "Wandering Rocks" as "both mechanical and maliciously ironic." If we filter the Poddle's metaphorical "tongue" through Hugo's assertions about the sewer's urban truth, then we have a heuristic for understanding the formal novelty of "Wandering Rocks" as a reimagining of the omniscient narrator through the material and collective constructions of modern urbanism.

The ironic tone of the chapter might easily be summed up in the description of the Poddle's tongue of liquid sewage: The river gives a raspberry to the cavalcade, announcing its subversive "fealty." Not content to stop at mocking authority, it mocks nearly every character it encounters. This ironic note sounded by the "tongue" bears a very strong family resemblance to the malicious irony and opacity of the headlines in "Aeolus." As Hart again points out, the Poddle River empties into the Liffey at Wellington Quay, not Wood Quay, as this line from "Wandering Rocks" would have it (Wellington Quay is about a half-kilometer downriver of Wood Quay; both run along the south bank of the Liffey, with Essex Quay separating them). Hart interprets the geographical imprecision of the line as one of Joyce's few factual feints in *Ulysses*. The viceregal cavalcade around which "Wandering Rocks" is organized, for example, actually took place on May 31, 1904, not June 16. While this is easily explicable as the author's need to "change some of the facts in order to accommodate his fiction," other factual changes, like moving the Poddle's mouth from Wellington to Wood Quay, have less to do with plot and more to do with symbolism ("Wandering" 196). Because the Dublin Corporation Cleansing Department Offices were located at 15–16 Wood Quay, Hart suggests, it makes sense to have the sewage emerge from just underneath the building; It produces "a more powerful image of unified sewage" (199).

More than an image of "unified sewage," however, the relocation of the Poddle's sluice gate to Wood Quay is one more way of rendering Dublin, in Michael Seidel's words, "as a city of traps, a city of irresolution, cul de sacs, accidents, missed connections and missed streetcars, misread signs, wrong turns, indignities, and sheer labyrinthine terror, a Minoan as much as a Greek adventure."[11] And the characters in "Wandering Rocks" seem as confused by Dublin's geography as the reader may be, as if Dublin suffered in both fiction and fact from a certain unreality. The Poddle River was, before the Dublin Corporation Waterworks Act of 1861, the source of much of Dublin's drinking water.[12] That a recent source of potable water should be, by 1904, reduced to "a tongue of liquid sewage" adds another indignity to Seidel's list and makes a complete mockery of the name of the institution dedicated to its maintenance, the Dublin Corporation Cleansing Department. Joyce's fictional relocation of the river's mouth thus creates not only an image of unified sewage but – as it evokes the Poddle's civic role through a long history – a tragicomic image of urban ecological degradation through time.

Under the sign of unified sewage emerges also a powerful image of the urban totality. Wood Quay was the site of the very first Viking settlement in Dublin in 841, just east of the point where the Poddle met the Liffey. Those early Norse settlers docked their ships in a body of stagnant water at the rivers' intersection that they called "Black Pool," a phrase taken from the Irish "Dubh Linn," which was borrowed from the Irish Christian monastery they found and conquered. So for Joyce fictionally to move the "tongue of liquid sewage" to a site that evokes the city's earliest origins is to give that tongue something rather specific, if maybe a little disappointing, to say: "Dubh Linn," or "Dublin."[13] Joyce, in effect, relocates the rivers' confluence in time as well as space, marking the beginning of the history of a place called Dublin in a real but long gone "black pool" that has since metempsychosed into a black tongue of liquid sewage.[14] That tongue speaks the etymology of the Hiberno-English word Dublin from its Irish origins; it speaks the ontology of the vital entity known as Dublin; likewise, it speaks a whole history of conquest (from the Celts to the Vikings to the Normans) and relativizes, in its long historical perspective, the pompousness, the ignorance, and above all the fleetingness of the authority represented in the viceregal cavalcade. Dublin speaks itself and its defiance from the river's mouth, mocking the cavalcade with sly civility.[15] Liquid sewage is granted being by Joyce's narrative, and it grants being to the city of Dublin, naming an organism but also giving it a voice.

In a manner typical of Joyce's scatological humor, "Wandering Rocks" situates the erstwhile omniscient narrator in a zone of grotesque embodiment in the form of a "tongue" of liquefied human excrement, which is really only to say that he literally humanizes it.[16] The networks of rivers, sewers, and canals that make up Dublin's circulatory system, when taken as a whole, present a plausible point of view from which the narrating voice of the chapter gains its multiple and simultaneous perspectives, and that point of view explains why "Wandering Rocks" can jump from one section to another without syntactic connection. The infrastructure of the city "lives" or "sees" each geographical point simultaneously. It is everywhere at once; it doesn't need *syntactic* connection because it has *infrastructural* connection. Words like "meanwhile," or phrases like "at the same time" are conspicuously absent from the episode not just to make it difficult to understand but to invoke the infrastructural narrator, from whose point of view such adverbial connectors would be superfluous or even meaningless. As if to remind us that the view is ubiquitous, the later sections of the episode occasionally break back to earlier ones, re-narrating events that are occurring simultaneously with the current section's action. Section one, for example, follows the movement through the city of Father Conmee: "At Newcomen bridge Father Conmee stepped into an outward bound tram for he disliked to traverse on foot the dingy way past Mud Island" (*U* 10.113–14). One hundred lines later in section two, focalized on Corny Kelleher, we see the same event repeated: "Father John Conmee stepped into the Dollymount tram on Newcomen bridge" (*U* 10.213–14). The technique produces the effects of simultaneity in a medium – print language – in which actual simultaneity is not possible. The intercutting of primary narrated events with repetitions of previously narrated events achieves the impression of simultaneity, and the image of the sewer as a unifying point of view for the episode proposes a perspective for such simultaneity.

The sewer's point of view is not humanly possible and thus appears improbably synoptic; it is, however, bounded by its human-built limits, its engineered corporality. The episode's narrator thus bears little resemblance to an omniscient narrator since it remains within the limited geographical scope of the networks of rivers and sewers that define the municipal boundaries of Dublin. The impression of omniscience is not superhuman in this case but rather non-human; it is, moreover, not even omniscience so much as the "stream of consciousness" of the sewer. To borrow a suggestive term from D. A. Miller's *The Novel and the Police*, "Wandering Rocks" may be said to operate on a principle of panoptical narration as opposed to omniscient narration.[17] Of course, unlike Jeremy Bentham's panopticon, the sewer is not a machine for seeing, but is descended from the utilitarian ideal of governmentality; and as an ubiquitous urban infrastructure it inadvertently offers a point of view no longer rooted in human subjectivity. As Ann Banfield points out, "Point of view in language in the sense of a spatial position is not a grammatical notion, but a pragmatic one. In language, it has been axiomatically taken as located in a speaker."[18] But in the literary experiment Joyce conducts across "Wandering Rocks," "[p]oint of view becomes a concept which can be independent of the speaker's role in communication" (*Unspeakable Sentences* 70). The narrator of the chapter is "not objective, centreless," but rather "subjective but subjectless … representing the perspective of no one."[19] This does not mean that the narrator is perspectiveless. It means rather that we have the perspective, wholly distinctive from omniscient narration, of the underground infrastructure of the city of Dublin; it means that the city is here a speaking character in the fiction. And it means that instead of an omniscient narrator, we encounter an infrastructural narrator.

More in the way of anecdotal evidence could be brought to bear on the argument that the sewer is a good place from which to think about narrative point of view in "Wandering Rocks." If, for example, we were to ask why Joyce chose to title *Ulysses* after the Latin translation of Homer's Greek epic, we might notice that ancient Rome was famous for its sewers and aqueducts, and disparaged for its lack of aesthetic and philosophical achievements when compared to its Greek precursors. We would note too that ancient Rome's most famous sewer, the Cloaca Maxima – in its time and still today considered an engineering marvel – "was central to the city: it began under the Argiletum, the street of the booksellers."[20] And we would note that the Cloaca Maxima's origin in the booksellers' street corresponds wonderfully to the tenth section of "Wandering Rocks," the exact center section of the nineteen sections comprising the episode, where Bloom reads over and finally buys *The Sweets of Sin* for Molly from the hawker's cart (*U* 10.637–41).

We might further note that *The Sweets of Sin*, a work of soft-pornographic pulp fiction, is diametrically opposed to the high-mindedness of an ambitious literary work like *Ulysses*. And yet *Ulysses* is justifiably famous – and in its time, infamous – for demolishing the traditional boundaries between high- and low-brow cultural forms (and sparking a landmark decision in U.S. legal history that distinguished between "obscenity" and a literary classic[21]). Following further on the notional link between Dublin's Poddle and Rome's Cloaca Maxima, we might turn to another distinctive feature of *Ulysses* – or even as is often noted, Joyce's oeuvre as a whole: what H.G. Wells, in his March 1917 review of *A Portrait of the Artist as a Young Man*, referred to as Joyce's "cloacal obsession":

Like Swift and another living Irish writer, Mr. Joyce has a cloacal obsession. He would bring back into the general picture of life aspects which modern drainage and modern decorum have taken out of ordinary intercourse and conversation.... We shall do Mr. Joyce an injustice if we attribute a normal sensory basis to him and then accuse him of deliberate offence.[22]

The source of Joyce's cloacal obsession was for Wells simply – almost self-evidently given the contemporary logic of national character – Joyce's Irishness, as if an Irish obsession with shit were a national characteristic along the same lines as a poetic sensibility or drunkenness. Indeed, what was at the time widely understood to be Joyce's obscenity in *Ulysses* – what Joseph Brooker calls the "complex offensiveness" of Joyce's writings, which had so many consequences for the circulation and publication of *Ulysses* – can be traced back as much to the so-called cloacal obsession as to the sexual explicitness of the novel.[23] Given the evidence of "Wandering Rocks" and "Aeolus," it may be that the cloacal obsession is itself no more an obsession with shit than it is an obsession with sewers – that is to say, an obsession with the forms of infrastructure as much as their contents.

A cloacal obsession like the one Wells describes would be a kind of explanation for the role of the sewer in "Wandering Rocks," and of the scene in "Calypso" that depicts Bloom shitting in the outhouse at 7 Eccles Street. But again, we need to understand this as Joyce's infrastructural obsession – actually truer to the Latin root *cloacae*, meaning sewer – with an emphasis, in Wells's words, on bringing "back into the general picture of life aspects which modern drainage and modern decorum have taken out of ordinary intercourse and conversation." Such a mission was in the service not merely of modernist innovation but of a new, more honest, more realistic kind of realism – one that attempted to leave nothing out, or, more to the point, that refused to leave out the things that nineteenth-century realism, by convention, refused to include.

Joyce had three things to say about Wells's review. The first two were confidences reported by Budgen. Joyce told him that Wells was "a very appreciative critic of my writings," but, apropos of the "cloacal obsession," that "it's Wells's countrymen who build water-closets wherever they go" (*Making* 108). So Joyce reassigned the cloacal obsession to an English imperial sensibility, dismissing it from his Irish colonial one. Thirdly, Joyce fictionalized his response in *Ulysses*, in the first serialized publication of "Aeolus," which appeared in *The Little Review* in October 1918, about eight months after Wells's review.[24] There Joyce rebutted Wells's accusation in print, through Professor MacHugh's joke about Roman, and, by extension, British imperialism:

> What was their [Roman] civilization? Vast, I allow: but vile. *Cloacae*: sewers. The jews in the wilderness and on the mountaintop said: *It is meet to be here. Let us build an altar to Jehovah.* The Roman, like the Englishman who follows in his footsteps, brought to every new shore on which he set his foot (on our shore he never set it) only his cloacal obsession. He gazed about him in his toga and he said: *It is meet to be here. Let us construct a watercloset.* (*U* 7.489–95)

The whole joke so resembles Wells's critique and Joyce's response to it that it must have been incorporated into *Ulysses* and put into MacHugh's mouth straight from Joyce's reading of and response to his own critical reception. Here again Joyce turns the polarity of the cloacal obsession around, imputing it to imperial utilitarianism rather than to some aspect of his Irish literary sensibility. But the truth of the problem more likely resides in a "both / and," not an "either / or." Roman and British imperialism were characterized by infrastructural development of conquered territory; and this was particularly true in the case of the British colonization of Ireland. In the Irish case, one feature of the colonized sensibility under such utilitarian rule might very well have been a kind of infrastructural obsession, or ambivalence. Certainly this appears to be true for Joyce, who included so much of it in *Ulysses* but who, at the same time, seemed compelled to denigrate it, as in MacHugh's joke.

In 1904, Dublin already had, according to Bruce Stewart, "one of the most advanced communications systems in Europe ... a fact which made its imprint on ... *Ulysses*, in the shape of trams and telephones"[25] One could add to Stewart's assertion the Vartry Waterworks, an ambitious and successful scheme completed in 1868 that replaced the Poddle's failing water supply with a new, more abundant one piped in from Wicklow; it is described eloquently in the later "Ithaca" episode of *Ulysses*.[26] Colonial Dublin may have been perceived as a second-rate backwater, but in fact it was at the cutting edge of European modernity and modernization. Joyce's modernist impulse in *Ulysses* was to acknowledge such infrastructural transformations – no matter how ambivalent he may have been about them – and to take them on board his fictional project. *Ulysses* allows the networks of modernity to change the ways a story about a modern polity can be told, as part of the utopian project of reimagining – in the strongest sense of the word – that polity. To borrow from the work of German architect Sigfried Giedion, the subterranean "everyday despised domains" of the late nineteenth-century urban world – those aspects of life that drainage and decorum had, for H. G. Wells, excluded from "ordinary intercourse and conversation" – actually "furnish … as in a delirium, the elements for a collective formation."[27] It was toward an imagination of a new "collective formation" in Giedion's sense that Joyce played with infrastructure in *Ulysses* as a model for narrative form.

Wells went on in his 1917 review of *A Portrait* to excuse Joyce's cloacal obsession, arguing in effect that its offensiveness was outweighed by the novel's literary merit. "The value of Mr. Joyce's book," he wrote, "has little to do with its incidental insanitary condition."[28] This is where Wells gets it precisely wrong, at least insofar as *Ulysses* is concerned. The modernist strengths of *Ulysses* live vibrantly in the contradictions and ambivalences of infrastructure, the basic material building blocks of civic life that were then largely considered unfit for inclusion in literary art. In infrastructure – and in the narrative innovations that Joyce cobbled together from his ambivalent consideration of infrastructure – lies a central aspect of the formal novelty and the stylistic experimentation of *Ulysses*. "Aeolus" and "Wandering Rocks" are both striking examples of the extent and range of such narrative innovation.

Notes

* Portions of this essay have been previously published, in *Public Works: Infrastructure, Irish Modernism, and the Postcolonial* (South Bend, IN: University of Notre Dame Press, 2010). I thank the publishers for their kind permission to reprint those passages here. I'd also like to thank the organizers and participants of the 2012 National Endowment for the Humanities Summer Seminar on *Ulysses* at Trinity College Dublin, whose help and insights have shaped the work presented here: Sara Bryant, James Clawson, Amy Clukey, Jennifer Dellner, Kevin Dettmar, Heather Fielding, Sarah Hardy, Emily James, Matthew Kochis, Mia McIver, Pat Moran, Patrick Mullen, Taura Napier, Adam Putz, Bonnie Roos, Paul K. Saint Amour, and Laura Winkiel.

1 Benedict Anderson, *Imagined Communities: Reflections on the Origin and Spread of Nationalism*, rev. ed. (London: Verso, 1991). Further references will be cited parenthetically in the text as *Imagined*.

2 Frank Budgen, *James Joyce and the Making of "Ulysses"* (Oxford: Oxford University Press, 1972), p. 123. Further references will be cited in the text as *Making*.

3 Declan Kiberd, *"Ulysses" and Us: The Art of Everyday Living* (London: Faber & Faber, 2010), p. 118.

4 James Joyce, *"Ulysses*: Episode VII," *The Little Review* 5 (October 1918): 26–51. The issue is available online at *The Modernist Journals Project*: http://dl.lib.brown.edu/mjp/render.php?view=mjp_object&id=1298921533562502, Accessed: March 2013.

5 See Harry Blamires, *The New Bloomsday Book: A Guide Through "Ulysses"*, 3rd ed. (New York: Routledge, 1996), p. 93.

6 For more about major and minor characters in nineteenth-century fiction, see Alex Woloch, *The One vs. The Many: Minor Characters and the Space of the Protagonist in the Novel* (Princeton, NJ: Princeton University Press, 2003).

7 Clive Hart, "Wandering Rocks," in *James Joyce's "Ulysses": Critical Essays*, eds. Clive Hart and David Hayman (Berkeley: University of California Press, 1974), p. 193. Further references will be cited parenthetically in the text as "Wandering."

8 Declan Kiberd, *Irish Classics* (Cambridge, MA: Harvard University Press, 2002), p. 468.

9 "L'égout, c'est la conscience de la ville." See Victor Hugo, *Les Misérables*, 4 vols. (Paris: Éditeurs Nelson, 1930), 4:191.

10 See Emily Gowers, "The Anatomy of Rome from Capitol to Cloaca," *The Journal of Roman Studies* 85 (1995): 31. Gowers quotes Hugo in English. The original French reads, "Un égout est un cynique. Il dit tout" (Hugo 189). Thanks to Karen Lloyd for directing me to Gowers's article.

11 Michael Seidel, *Epic Geography: James Joyce's "Ulysses"* (Princeton, NJ: Princeton University Press, 1976), p. 183.

12 Joseph Brady, "Dublin at the Turn of the Century," in *Dublin through Space and Time*, eds. Joseph Brady and Anngret Simms (Dublin: Four Courts Press, 2001), pp. 221–81. See especially pp. 238–41.

13 See Chris Stillman, Robert Barklie, and Cathy Johnson, "Viking Iron-Smelting in Dublin's Temple Bar West," *Geology Today* 19 (November/December 2003): 216.

14 For more about the play between time and space in "Wandering Rocks," see Luke Gibbons, "Spaces of Time through Times of Space: Joyce, Ireland, and Colonial Modernity," *Field Day Review* 1 (2005): 71–86.

15 The term is Homi Bhabha's, from his "Sly Civility," *October* 34 (Autumn 1985): 71–80. See especially pp. 77–78, in which Bhabha quotes the frustration of missionaries toward recalcitrant natives who persist in their own religious beliefs by reinterpreting Christianity as capacious enough to accommodate them.

16 For more on the myths and meanings of the sewer, not in Dublin but in a comparative study of Paris and London, see David L. Pike, *Subterranean Cities: The World Beneath Paris and London, 1800–1945* (Ithaca, NY: Cornell University Press, 2005), especially ch. 3, "Charon's Bark." See also, by the same author, *Metropolis on the Styx: The Underworlds of Modern Urban Culture, 1800–2001* (Ithaca, NY: Cornell University Press, 2007).

17 D. A. Miller, *The Novel and the Police* (Berkeley: University of California Press, 1988), p. 24.

18 Ann Banfield, *Unspeakable Sentences: Narration and Representation in the Language of Fiction* (London: Routledge and Kegan Paul, 1982), p. 69. Further references will be cited parenthetically in the text as *Unspeakable Sentences*.

19 Ann Banfield, "L'Imparfait de l'Objectif: The Imperfect of the Object Glass," *Camera Obscura* 24 (Fall 1990): 77.

20 Gowers, "Anatomy," p. 25.

21 See Jeffrey Segall, *Joyce in America: Cultural Politics and the Trials of "Ulysses"* (Berkeley: University of California Press, 1993).

22 H. G. Wells, "James Joyce," *Nation* 20 (February 24, 1917): 710, 712.

23 Joseph Brooker, *Joyce's Critics: Transitions in Reading and Culture* (Madison: University of Wisconsin Press, 2004), p. 17.

24 *U* VII. MacHugh's joke appears on page 37 of the magazine and is nearly identical to the book version.

25 Bruce Stewart, "James Joyce," in *The Cambridge Companion to the Irish Novel*, ed. John Wilson Foster (Cambridge: Cambridge University Press, 2006), p. 133.

26 See Michael Rubenstein, *Public Works: Infrastructure, Irish Modernism, and the Postcolonial* (Notre Dame, IN: University of Notre Dame Press, 2010), pp. 43–92.

27 Sigfried Giedion, *Bauen in Frankreich* (Leipzig and Berlin: Klinkhardt & Biermann, 1928). As Quoted in Walter Benjamin, *The Arcades Project* (Cambridge, MA: Harvard University Press, 1999), p. 390.

28 H. G. Wells, "James Joyce" *Nation* 20 (24 February 1917), http://www.tnr.com/book/review/james-joyce, Accessed: March 2013.

CHAPTER 9

Memory: "Sirens"

Marjorie Howes

"Sirens" begins by "remembering" events that haven't happened yet, and by offering readers a passage we can't read yet. The first sixty-three lines only become intelligible in retrospect, when we have read the whole episode, returned to those lines, and realized that they are composed of fragments culled from the rest of "Sirens." This bit of narrative trickery, which encourages readers to reevaluate a passage in light of later textual moments, illustrates what Hugh Kenner calls the "aesthetic of delay" in *Ulysses*.[1] It suggests, among other things, Joyce's fascination with the complexities of memory. He was famous among his acquaintances for his retentive memory, and, having left Ireland at a young age, he spent the rest of his life drawing on his memories of Ireland for his work. But memory was not simply a matter of retention or retrieval for Joyce; he was deeply interested in questions of what memory is and how it works. The history of Western thought has produced many competing ideas about these questions, and Joyce's works are full of them.[2] Memory can be thought of in a number of different ways: a conscious art, a voluntary act of storage and retrieval, an invention in the service of the present, a necessarily incomplete delving into the recesses of the unconscious mind, or an involuntary experience of an assault by the past. Some kinds of memory are individual; others are collective or cultural. Some inhabit the mind, while others are lodged in the body or in physical objects. One of the questions *Ulysses* returns to over and over again, in a number of registers, is the question of the present's relationship to the past. Is the past enabling or crippling? Are memories painful or pleasurable? Easily accessible or deeply buried? How can individuals come to terms with the past?

Memory is one of the sirens in "Sirens," both alluring and dangerous. This eleventh episode is full of people and things designed to seduce. Music is perhaps the most obvious, and much scholarship has understandably seen it as central to both the formal qualities and thematic concerns of the episode.[3] Other sirens include the barmaids, alcohol, commodity culture, Blazes Boylan, and Irish nationalism. Joyce chose to foreground memory in an episode focused, in important ways, around seduction to emphasize the temporal complexities of memory, which have as much to do with imagination, desire, and the future as they do with the past. This chapter proposes to explore some of the major preoccupations of "Sirens" through the lens of memory. These preoccupations are all related, but we can separate them somewhat clumsily into narrative technique, individual identity and subjectivity, and community and collective memory.

As *Ulysses* proceeds, the narrative becomes increasingly self-referential, returning to earlier events and phrases and amplifying them, so that readers can only make sense of the novel going forward by going back and remembering what came before. "Sirens" is arguably the first chapter to embody this principle in a systematic way. One aspect of it appears in the opening; another appears in the repeated use of a kind of shorthand to recall moments that were originally narrated more fully. Many instances of this method are quite local, designed to highlight the principle itself rather than the content of what is being remembered:

> – God, do you remember? Ben bulky Dollard said, turning from the punished keyboard. And by Japers I had no wedding garment.
> They laughed all three. He had no wed. All trio laughed. No wedding garment. (*U* 11.472–5)

The last three sentences in this quote deliver no new information; instead they remember, repeat and rearrange parts of the initial statements. Other examples call attention to their redundancy even more explicitly, as when the narrative returns to the famous opening line of "Calypso": "As said before he ate with relish the inner organs, nutty gizzards, fried cods' roes .... Bloom ate liv as said before" (*U* 11.519–20, 569).

These small examples illustrate a counterpoint to the aesthetic of delay; to tweak Kenner's argument slightly, we might call it the aesthetic of parallax.[4] The aesthetic of delay prompts the reader to revisit passages and solve riddles in light of later information, while the aesthetic of parallax creates textual moments that are only intelligible in relation to what has been said before. In each case, a particular passage demands to be interpreted in relation to other passages – either later passages (delay), or earlier passages (parallax). Taken together, they suggest a model of reading *Ulysses* that is non-linear and always in process. Reading the novel can only be rereading, a returning to the text armed with the memories of earlier readings. And no reading can ever be final or definitive, because each one will send us back to the beginning – precisely the kind of loop suggested by the opening of "Sirens." Within the larger novel too, reading tends to give way to rereading: In "Calypso" Bloom reads Milly's letter not once, but a total of four times, and in "Lotus Eaters" he reads Martha's letter twice.

Retelling goes along with rereading. Many things that happen in *Ulysses* are narrated more than once. In "Sirens" the same minor story about Ben Dollard borrowing a pair of tight trousers from the Blooms is told twice, from two different points of view, in the space of three pages (*U* 11.472–562). There is no final or definitive narration, only endlessly proliferating opportunities to re-narrate what has gone before. *Ulysses* is also famous for its massive numbers of allusions to other literary and cultural texts, and for its multitude of accurate references to real people, places, and events around Dublin in 1904. A number of scholars have argued that Joyce's method, and his conception of literature, relied more on indebtedness, citation, and plagiarism than on notions of individuality or creativity. Joyce, according to this line of thinking, is remembering, rearranging, and repeating elements from his own works and from the history of Western culture and history.[5] Ironically, then, part of Joyce's great originality may have been to flaunt his lack of originality and his dependence on his various sources.

The narrative methods outlined above are not simply functions of individual characters' minds. This is clear, for example, when the barmaids make fun of a local chemist with his "greasy eyes" (*U* 11.169) and the narrative somewhat cruelly transfers this joke to Bloom, who has not yet entered the hotel: "Married to Bloom, to greaseabloom" (*U* 11.180). However, Joyce does use the interweaving of memory, narrative, and temporality to comment on individual characters' identity and subjectivity. At one point the narrative (or possibly Bloom – it could be either) remembers: "Mrs Marion. Met him pike hoses. Smell of burn. Of Paul de Kock. Nice name he" (*U* 11.500–01). This passage consists entirely of bits that first occur in the fourth episode, "Calypso." It functions as a summary and reminder of that chapter, while at the same time offering the reader important clues about how to read "Sirens." In "Calypso," Bloom first learns that Molly will have a sexual encounter with Blazes Boylan at four o'clock that day; "Sirens" takes place shortly before and shortly after that fateful hour. Here we watch as Bloom makes a transition from anxiously anticipating Molly's infidelity to sadly acknowledging that it has already begun; the episode's last word is *"Done"* (*U* 11.1294). The fragments juxtapose references to Boylan's boldness and Molly's wayward desires with references to the Blooms' relationship and domestic life – repeating, on a small scale, the larger structures of the novel's plot.

By foregrounding Molly's adultery, the fragments also help readers understand why "Sirens" is obsessed with clocks and time. Bloom thinks repeatedly about the time: "Not yet. At four, she said. Time ever passing. Clockhands turning" (*U* 11.187–88); "At four. Near now.... At four she" (*U* 11.305, 309); "Not yet. At four she. Who said four?" (*U* 11.352); "At four. Has he forgotten?" (*U* 11.392); "Four now" (*U* 11.445). In fact, the episode as a whole, rather than just Bloom, is preoccupied with time and clocks: "Clock whirred.... Clock clacked.... Clock clacked.... –What time is that? asked Blazes Boylan. Four?" (*U* 11.380–85). Even Miss Douce's risqué display of her garter is described as the striking of a bell on a clock: "Let's hear the time .... *Sonnez la cloche*" (11.389, 404). The inexorable march of empty, homogeneous clock time signals the inevitability of Molly's unfaithfulness – the moment Bloom is both waiting for and dreading. In a sense, he is remembering it before it happens.

The present moment of the episode combines memory and anticipation – looking back and looking forward – on a thematic and linguistic level as well as a narrative one. "Sirens" is littered with references to the act of remembering. For example, they crop up repeatedly as the men in the bar of the Ormond Hotel tell the story of Ben Dollard and the tight trousers: "Poor old Goodwin was the pianist that night, Father Cowley reminded them.... God, do you remember? ... I remember those tight trousers too.... Do you remember? ... Remember? Ben remembered, his broad visage wondering" (*U* 11.466–90). References to anticipation or waiting are equally numerous. Many of them cluster around passages involving Pat, the waiter: "Pat is a waiter who waits while you wait. Hee hee hee hee. He waits while you wait. Hee hee. A waiter is he. Hee hee hee hee. He waits while you wait. While you wait if you wait he will wait while you wait" (*U* 11.916–18). Such references verge on nonsense; they certainly do little to advance the narrative in conventional ways. Their main purpose is to emphasize Bloom's temporal predicament in "Sirens" since he is trapped between memories he cannot escape and an impending event that appears similarly inevitable: "Wish they'd sing more. Keep my mind off" (*U* 11.914).

Memory can play the siren in ways that prove damaging. Other characters succumb to memories that trap them in nostalgia, sentimentality, and falsehood. Richie Goulding, for example, remembers his brother-in-law Simon Dedalus singing some years ago: "Richie ... descanted on that man's glorious voice. He remembered one night long ago. Never forget that night" (*U* 11.778–79). Richie lives in the past: "Never would Richie forget that night. As long as he lived: never" (*U* 11.623). His present existence is full of failure and falsehood, as Bloom thinks scornfully: "Coming out with a whopper now. Rhapsodies about damn all. Believes his own lies. Does really. Wonderful liar. But want a good memory .... Rollicking Richie once. Jokes old stale now" (*U* 11.626–27, 646–47). For Richie, memory is a siren that falsifies the past and impoverishes the present and Bloom sees in him the "Face of the all is lost" (*U* 11.646). Another character whose pretentious memory of past glory provokes scorn is Tom Kernan, who praises Ben Dollard's singing of "The Croppy Boy" for its "*trenchant rendering*" and its "*retrospective arrangement*" (*U* 6.147, 150). The men attending Dignam's funeral poke fun at him for his pseudo-elegant sentimentality: " – *Trenchant*, Mr Power said laughing. He's dead nuts on that. And the *retrospective arrangement*" (*U* 6.149–50). In "Sirens" Kernan – described as "Tomgin Kernan" (*U* 11.1148) with his "ginhot words" (*U* 11.926) – is seen in the Ormond bar "harking back in a retrospective sort of arrangement" (*U* 11.798) and complimenting Simon on his "trenchant rendition of that ballad" (*U* 11.1148).

This kind of harking back is at once dishonest and sentimental: It casts a false glamour over the past and indulges in cheap emotion. Such shallowness is an important theme in "Sirens." The bar is full of shiny surfaces like the "barmirror gildedlettered where hock and claret glasses shimmered" (*U* 11.118–19), "mirrors, gilded arch for ginger ale, hock and claret glasses shimmering" (*U* 11.421–22), the piano's keys "[b]rightly ... all twinkling" (*U* 11.324), and Miss Douce's "[s]parkling bronze azure" eyes (*U* 11.394). And the barmaids – whose unguarded speech betrays their relative lack of education – aspire to more sophisticated phrasing like "[e]xquisite contrast," "impertinent insolence," and "essence of vulgarity" (*U* 11.68, 99, 418) when they're paying attention and trying to impress. Their clothes also embody their aspirations to greater elegance and higher class status than they actually possess. They are, as Bloom observes, "Got up to kill: on eighteen bob a week" (*U* 11.1076–77). The deceptive object world the barmaids inhabit includes the shell Miss Douce has brought from her vacation on the beach.[6] We buy souvenirs because we imagine these objects will help us remember experiences: "She had a gorgeous, simply gorgeous, time. And look at the lovely shell she brought" (*U* 11.921–22). But what they really embody is the present, rather than the past: "The sea they think they hear. Singing. A roar. The blood it is. Souse in the ear sometimes" (*U* 11.945–46). The shell becomes a misleading siren that threatens to make listeners drunk.

This is not to say that *Ulysses* privileges real elegance and high culture; on the contrary, the novel often revels in bad jokes, low humor, popular culture, and even junk and trash. And Joyce's tone is often hard to judge: Are we to scorn the barmaids for their banality and their pretensions or sympathize with them because of their limited social and political options? Mark Osteen argues that "their flirting reveals through the veil of giggles a desperate longing to escape from their jobs and lonely lives" (*Economy* 283). Miss Kennedy sadly leaves the window where she was watching the viceregal cavalcade pass, thinking of male privilege: "It's them has the fine times, sadly then she said" (*U* 11.84). Joyce agreed about the sexist nature of Irish society, writing to Nora in a 1904 letter:

> My mother was slowly killed, I think, by my father's ill-treatment, by years of trouble, and by my cynical frankness of conduct. When I looked on her face as she lay in her coffin – a face grey and wasted with cancer – I understood that I was looking on the face of a victim and I cursed the system which had made her a victim. (*JJ* 169)

When the novel reports that "Miss Douce's brave eyes, unregarded, turned from the crossblind" (*U* 11.460), is the adjective "brave" applied to her by the narrative, or by her own mind? Is it ironic or not? In contrast to Osteen, Joseph Valente suggests that the exuberance of the barmaids' laughter subverts, albeit temporarily, the patriarchal order of representation.[7] And Derek Attridge observes that Joyce's syntax gives individual body parts independent agency in lines like "Her wet lips tittered" (*U* 11.76). As a result, he argues, "Sirens" seeks to "liberate the body from a dictatorial and englobing will and allow its organs their own energies and proclivities."[8] Debates over the implications of the novel's representations of women, and the forms of memory and desire they involve, will no doubt continue.

Bloom is more tempted by the shallow sentimentality of Richie's self-pity than by the episode's other sirens. As he leaves the Ormond, the narrative describes him as "I feel so lonely Bloom" (*U* 11.1136–37), and he laments that Molly's unfaithfulness is inevitable: "As easy stop the sea. Yes: all is lost" (*U* 11.641). But throughout the episode, if Bloom remembers what four o'clock will mean, he also remembers happier times with Molly in the past. While his memory registers his loss and Molly's transgression, it also allows him to reclaim her in a way. At one point, for example, Bloom thinks back to the night he and Molly met: "First night when first I saw her at Mat Dillon's in Terenure. Yellow, black lace she wore. Musical chairs. We two the last. Fate. After her. Fate" (*U* 11.725–26). This memory returns Bloom to the very beginning of their romance, and it converts inevitability into his ally rather than his enemy. A similar passage continues this process of reclamation and conversion: "Singing. *Waiting* she sang. I turned her music.... First I saw. She thanked me. Why did she me? Fate" (*U* 11.730–32). Here again, fate determines the Blooms' marriage, rather than Molly's adultery; in addition, waiting has been transformed from painful anticipation of adultery into part of their alluring first encounter. Music itself, often a dangerous siren in this episode, can become comforting when allied with memory:

> Through the hush of air a voice sang to them, low, not rain, not leaves in murmur, like no voice of strings or reeds or whatdoyoucallthem dulcimers touching their still ears with words, still hearts of their each his remembered lives. Good, good to hear. (*U* 11.674–77)

The "still hearts" of "remembered lives" offer, at least temporarily, a refuge from the pain of the present.

For Bloom, then, memory represents a way of both thwarting and fulfilling desire: It offers traumatic reminders of what he has lost and what will happen during "Sirens," but it also provides solace and support in the present. This dual function is central to Bloom's unique heroism. Joyce had little interest in conventional forms of masculinity, and much has been written about how Bloom might embody alternatives.[9] Hugh Kenner puts it this way: "His distinction is to have been fit to live in Ireland without malice, without violence, without hate" (Kenner 1). Upon returning home, Odysseus slaughtered the suitors; Bloom's version of this overcoming is that he achieves a degree of emotional tranquility and acceptance, feeling "more abnegation than jealousy, less envy than equanimity" (*U* 17.2195). In contrast to Boylan, who is a conventional and fairly vulgar "conquering hero" (*U* 11.340), Bloom is an "unconquered hero" (*U* 11.342), vulnerable but resilient, and he is able to analyze and resist the various siren songs in the episode.

Nationalism also involves the seductions of collective memory; these are most clearly embodied in Ben Dollard's singing of "The Croppy Boy." The song chronicles the story of a young Irish rebel whose father and brothers have all been killed, leaving him the "Last of his name and race" (*U* 11.1064–65). He goes to a priest for confession, but the priest turns out to be a British soldier in disguise, and the croppy boy is captured and executed. The final lines ask that listeners remember him: "Good people who live in peace and joy, / Breathe a prayer and a tear for the Croppy Boy."[10] A familiar ballad to all the listeners in the Ormond, the song represents a collective memory they all share. "They know it all by heart" (*U* 11.1082–83), Bloom observes. Not only is the song about a nationalist rebel, it also embodies a particular model of nationalism, one that sees itself not as a rupture with the past and a new beginning, but as the reawakening or return of an identity and tradition that has been suppressed. Such nationalism is, in Benedict Anderson's term, genealogical, seeing itself "as the expression of an historical tradition of serial continuity."[11] For Anderson, and other theorists of the nation, this kind of national belonging requires the creation of collective memories, like the injunction to remember the croppy boy. More specifically, it requires a combination of remembering and forgetting, in which national community is enabled by a shared forgetting of divisiveness and violence.[12]

Such memories are therefore as much invention as recollection, and they elide as much as they reveal. This makes the form of collectivity they embody an alluring but potentially damaging siren. In the bar, listeners are "All lost in pity for croppy" (*U* 11.1113), and Joyce's phrasing both indicates community and links this community to the siren-like nostalgia of the episode's other songs in which "all is lost" is a major theme: "Thou lost one. All songs on that theme" (*U* 11.802). Bloom characterizes such sentimentality this way: "Cowley, he stuns himself with it: kind of drunkenness.... Thinking strictly prohibited" (*U* 11.1191–94). He also links it to his earlier thoughts on the narcotic effects of religion in "Lotus Eaters": "Good idea the Latin. Stupefies them first" (*U* 5.350–51). In "Sirens" he muses, "Latin again. That holds them like birdlime" (*U* 11.1034). This national belonging renders its adherents drugged, senseless, and trapped.

Joyce had little sympathy for the sentimental armchair nationalism implied by the combination of the prayer and the tear. Neither does Bloom, who thinks, "Thrill now. Pity they feel. To wipe away a tear for martyrs that want to, dying to, die" (*U* 11.1101–02). As this quote suggests, another aspect of Joyce's critique of Irish nationalism was that it sentimentalized and consented to violence, forgetting rather than acknowledging its true ugliness and cost, assuming blithely that martyrs want to die and that their deaths are sad but unavoidable: "The chords consented. Very sad thing. But had to be" (*U* 11.1121). The novel makes the same point, using a different narrative technique, when it describes the execution of Robert Emmett in "Cyclops" (*U* 12.525–678). Bloom is the only person within hearing who is not seduced by the song; he determines to "Get out before the end" (*U* 11.1122) and thinks, "Breathe a prayer, drop a tear. All the same he must have been a bit of a natural not to see it was a yeoman cap" (*U* 11.1248–49), suggesting that the nationalist martyr met his demise because of his own ignorance.

But Joyce's engagement with Irish nationalism is more complex than mere critique. For some time now, scholars have recognized that Joyce was also seriously interested in struggles against imperialism, in various forms

of national community and in the kinds of collective memory that enabled
them.[13] *Ulysses* is full of critical references to British imperialism, which
Joyce often compares to the Roman Empire. Stephen names the "imperial
British state" as one of the "two masters" he is forced to serve (*U* 1.643,
638), and thinks of the Englishman Haines as "The seas' ruler" (*U* 1.574).
In "Aeolus," Professor McHugh characterizes imperial Rome's civilization
as "Vast … but vile," continuing, "The Roman, like the Englishman who
follows in his footsteps, brought to every new shore on which he set his
foot … only his cloacal obsession" (*U* 7.489, 491–93). Joyce also proposes
a corollary to his linking of the English and Roman empires in a comparison between the Irish and the Jews, two peoples who were oppressed
by more powerful but less spiritual peoples than themselves. The physical
landscape of the novel features many buildings, monuments, streets, and
other sites that embody both imperialist and nationalist history. Vincent
Cheng points out that "a ramble through the streets of Dublin or through
any episode of *Ulysses* […] is an object lesson in the omnipresent history
of imperial domination and nationalist insurrection" (*Race and Empire*
169). Collective memories of dispossession and anti-colonial resistance are
lodged in individual cultural artifacts like the song, in other cultural traditions, and in the surrounding geography.

Bloom is critical of the croppy boy and the sentimentality of the ballad.
But "Sirens" makes another point about Bloom in relation to the croppy
as well. In some respects, Bloom and the boy inhabit similar situations.
Both are lonely, both have been betrayed, and Bloom thinks, "I too. Last
of my race" (*U* 11.1066). In the song, the croppy boy finishes his confession and tells the priest "*Bless me and let me go*" (*U* 11.1074); meanwhile
"Bloom looked, unblessed to go" (*U* 11.1076). Unlike the croppy, Bloom,
the "unblessed," is able to extricate himself from the scene. He becomes a
more successful version of the croppy, one who survives rather than dies.
Once again, Bloom is an "unconquered hero," a hero by virtue of the fact
that he does not succumb to sentimentality or despair. The nationalist
tradition represented by the ballad, while it is rejected by Bloom, is also
rewritten into a discourse that enables him to leave the siren songs of the
episode behind.

The complex engagement with the traditions and collective memories of Irish nationalism in "Sirens" is also evident in the final scene, after
Bloom has left the Ormond. On the street, he pauses and looks into the
window of an antique shop:

> In Lionel Marks's antique saleshop window haughty Henry Lionel Leopold
> dear Henry Flower earnestly Mr Leopold Bloom envisaged battered

candlesticks melodeon oozing maggoty blowbags. Bargain: six bob. Might learn to play. Cheap. Let her pass. Course everything is dear if you don't want it. That's what good salesman is. Make you buy what he wants to sell. (*U* 11.1261–66)

The spell of the sirens in the bar has been quite broken; the elegant appearances are gone, and neither memory nor desire creates pleasing illusions. The items in the window appear as junk rather than as alluring objects. The seductive charms of music and flirtatious barmaids have given way to the melodeon that is decaying like a dead body and the "frowsy whore" who "[l]ooks a fright in the day" (*U* 11.1252, 1259). A siren is now just a "good salesman." In addition, Bloom needs to fart, and the narrative faithfully reproduces this thoroughly unromantic, unglamorous sound.

Amid all this demystifying and deglamorizing, Bloom sees something else in the window as well: "Bloom viewed a gallant pictured hero in Lionel Marks's window. Robert Emmet's last words" (*U* 11.1274–75). Robert Emmet led a failed Irish rebellion in 1803 and was publicly executed. His famous last words came from the speech he made to the court that condemned him to die, which ended "Let no man write my epitaph.... When my country takes her place among the nations of the earth then and not till then, let my epitaph be written. I have done" (*Annotated* 310). The final lines of "Sirens" weave together the sounds of Bloom passing gas, the sounds of a passing tram, and Emmet's words. Bloom's fart has often been interpreted by scholars as a firm and vulgar dismissal of Irish nationalism as represented by Emmet. But Emer Nolan has offered a more nuanced view, arguing that "Bloom, although deliberately separating himself from the group and their activities, remains dependent on the temporal structures they provide" (*Nationalism* 63). As with "The Croppy Boy," Bloom's relationship to the siren song of nationalism is more complicated than simple critique or rejection.

In the case of Emmet's last words, however, the kind of nationalism they embody has a very different temporal structure from the backward-looking command to remember illustrated by the song. The croppy boy functions as a shared memory for the men in the bar – one that creates belonging but also elides violence through sentimentality. Emmet is also remembered as a nationalist hero in Ireland. But he is most famous for his last words; the memories nationalists share of him are, above all, memories of his insistence on futurity. Emmet refuses his epitaph – which might involve prayers, tears, and words – until Ireland is free. Like the process of narrating or reading *Ulysses*, the blank epitaph perpetually defers a final statement. The setting in which Bloom views Emmet's words can be taken as a dismissal of them, but it can also be read as a refusal of the falsifying and pseudo-glamorous setting of the bar and a more balanced assessment of the way nationalism and its collective memories incorporate both the noble and the ignoble. Emmet dies, as Lenehan quips of Moses, "with a great future behind him" (*U* 7.875–76); this remark is funny and, in another way, rather profound.

In these two temporal structures we can find echoes of the aesthetic of delay and the aesthetic of parallax. The aesthetic of delay looks back, using new passages to answer past questions. The aesthetic of parallax, on the other hand, looks forward, in the sense that it generates new mysteries that the reader must elucidate by remembering what has gone before. We can also see connections with the ambiguities of individual memory, which can mire people in the past or empower them in the present. In exploring the complexities of memory in these various registers, "Sirens" weaves together past and future, memory and desire, reading back and reading forward. Among the many siren songs in the episode, the most powerful, the most fascinating, and the most complex is that of memory itself. In *Ulysses*, such careful attention to the past proves a useful preparation for the difficult episodes ahead.

Notes

1 Hugh Kenner, "*Ulysses*," rev. ed. (Baltimore, MD: Johns Hopkins University Press, 1987), pp. 72–82. Kenner characterizes the aesthetic of delay as "producing the simplest facts by parallax, one element now, one later, and leaving large orders of fact to be assembled late or another time or never" (81). Further references to this text will be cited parenthetically as Kenner.

2 In *Joyce's Book of Memory* (Durham and London: Duke University Press, 1999), John Rickard argues at length that *Ulysses* stages a series of conflicts between modes and models of memory. For effective overviews of different models of memory, see Michael Rossington and Anne Whitehead, eds., *Theories of Memory: A Reader* (Edinburgh: Edinburgh University Press, 2007), and Susannah Radstone and Bill Schwarz, eds., *Memory: Histories, Theories, Debates* (New York: Fordham University Press, 2010).

3 See, for example, Sebastian Knowles, ed., *Bronze by Gold: The Music of Joyce* (New York and London: Garland Publishing, 1999); "Lorraine Wood, Joyce's Ineluctable Modality: (Re)Reading the Structure of 'Sirens,'" *Joyce Studies Annual* (2007): 67–91; Jon D. Green, "The Sounds of Silence in 'Sirens': Joyce's Verbal Music of the Mind," *JJQ* 39 (Spring 2002): 489–508; and Zack Bowen, *Bloom's Old Sweet Song: Essays on Joyce and Music* (Gainesville: University of Florida Press, 1995).

4 The *Oxford English Dictionary Online* defines parallax as the "difference or change in the apparent position or direction of an object as seen from two

different points. Parallax involves the same object seen more than once, from different points of view." http://www.oed.com.proxy.bc.edu/

5 For example, see Cheryl Herr, *Joyce's Anatomy of Culture* (Urbana: University of Illinois Press, 1986); Mark Osteen, *The Economy of "Ulysses": Making Both Ends Meet* (Syracuse, NY: Syracuse University Press, 1995); and Eloise Knowlton, *Joyce, Joyceans, and the Rhetoric of Citation* (Gainesville: University of Florida Press, 1998). Further references to Osteen's book will be cited parenthetically as *Economy*.

6 For a longer discussion of objects and the curious lives throughout *Ulysses*, see Chapter 14.

7 See Joseph Valente, "Who Made the Tune: Becoming-Woman in 'Sirens,'" *JJQ* 30 (Winter 1993): 191–208.

8 Derek Attridge, *Peculiar Language: Literature as Difference: From the Renaissance to James Joyce* (London: Methuen, 1988), p. 167.

9 On masculinity, see, for example, *Masculinities in Joyce: Postcolonial Constructions*, eds. Christine van Boheemen and Colleen Lamos *European Joyce Studies* **10** (2001); and Joseph Valente, "'Neither Fish nor Flesh'; or How 'Cyclops' Stages the Double-Bind of Irish Manhood," in *Semicolonial Joyce*, eds. Derek Attridge and Marjorie Howes (Cambridge: Cambridge University Press, 2000), pp. 96–127.

10 Don Gifford, *"Ulysses" Annotated* (Berkeley: University of California Press, 1988), p. 293. Further references to this text will be cited parenthetically as *Annotated*.

11 Benedict Anderson, *Imagined Communities: Reflections on the Origin and Spread of Nationalism* (1983), rev. ed., (London and New York: Verso, 1991), p. 195.

12 See also Ernest Renan's "What is a Nation?" http://ig.cs.tu-berlin.de/oldstatic/w2001/eu1/dokumente/Basistexte/Renan1882EN-Nation.pdf.

13 See Vincent Cheng, *Joyce, Race, and Empire* (Cambridge: Cambridge University Press, 1995); Enda Duffy, *The Subaltern "Ulysses"* (Minneapolis: University of Minnesota Press, 1994); Emer Nolan, *James Joyce and Nationalism* (London: Routledge, 1995); *Semicolonial Joyce*; and David Lloyd, "Adulteration and the Nation," in *Anomalous States: Irish Writing and the Post-Colonial Moment* (Durham, NC: Duke University Press, 1993), pp. 88–124. Cheng's work will be cited parenthetically as *Race and Empire*, Nolan's as *Nationalism*.

CHAPTER 10

Interruption: "Cyclops" and "Nausicaa"

Sean Latham

Something strange happens at the start of the twelfth episode. Departing from the stream of consciousness that had been pushed nearly to its breaking point in the intricately wrought fugal patterns of "Sirens," we encounter something comfortingly familiar to novel readers yet utterly unique in all of Joyce's work: a retrospective, first-person narrator. Here *Ulysses's* carefully organized temporal pattern unravels since this anonymous narrator – typically referred to as "the nameless one" or "the dun" – recounts to an equally anonymous audience the events that took place in Barney Kiernan's pub some time (maybe hours, maybe days) after they actually occurred on June 16, 1904.[1] And this temporal interruption mirrors a stylistic one, as a series of bewildering passages Joyce critics call "interpolations" erupt in the midst of the narrator's sometimes witty, insistently offensive, and often libelous account of a fight that nearly breaks out between Bloom and yet another anonymous character referred to only as "the citizen."

Ulysses, of course, is a book of constant interruptions, which is one reason it can be so difficult to read. The opening conversation atop the Martello tower, for example, is strangely interrupted by the one-word sentence "Chrysostomos," arguably the book's very first interpolation and a phrase that we only retrospectively understand is the first rivulet of what will become Stephen's stream of consciousness (*U* 1.26). As Hugh Kenner argues, even the style of "Telemachus" is self-interrupting, split between what he accurately calls "unemphatic novelese" on the one hand and the distinctively fractured language of interiority on the other.[2] These interruptions multiply wildly through the rest of the book as new "technics" for each episode. This constant succession of stylistic interruptions so characteristic of what Karen Lawrence calls the book's "odyssey of style," might seem hopelessly chaotic were the novel not so tightly wound about the events of that single June day.[3] Even at the level of plot, Stephen's story is abruptly interrupted by Bloom, who is himself now interrupted in "Cyclops" in ways that will ramify throughout the rest of the book. As we overhear the story of Bloom's hasty retreat from Barney Kiernan's pub and then in "Nausicaa" plunge into the consciousness of an entirely new character named Gerty McDowell, a first-time reader might well wonder if Bloom and Stephen have both been abandoned, the book morphing into a Dublin odyssey that, like Joyce's short stories, moves deftly between a shifting array of characters.

Critics have long recognized and debated the nature of the disruptive change in *Ulysses* that occurs when we arrive at "Cyclops." Michael Groden calls this episode part of the book's "middle stage," marking the moment when Joyce first abandons the mélange of third-person narration and stream of consciousness that characterizes the "initial style."[4] Based on his careful reading of the manuscript pages, Groden contends that here "one *Ulysses* ended, and another one began."[5] As Chapter 1 suggests, the discovery of new manuscript materials (now held by the National Library of Ireland) has complicated, but not drastically changed this basic understanding of the book's larger development. And the drafts for the episode themselves reveal the surprising fact that Joyce began his work on "Cyclops" by abandoning the initial style and experimenting with one of the parodic interpolations, the scene that will develop into the initial description of the citizen in the pub: "In Inisfail the fair there lies a land, the land of holy Michan" (*U* 12.68). Joyce's first conception of the episode, in other words, begins with an interruption and only later does he build around it fragments of more familiar dialogue before interrupting himself again to embed it all within the story related by the episode's nameless narrator. Unfortunately, the early manuscripts for "Nausicaa" have not survived, but the "exaggeration" Joyce identifies as essential to "Cyclops" clearly persists in this episode too, the first half of which reads like a remix of earlier stream-of-consciousness passages with the satiric excess of a single, inflated interpolation.[6] The interruptions of these two central episodes thus compound with one another to crowd out the novelistic trajectory of Bloom and Stephen, replacing it instead with new voices, new styles, and new histories. Indeed, when Bloom finally reappears at the end of "Nausicaa," he is now the one interrupting the story, and our eventual return to him proves anything but an easy homecoming.

Our departure from Bloom's stream of consciousness at the end of "Sirens" is abrupt, and is even marked by the episode's final word: "*Done*" (*U* 11.1294). Here the next phase of *Ulysses* begins – not just with the shift toward an anonymous narrator but in the baffling introduction of a legal contract that quickly shoulders this new voice aside. Dropped into the text without transition or introduction, it initially appears that this document might be simply a quotation or reproduction of the actual agreement between Herzog and Geraghty, something similar to the letters from Milly and Martha Clifford that Bloom read earlier in the day or to the strange hangman's letter that will shortly grab the men's attention in the bar. The text, however, is not set aside as an embedded quotation with inverted commas or italics, and its legalese is baroque – the often dense prose of a real contract exaggerated into a maddening, essentially unreadable single sentence. Even more curiously, the characters and narrator alike are unaware of this document: It hovers in the text but doesn't actually appear to be a part of the narrative world. It instead inhabits a space somewhere between the reader and the Dublin of 1904, the creation perhaps of another, more obscure narrator David Hayman calls the "arranger": "a figure or a presence that can be identified neither with the author nor with his narrators" but to whom we can attribute "just about any intrusive or arbitrary phenomenon."[7] If there is another narrative agent interrupting the text as Hayman suggests, then its aim here is clearly satiric since, like those equally unmoored headlines in "Aeolus," the interpolations comment, often hilariously, on the episode's events.

When Bloom arrives at Barney Kiernan's, for example, he is hailed in language evocative of the Irish Revival's neo-mythology: "Who comes through Michan's land, bedight in sable armour? O'Bloom, the son of Rory: it is he" (*U* 12.215–16). Neither the men in the pub nor the episode's narrator would express themselves this way, and we know by now that such language doesn't belong to Bloom. Instead, like many (although not all) of the interpolations in the first half of "Cyclops," it seems to be a broad parody of the work of Revivalists like Yeats, O'Grady, and Lady Gregory, who sought to reconstruct an ancient Irish past by editing collections of myths and folktales. As Andrew Gibson notes in his careful reading of this episode's politics, such passages "mak[e] light of a whole mode of discourse that speciously presented itself as a form of historiography."[8] The long catalogs of people, the recitation of places, and the rehearsal of topographic mythologies (part of the bardic tradition called *dindsenchas*), all evoke the romanticism of the Celtic Twilight only to expose it as vapid and, on the pages of "Cyclops," entirely removed from modern Dublin. History returns here, but in the way Karl Marx describes Louis Napoleon's recycling of Bonapartist France: it's now a farce rather than a tragedy.

This satiric evocation of Irish myth even threatens to disrupt the larger symbolic patterns of *Ulysses* itself. These short passages, after all, operate much like the Homeric titles and parallels that pervade the rest of the book: pieces of ancient epic tessellated around the everyday events of an urban, colonial modernity. As "Cyclops" launches its critique of Revivalist historiography and its fascination with mythical heroes and symbols, it thus also takes aim at what T. S. Eliot famously said was *Ulysses's* most important contribution: the "mythical method," in which the Homeric parallels offer a way of "controlling, of ordering, of giving shape" to modernity's "immense panorama of futility and anarchy."[9] There is more at stake here, in other words, than just a parody of the Revival because Joyce actually begins to interrupt the overarching symbolic structures of the book itself.

Such interruptions are not simply formal or symbolic but instead raise questions about the nascent formation of postcolonial identity in a city just a decade away from the bloody uprising that will eventually lead to independence and civil war. Consider, for example, that final encounter between Bloom and the citizen, an incident that has a clear Homeric analogue: As Odysseus takes to his boat to escape the one-eyed giant he has blinded, he taunts the creature and reveals his own name, which he had so far kept secret by calling himself "Noman." Wounded and furious, the creature calls out to his father, the god of the sea, asking him to curse the sailor so that he will "lose all companions, and return / under strange sail to bitter days at home."[10] This prayer is answered, and Odysseus's crew is soon slaughtered, his boat destroyed, and his home overrun with suitors. Although the day of June 16 is now waning in the novel, Bloom also still faces his greatest trials before he can make his way back to a home and marital bed that still bear the impressions of another man's body.

It's easy to see the citizen and the cyclops alike as dismal monsters, embodiments of senseless violence and dull-witted hatred. When read aslant, however, as the parodic interruptions of the episode invite us to do, both can also become more sympathetic figures who have been subject to constant derision, frustration, and disappointment. The nameless narrator, after all, has little sympathy for the largely impotent champion of Irish independence, and the final attack on Bloom sparks the most striking interpolation in the entire episode – the description of an earthquake that destroys the center of Dublin:

> The epicentre appears to have been that part of the metropolis which constitutes the Inn's Quay ward and parish of Saint Michan covering a surface of fortyone acres, two roods and one square pole or perch. All the lordly residences in the vicinity of the palace of justice were demolished and that

noble edifice itself, in which at the time of the catastrophe important legal debates were in progress, is literally a mass of ruins beneath which it is to be feared all the occupants have been buried alive." (*U* 12.1862–69)

No mere comic intrusion into the narrative by a sneering arranger, this is the moment when Dublin's future invades and interrupts that otherwise placid summer day in 1904. As Enda Duffy argues, the scene of destruction mirrors the city's devastation by the British military in response to the nationalist uprising of Easter 1916. "Even the biscuit tin used as a missile ... is a clue," he writes, since "Jacob's biscuit factory, where the tin originated, was one of the strongholds occupied by the rebels."[11] Unlike the symbolic geography in the earliest interpolations that evoke Revivalist fantasies about the past, this one now looks to the future, representing the violence and smoldering ruin that will soon follow the dream Bloom and the citizen share for an autonomously governed Ireland.

This climatic moment of interruption thus shapes our reading of both "Cyclops" and *Ulysses* as a whole. It emphasizes that the citizen's vision of violent revolt will win out over Bloom's liberal pacifism and that the cultural as well as the political structures of 1904 are already archaic, caught here in narrative amber just before they too will be violently disrupted by revolt, military occupation, and then guerilla and civil war. Declan Kiberd argues that the interruptions in this episode offer a way to represent "the instability of Irish literary tradition" and perhaps even the impossibility of fashioning a pure or authentic Irish identity since this "scene set in Little Britain Street indicts an Ireland which is hardly its own authentic self so much as a not-England."[12] The past and the future are thus constantly interrupting one another in "Cyclops," defying one of the novel's most basic functions as a genre: the ability to craft stable yet changeable identities within a fixed time and space. That novel and its vision of a liberal, humanist world does not survive "Cyclops" and, significantly, neither does Bloom nor the stream-of-consciousness narrative that constitutes Naturalism's own dying gasp in the book. The citizen's biscuit tin misses its target, but Bloom nevertheless departs the story world as we watch him "amid clouds of angels ascend to the glory of the brightness at an angle of fortyfive degrees over Donohoe's in Little Green street like a shot off a shovel" (*U* 12.1916–18). Transported to heaven, the Bloom from the first half of the book cannot fit its second half. Just as Odysseus arrogantly thought himself safe after escaping the cyclops only to encounter a more desperate ruin, so too does Bloom leave Barney Kiernan's filled with a false sense of security. The interpolations that puncture his narrative world, after all, will finally rend its fabric entirely, so that when our

Irish Odysseus does eventually return to *Ulysses*, it will be to interrupt the story of Gerty McDowell.

Between "Cyclops" and "Nausicaa" we encounter a significant temporal gap that initially appears to swallow Bloom. The events at Barney Kiernan's pub likely conclude around six in the evening, yet "Nausicaa" begins at eight o'clock, an interruption noted in Joyce's schema but also emphasized by the sunset at the episode's start, the beginning of the service at Mary, Star of the Sea Church, and finally the sounding of the cuckoo clock in the final pages. Two hours suddenly go missing. Into this disquieting fissure there emerges a new narrative consciousness, yet another interruption that might make a novice reader wonder if the book had begun to abandon Bloom and his odyssey entirely.

As was the case in "Cyclops," furthermore, Joyce's attention turns again to the Revival, this time to the symbolic figure of a beautiful young girl or "colleen" who typically serves as a metaphor for Irish kingship and sovereignty.[13] For those familiar with Joyce's work, this scene on the beach evokes Stephen's famous epiphany when he encounters a similar figure in *A Portrait of the Artist as a Young Man*. There he sees a girl wading in the sea: "She was alone and still, gazing out to sea; and when she felt his presence and the worship of his eyes her eyes turned to him in quiet sufferance of his gaze, without shame or wantonness" (*P* 171). In response, Stephen resolves to become an artist, "[t]o live, to err, to fall, to triumph, to recreate life out of life" (*P* 172). Elsewhere in that book, the young man declares his aim as a postcolonial artist, seeking "to forge in the smithy of [his] soul the uncreated conscience" of the "batlike soul" of Ireland (*P* 253, 221). Entangled in the language, ideology, and poverty of imperialism, the colleen becomes for Stephen the very symbol of a nation he hopes to create. In *A Portrait*, this girl remains troublingly silent as she is reduced to a mere symbol for the male artist who grants her no space or possibility for an identity of her own. When Joyce replays this scene in "Nausicaa," therefore, he interrupts not just Bloom's trip through Dublin, but his own earlier sexist tropes and those of the Revival more generally, which enfold the colleen in silence so they can speak for her. As the stream-of-consciousness narrative returns in this episode, we thus encounter Joyce's first sustained engagement of a woman's interior life since he left Polly Mooney and Eveline to their enigmatic silences in *Dubliners*.

Early readers and critics often treated Gerty McDowell's intrusion in the text as just another bit of gigantism carried over from "Cyclops," an essentially satiric rendering of a girl's consciousness that is littered with snippets from fashion magazines and sentimental novels. "It was Madame Vera Verity, directress of the Woman Beautiful page of the Princess Novelette," Gerty thinks, "who had first advised her to try eybrowleine which gave that haunting expression to the eyes, so becoming in leaders of fashion" (*U* 13.109–12). In this passage it is almost impossible to disentangle Gerty's thoughts from the advertising slogans and brand names that so powerfully shape her own self-perception. There appears to be almost no room here for anything except the most degraded form of subjectivity and desire, as Suzette Henke argues when she claims that the girl is "doomed to construct a media-controlled self-image."[14] Seen this way, her encounter with Bloom on the beach can be nothing more than a sordid, even misogynist act as she fashions a sexuality "designed to attract the male consumer."[15] Such readings become even more convincing when we later measure this episode against the more human and more humane portrait of Molly Bloom that not only ends but also rewrites so much of *Ulysses*.

So is Gerty anything more than a condescending parody or an ideological critique? In his reading of the episode, Andrew Gibson articulates an alternative view of the girl, arguing that Joyce deploys the form and structure of magazines in this episode in order to construct a "representative of Irish girlhood on the threshold of modern consciousness" (*Joyce's Revenge* 142). Her identity here thus emerges at the intersection of discontinuous media fragments, making her less a parody than a kind of pastiche – a subject fractured by modernity and struggling to assemble a new kind of self from the often meager but still powerful resources surrounding her. Her identity, in other words, is in process, taking shape at the discontinuous interfaces between religion, sentimental fiction, nationalism, and fashion magazines. And when we read the episode looking for these sites of dissonant interface, they begin to multiply. She can on the one hand, for example, imagine herself "[a] sterling good daughter ... just like a second mother in the house," and then almost immediately wish the girls "would take their squalling baby home out of that and not get on her nerves, no hour to be out, and the little brats of twins" (*U* 13.325–26, 404–06).

When the talk turns to Gerty's failed romance with "Reggy Wylie T. C. D.," we see this same process at work (*U* 13.196). Initially, she becomes ensnared in the language of sentimentalism and romance, so that when Edy asks if she is "heartbroken," Gerty laments that "he would never understand what he had meant to her and for an instant there was in the blue eyes a quick stinging of tears" (*U* 13.577, 585–86). Crucially, this moment takes place beneath the looming edifice of the Catholic church, the evening mass literally interrupting the text at times: Cissy

> took off the twins' caps and tidied their hair to make herself attractive of course and Canon O'Hanlon stood up with his cope poking up at his neck and Father Conroy handed him the card to read off and he read out *Panem de coelo praestitisti eis* and Edy and Cissy were talking about the time all the time. (*U* 13.571–75)

Sentimental fiction and the Church initially appear to conspire in regulating Gerty's sexual desires, directing her toward passivity and constraint. Were the episode to end here, she might indeed be no different than Eveline, whose story ends in *Dubliners* when she literally exhausts these same cultural resources and thus stands erotically, psychically, and ideologically paralyzed in her attempt to flee the city.

Similar scenes of paralysis pervade Joyce's other works, most notable among them the young Stephen Dedalus of *A Portrait* who, like Gerty, struggles with the inadequate languages of home, nation, and religion. He manages, however, to fracture these discourses and then reassemble from their pieces the eccentric aesthetic theory that helps pave the way for his eventual exile from Dublin. Lacking Stephen's education, Gerty's resources are different, but her will to make something more of them is equally charged. Thus even in the shadow of the Church and entangled in the emotive language of sentimental fiction, she thinks "As for Mr Reggy with his swank and his bit of money she could just chuck him aside as if he was so much filth ... so they could put that in their pipe and smoke it" (*U* 13.593–95, 604). Critics do not lavish the care on these passages that they do on Stephen's aesthetic theory – both in *A Portrait* and in "Scylla and Charybdis" – but something very similar happens here: Gerty gathers from the orts and fragments of culture around her a language for self-possessed desire. Like Stephen's, it might be secondhand, even a little tattered, but it does point the way toward something beyond the terror of sin and the disempowering stereotypes of the novelettes.

This assemblage of resources within Gerty's mind changes *Ulysses* fundamentally by interrupting the illusion of authenticity that Joyce himself felt had begun to ossify in the novel's first part. In a 1919 letter to Harriet Shaw Weaver, written as he was working on "Cyclops," Joyce noted that "each successive episode, dealing with some province of artistic culture (rhetoric or music or dialectic), leaves behind it a burnt up field" (*Letters I* 129). When Bloom returns with his familiar stream-of-consciousness style at the midpoint of "Nausicaa," we realize that this character and the mode of representation that has given him shape have both been badly singed indeed – that both are now themselves interruptions or intrusions in the book. We cannot return to this character as our modern Odysseus because this book is no longer simply about him, his journey through the day, or his eventual homecoming. This might well explain, in fact, why the epic arc eventually falters, why Stephen refuses to stay at Eccles Street, and why the suitors remain – potent and unvanquished – in Molly's memory at the book's end.

In this episode, *Ulysses* becomes a self-interrupting text that fashions mobile identities, politics, and pleasures amid a welter of conflicting rhetorics. Bloom's brief return in "Nausicaa" is thus more a curtain call than a triumph, and so we shouldn't be surprised that he spends the final pages of the episode wondering if he will return: "Must come back. Murderers do. Will I?" (*U* 13.1254–55). Before dozing off on the beach (completing the cycle that saw him awake that morning), he uses a stick to draw a message in the sand: "I.... AM. A." he writes, before erasing the letters (*U* 13.1258, 1264). This famously incomplete sentence embodies the larger interruptions that have now set *Ulysses* on a fundamentally new path. Himself as partial and contradictory as Gerty, Bloom lapses here into a silence that will now be filled with a growing cacophony of styles, all struggling to complete or at least continue this final ellipsis.

Bloom's fragmentation is not just an effect of style or ideology; it also constitutes a deep engagement with the rapidly changing role of the novel as a printed form amid the dazzling new media of the Edisonian era. Although Joyce's schemas do not correlate media forms with each of the episodes, it's nevertheless easy to imagine an additional column that might contain pairings like these:

Episode	Medium
"Sirens"	phonograph
"Cyclops"	newspaper
"Nausicaa"	cinema
"Oxen of the Sun"	book
"Circe"	theatre

In these episodes, Joyce interrupts himself by no longer treating other media as simply part of the content or setting of his work (as in the "Aelous" episode); instead he seeks to understand them as alternative realisms capable of fashioning new kinds of subjectivity and experience.

The late nineteenth and early twentieth centuries witnessed a revolution in mass media. In print culture, innovative technologies, efficiently organized transportation networks, widespread educational reforms, and new labor laws all combined to transform magazines, newspapers, and the book trade. The rapid growth in literacy rates coupled with the expansion of leisure time generated a massive new audience for reading material that was subsidized by the burgeoning advertising industry. For the first time, images could be reproduced cheaply and with relative ease – images that new consumer-oriented industries used to market their goods. These advertisements, in turn, subsidized the costs of printing, lowering the price of magazines and other periodicals to put them in easy reach of readers like Gerty McDowell. Bloom, of course, is an advertising agent, and he spends a significant part of his day tracking down an image of crossed keys for use in one of the many advertisements that proliferated across hoardings, newsstands, cafés, trams, and other such urban spaces.

As we have seen, there are many ways to understand the interpolations in "Cyclops" – as parodies of Revival mythology, as a critique of the stream of consciousness, and as a commentary on the fragmentation of Irish cultural history. Seen from within the horizon of the period's new media, however, they also look like advertisements. Rather than literally interpolating ads, however, Joyce instead reproduces their *effects* as new media forms: intrusive interruptions on the page structured around often absurdly exaggerated rhetoric that readers learn to treat with distrust or suspicion. As is the case with an ad that appears on a page of newsprint or in a magazine, furthermore, these fragments of text are discontinuous, cut lose from any clear connection to the stories or events being narrated elsewhere on the page. Reading "Cyclops" thus mirrors the process of reading the ad-laden pages of a magazine or newspaper. Joyce here engages with the new media not as something that can be simply incorporated into the novel (as the hangman's letter is), but as itself a new way of shaping the processes of reading, reception, and interpretation. Thus the interpolations become not just a new style or technic, but the site of a contest between the novel and the emergent media forms now competing with it.

A similar kind of "mediamorphosis" takes place in "Nausicaa" as well, an episode that even more vividly insists on the powers of the Edisonian revolution to remake the very process of perception and subject formation.[16] Although Gerty's portion of the narrative draws heavily on the rhetoric of advertising, the form itself derives from an early precursor to cinema called the mutoscope – a device Bloom immediately calls to mind just after Gerty leaves: "Mutoscope pictures in Capel street: for men only. Peeping Tom. Willy's hat and what the girls did with it. Do they snapshot those girls or is it all a fake?" (*U* 13.794–96). Typically confined to fairs, sideshows, and other marginal sites, these machines played very short films to a single viewer who manually turned a crank to move the film reels while peering into an eyepiece. Many of these films were voyeuristic, offering views through keyholes into bedrooms, boudoirs, or changing rooms, and they had titles like "Late Night in the Bedroom" and "What the Butler Saw." Thematically, the silent, masturbatory encounter on the beach in "Nausicaa" thus deliberately evokes these early films while explaining the gap that remains between Bloom and Gerty. Indeed, for a number of critics the cinematic nature of the episode locks Gerty herself into the hazardous trap of what Laura Mulvey calls the "determining male gaze" that "projects its fantasies onto the female figure," who is herself reduced to a position of "*to be looked-at-ness.*"[17] Gerty, in such readings, becomes both objectified and narcissistic, her identity further diminished by her inability to see herself as anything other than an object of an oppressive male gaze.[18]

The mutoscope, however, is not simply a thematic component of this episode, but a formal one as well since the style evokes the machine's uncanny abilities to interrupt the realism of the image by accelerating or dilating time. Turning the crank manually, viewers could decide how quickly or slowly the film and its images moved. This helps explain the disorienting effects of the episode's technic – "tumescence detumescence," a term that evokes not just Bloom's sexual arousal but also the expanding and contracting temporal flow of the narrative. As Katherine Mullin argues, Joyce writes this episode (and the fireworks scene, in particular) "not in real time but rather in 'reel time'": Gerty's "coloured narrative simulates the salacious slowing down of the mutoscope reel and the deconstruction of movement into a series of photographs."[19] This distinctly mechanical temporality, furthermore, finds its correlate in Bloom's stopped watch, another interruption of "real time" that opens a space for thoughts of Molly's adulterous encounter with Boylan to enter his mind. Significantly, they do so in a mutoscopic fashion, slowed down into a series of painful, staccato images and words that evoke cinema's decompositional powers:

> Was that just when he, she?
> O, he did. Into her. She did. Done.
> Ah! (*U* 13.848–50)

Here Joyce's experiments with "mediamorphosis" create a full circuit between the new media of the Edisonian era and the distinctly novelistic style we call stream of consciousness. Bloom's mind becomes itself a cinematic device capable of interrupting the external and internal worlds alike, rewriting – even rewiring – perception, memory, and thought. "Do they snapshot those girls, or is it all a fake?" he wonders. In perhaps his greatest feat of self-interruption, Joyce dismantles this binary distinction between the authentic and the mediated to reveal their newly emergent interdependence.

In "Cyclops" and "Nausicaa" Joyce does more than simply interrupt *Ulysses*; he also makes interruption itself an integral part of his aesthetic. From the moment the nameless narrator usurps the stream-of-consciousness style, it becomes clear that we have entered into a different kind of book. Other forms of media begin to unmake the novel as well as the psychological, subjective, and representation patterns upon which the genre traditionally depended. This is, we discover, no longer Bloom's story – or at least no longer just Bloom's story – but instead an experiment with the very materials of language itself, an event that spills over into the cacophonous brilliance of "Oxen in the Sun." Replaying, in some ways, the drunken pub culture of "Cyclops," this subsequent episode transforms the entire history of the English language into a succession of baffling interpolations and interruptions. No longer set aside from the narrative, as was the case in "Cyclops," these intrusions become the book itself.

The first readers of *Ulysses*, however, who followed the book through its serial appearance in *The Little Review* from March 1918 to December 1920, did not get to see much of this next installment because the book was interrupted by the United States government. On September 20, 1920, the New York Society for the Suppression of Vice filed a complaint about the July–August issue of *The Little Review* in which a portion of "Nausicaa" had appeared. Four previous issues of the magazine had already been seized by the U.S. Postal Service, which deemed them indecent and unfit for passage through the mail. This time, however, Anderson and Heap faced criminal charges and on February 21 were convicted of publishing obscene material, a verdict that set in place a decade-long ban on *Ulysses* in the United States.[20] Here Joyce's aesthetic of interruption turned back on itself, disrupting the circulation of a book that pressed against the legal and social boundaries of narrative itself. Like Bloom, who scrawls that enigmatic "I. AM. A." on the beach, Joyce's book ended, for the moment, in an ellipsis. Modern readers holding the full book in their hands will not find this interruption on the novel's pages; its consequences, however, radiate out beyond the end of "Nausicaa" into a series of ever more explosive interpolations ranging from the talking objects of "Circe" through the catechistic examiner of "Ithaca," to the voice of Molly Bloom that so brilliantly interrupts and rewrites *Ulysses* as a whole.

Notes

1 In more precise narratological terms, story time (the actual order of events in *Ulysses*) becomes dissociated from discourse time (the order of their telling). David Hayman first called attention to this rupture, suggesting that "the reader is transported at an unspecified hour to an unnamed pub where he listens silently to the porterous voice of an insistent and self-assertive clown." David Hayman, "Cyclops," in *James Joyce's "Ulysses": Critical Essays*, eds. Clive Hart and David Hayman (Berkeley: University of California Press), p. 243.

2 Hugh Kenner, *Joyce's Voices* (Berkeley: University of California Press, 1978), p. 70. For a more detailed discussion of the self-interrupting fits and starts of the early episodes, see Chapter 4.

3 Karen Lawrence, *The Odyssey of Style in "Ulysses"* (Princeton, NJ: Princeton University Press, 1981), n.p.

4 Joyce attempted to justify the shift in a letter he wrote to his confused patron and supporter, Harriet Shaw Weaver: "I understand that you may begin to regard the various styles of the episodes with dismay and prefer the initial style much as the wanderer did who longed for the rock of Ithaca. But in the compass of one day to compress all these wanderings and clothe them in the form of this day is for me only possible by such variation which, I beg you to believe, is not capricious" (*Letters I* 129). For the description of the "stages" of composition, see Michael Groden, *"Ulysses" in Progress* (Princeton, NJ: Princeton University Press, 1977).

5 Michael Groden, "Joyce at Work on 'Cyclops': Toward a Biography of *Ulysses*," *JJQ* 44 (Winter 2007): 220.

6 Joyce's Linati schema lists "exaggeration" as one of the episode's "Symbols."

7 David Hayman, *"Ulysses": The Mechanics of Meaning* (Englewood Cliffs, NJ: Prentice-Hall, Inc., 1970), pp. 84, 125.

8 Andrew Gibson, *Joyce's Revenge: History, Politics, and Aesthetics in "Ulysses"* (Oxford: Oxford University Press, 2002), p. 117. Len Platt makes an even more aggressive claim, arguing that Joyce's response to the Revival, "far from being marginal, is actually fundamental to the quality of *Ulysses*, to the kind of text that *Ulysses* is." Len Platt, *Joyce and the Anglo-Irish: A Study of Joyce and the Literary Revival* (Amsterdam: Rodopi, 1998), p. 8. Further references to Gibson's work will be cited parenthetically as *Joyce's Revenge*.

9 T. S. Eliot, "*Ulysses*, Order and Myth," *Dial* 75 (November 1923): 483.

10 Homer, *The Odyssey*, trans. Robert Fitzgerald (New York: Doubleday, 1961), p.173.

11 Enda Duffy, *The Subaltern "Ulysses"* (Minneapolis: University of Minnesota Press, 1994), p. 124.

12 Declan Kiberd, *"Ulysses" and Us: The Art of Everyday Life in Joyce's Masterpiece* (New York: Norton, 2009), pp. 185, 186.

13 Yeats's intensely nationalist play, *Cathleen ni Houlihan*, draws on the traditional image of the *shan van vocht* or "poor old woman" as a symbol for Ireland in a state of political and social decay. As the young men in the play go off to fight for independence, however, she is transformed into "a young girl" with "the walk of a queen." W. B. Yeats, *"Cathleen ni Houlihan,"* in *Yeats's Poetry, Drama, and Prose*, ed. James Pethica (New York: Norton, 2000), p. 140. Joyce likely parodies this symbolic embodiment of nationalism in "Nausicaa." For more on his negotiation of this mythic image, see Layne Parish Craig, "'A Type of Her Race and His Own': The Celtic Sovereignty Goddess Tradition in *A Portrait of the Artist as a Young Man*," *JJQ* 45 (Fall 2007): 69–83.

14 Suzette Henke, *James Joyce and the Politics of Desire* (New York: Routledge, 1990), p. 138.

15 Gary Leonard, "The Virgin Mary and the Urge in Gerty: The Packaging of Desire in the 'Nausicaa' Chapter of *Ulysses*," *University of Hartford Studies in Literature* 23 (1991): 4.

16 The term "mediamorphosis" was coined by Roger Fidler to describe "a unified way of thinking about the technological evolution of communication media" so that "as each new form emerges and develops, it influences, over time and to varying degrees, the development of every other existing form." See Roger Fidler, *Mediamorphosis: Understanding the New Media* (Thousand Oaks, CA: Pine Forge Press, 1997), p. 23–24.

17 Laura Mulvey, "Visual Pleasure and Narrative Cinema," in *Issues in Feminist Film Criticism*, ed. Patricia Erens (Bloomington: Indiana University Press, 1990), p. 33.

18 Gerty's relation to the male gaze has been the subject of considerable debate among scholars. For an alternative to Henke's influential view that also offers a useful overview of the topic, see Philip Sicker, "Unveiling Desire: Pleasure, Power and Masquerade in Joyce's 'Nausicaa' Episode," *Joyce Studies Annual* 14 (Summer 2003): 92–131.

19 Katherine Mullin, *James Joyce, Sexuality and Social Purity* (Cambridge: Cambridge University Press, 2003), p. 155.

20 For the most detailed description of Joyce's struggle against American obscenity laws, see Paul Vanderham, *James Joyce and Censorship: The Trials of "Ulysses"* (New York: New York University Press, 1997).

CHAPTER 11

Difficulty: "Oxen of the Sun" and "Circe"

Cheryl Temple Herr

Whatever meanings we may discover in *Ulysses*, we must begin with the fact that the work represents the past – even for Joyce, even when he was writing it. From the perspective of 1914–21, the years of composition cited on the final page of the final episode, 1904 is rather remote. From the perspective of today's reader, 1904 is ancient history – not the unverifiable mythos of *Finnegans Wake*, but nonetheless a distant dream. Multiplying that sense of removal is the grounding of *Ulysses* not so much in the well-known narrative of the *Odyssey*, but more in a Homeric world that has suffered many dislocations and transpositions between a notionally original epic and the Irish story of Bloom, Stephen, and Molly. In composing this temporal layering, Joyce tightly controlled the immediate time frame of his 1922 novel. This concentration of several eras into the story of a single day has made the work a surprisingly manageable script for live readings when Bloomsday rolls around each year. Here is a text that we can keep pace with and that keeps pace with our own sense of regulated, clockwise existence, despite – or possibly because of – its temporal depth.

That said, a significant impediment to this comfortable sense of lived time occurs when readers arrive at "Oxen of the Sun" and "Circe." These episodes present specific problems. Their length makes it hard for a first-time reader to sustain the connections that Joyce wants us to follow. The episodes submerge action in prolific detail. By way of comedy, farce, and irony, they bring into question the narrative's attitude toward characters that heretofore we have been asked to take fairly seriously. Their content threatens to exceed their allotment of time in the day that we are tracking.

For many practical purposes, "Oxen of the Sun" and "Circe" can be considered a single unit of *Ulysses*. Together they carry readers from day to night, from the twilight of "Nausicaa" to the midnight closure of Bloomsday proper. In spite of their formal differences, these episodes together comprise the final and most arduous adventures in Joyce's rearrangement of the Homeric narrative. Furthermore, Joyce devoted the full calendar year of 1920 to writing them, and his correspondence shows that it was hard for him to resist elaborating and embroidering his plan. Joyce himself suffered a great deal while writing these sections because of the demands he placed on himself in plotting their extravagances of formal structure and fine detail.

Another reason to think of these episodes as a unit is that they are the ones most clearly devoted to the beginnings of life and thus of meaning, of language, and – as Giambattista Vico and then Joyce would have it – of the Irish nation. In episode 14, Mina Purefoy gives birth to her ninth living child; and among the many frantic events in episode 15, Leopold Bloom, claiming his androgynous identity, is delivered of eight metallic children. Mrs. Purefoy, of course, is suffering through a long and difficult delivery, while Bloom's pregnancy and delivery occur in a flash. In both cases, the momentous mystery of childbirth was difficult for Joyce to present head-on. Stephen Dedalus thus pontificates to the group at the hospital, "In woman's womb word is made flesh but in the spirit of the maker all flesh that passes becomes the word that shall not pass away" (*U* 14.292–94). This drunken boast illustrates both the artist's insecurities and his aspirations.

Finally, these episodes connect the origins of life to the inevitability of death through the figure of Rudy. The loss to Molly and Leopold of their newborn son has altered their lives in ways that it takes all of *Ulysses* to address. The animal themes in both "Oxen" and "Circe" specifically provide a framework for Joyce's many references to butchers, cattle, foot-and-mouth disease, meat, and slaughterhouses. Bloom has long wondered whether Rudy's death was somehow his fault, and this guilt complicates his emotional life considerably. At the time of Rudy's birth and death, the Blooms lived in the City Arms Hotel "(in the cattle district in northwest Dublin), where Bloom worked for Joe Cuffe, ... the cattleman."[1] Parliamentary investigations in London and Dublin had studied increased infant mortality in the environs of abattoirs and cattle markets. In "Oxen," the narrative comically describes Stephen as "intimately acquainted with the minutiae of the municipal abbatoir" (*U* 14.1294), and Mulligan has blamed the mortality rate in general on "the sanitary conditions" suffered by Dublin's "greylunged citizens" (*U* 14.1243, 1244), including their exposure to "the suspended carcases of dead animals" (*U* 14.1248). Thus Rudy's death could well have been part of the much larger challenge to social hygiene that Dublin's cattle trade had long presented. Such an argument would require more space to pursue, but my point is that although *Ulysses* can be made manageable for the novice reader in many ways (summary, explication, remediation), a one-on-one grappling with episodes 14 and 15 always demands a certain willingness to face tribulations and perhaps even to suffer through them for a time.

"Oxen of the Sun"

While writing *Ulysses*, Joyce often wrote to his Aunt Josephine for details about Dublin that would help him capture Irish life in a rich and realistic tapestry. During the time that he was working on "Oxen of the Sun" and the prior episode, he curtly wrote:

> Dear Aunt Josephine: ... I want that information about the Star of the Sea Church, has it ivy on its seafront, are there trees in Leahy's terrace at the side or near, if so, what, are there steps leading down to the beach? I also want all the information you can give, tittletattle, facts etc about Hollis Street maternity hospital. Two chapters of my book remain unfinished till I have these. (*SL* 248)

Joyce disliked waiting for information and also for praise. Once the book was published in 1922, he was surprised that his aunt had not yet congratulated him for his great accomplishment. Hurt, he chided her: "You say there is a lot of it you don't understand. I told you to read the *Odyssey* first" (*SL* 293).

Indeed, Joyce had asked her to familiarize herself with the *Odyssey* before the publication of *Ulysses*, but she seems not to have followed his instructions. Now he brusquely advised her to purchase a copy of Charles Lamb's volume *Adventures of Ulysses* – a staple text from its publication in 1808 onward – which Joyce condescendingly described as "Homer's story told in simple English much abbreviated" (*SL* 293). Lamb's small book happened to be the text through which schoolboy Joyce was first exposed to Homer. Despite his rather rude suggestion that Josephine should turn from Homer to a child's textbook, Joyce appears to have had a great fondness for Lamb's summary treatment. Certainly Lamb emphasizes action: He always tells us in no uncertain terms what Ulysses and his men are doing. Given how often Joyce scholars have debated what is actually happening on certain pages of *Ulysses*, one can appreciate Lamb's narrative all the more. Joyce, of course, played fast and loose not only with details of action but also with the order of Ulysses' trials, which were further transposed to accommodate the story in the Dublin of 1904. Still, Joyce seems to have believed that a reading of Lamb could take care of his aunt's problems in approaching his own unusual work. The take-away from this example, an instance that could be multiplied many times, is that he was a poor judge of what the ordinary reader could or would interpret without difficulty.

At the end of the day, the fundamental events that occur in "Oxen of the Sun" are straightforward enough. Reluctant to return home, Bloom goes to the Holles Street hospital to see whether Mina Purefoy, who has been in labor for three days, has given birth. There he joins a group of medical students who drink with abandon while discussing questions of birth, disease, theology, and death. A seriously inebriated Stephen Dedalus lingers at the hospital, perhaps because he has no home to which to return that evening. Recall that in the part of the Homeric narrative that underwrote Joyce's "Oxen of the Sun" episode, the crew, starving and becalmed, violate the Sun God's injunction not to tamper with his beloved cattle. When Odysseus, who has become the de facto parental figure in the narrative, temporarily leaves their immediate vicinity, the famished sailors barbecue the cattle and have a good feed. In *Ulysses*, the students' carousing at the hospital clearly refers to the crew's transgressive feasting. After the Purefoy child is born, the men pour noisily into the street. Bloom follows Stephen, apparently with the aim of keeping the young man's money from being stolen.

Joyce's dismissal of his aunt's puzzled response to *Ulysses* aside, while writing "Oxen" he seems to have been anxious about the episode's length. He confided his concern to his friend Frank Budgen while describing his central concept for restaging "Oxen of the Sun": "the crime committed against fecundity by sterilizing the act of coition" (*SL* 251). Joyce surely relished identifying the violation of the Sun God's oxen as the copious and routine spilling of sperm by Stephen, Bloom, and the Holles Street medical students, whether in routine masturbation or in the arms of prostitutes. Rather than unpack for Budgen this comic attention to non-procreative sex, Joyce briskly foresees a chapter of nine parts that would move from "a Sallustian-Tacitean prelude (the unfertilized ovum)" through stylistic references to Anglo-Saxon alliterative poetry, Mandeville, Malory, Elizabethan chronicles, Milton, Burton, Bunyan, Pepys, Defoe, Addison and Steele, and so on through to "a frightful jumble of Pidgin English, nigger English, Cockney, Irish, Bowery slang and broken doggerel" (*SL* 251, 252). He ends this précis with a succinct summary that is also a thrown gauntlet: "Bloom is the spermatozoon, the hospital the womb, the nurse the ovum, Stephen the embryo. How's that for high?" (*SL* 252). Joyce's description suggests his barely repressed concern over the extent of his experimentation in "Oxen" and over the increasing liberties that he was taking in the name of stylistic innovation as Bloom's day turned into Bloom's evening.

We need to remember that however much he professed wanting to display his skills and ingenuity, at this point in his writing of *Ulysses* Joyce also had certain critical tasks to accomplish. He had to move his narrative forward, to maintain a semblance of the Homeric connection in his novel, and to find a way to justify to his supporters *why it was taking so long* to complete *Ulysses*. It was to this pressured situation that Joyce added the job of imitating a host of prose rhythms for his selective history of English style. At the same time, he notes to Budgen his desire to have the episode represent "faunal evolution in general" (*SL* 252). We are left not with birth itself as the center of the action, but rather with homologies and analogies, misbirths and pathologies, drunkenness and anxiety. Genetic scholars have shown us that from this point in *Ulysses* onward, Joyce's creative process continued to become more deeply invested in intertextuality and in layered temporalities. Jedd Deppman, discussing the far horizon of *Finnegans Wake*, therefore speaks of Joyce's "hubristic multitasking."[2] For Joyce, evoking time past and time present increasingly meant creating the "hermeneutically excessive circumstance" ("Chapter in Composition" 333).

Regarding multiple time frames, note that for Mina Purefoy, the actual gestation of her child had been accomplished over the nine months preceding June 16. This fictional fact sits uneasily with Joyce's effort to mimic, by way of linguistic contractions, the birthing process as such. The reader begins to see – and this is crucial to understanding "Oxen of the Sun" – the rigorously controlled clock-time of Bloomsday breaking apart and overlapping so that competing nighttime chronologies seemingly distort the go-ahead daytime narrative. One of these chronologies has to do simply with the late evening hours of June 16, 1904. But another quite complicated sequence deals with the prior, notional, and primordial "faunal evolution" and the forced analogy to a history of English literary prose style that looks backward to the Purefoy child's development. These schemes strive to communicate some of the events at Holles Street while composing what we might call the nocturnal tempo for both "Oxen" and "Circe."

"Oxen" begins with an incantation: Both here and in the body of the chapter the baby's birth is announced more than once. The staccato effect of these announcements slows the reader's perception of time's passing. We both see and feel that the gathered merrymakers are losing track of time. A key sentence in setting up that temporal retardation follows from the incantation:

> Universally that person's acumen is esteemed very little perceptive concerning whatsoever matters are being held as most profitably by mortals with sapience endowed to be studied who is ignorant of that which the most in

doctrine erudite and certainly by reason of that in them high mind's orna-
ment deserving of veneration constantly maintain when by general consent
they affirm that other circumstances being equal by no exterior splendour
is the prosperity of a nation more efficaciously asserted than by the measure
of how far forward may have progressed the tribute of its solicitude for that
proliferent continuance which of evils the original if it be absent when for-
tunately present constitutes the certain sign of omnipollent nature's incor-
rupted benefaction. (*U* 14.07–17)

For Joyce, the long sentence with little or no internal punctuation became
a favorite comedic device strongly associated with dreams and night-time
activity, but the point made in this ponderous statement is serious enough:
In a nation for which the mid-nineteenth-century famines were still a
source of mourning and shame, demographic regrowth was desirable.
Everyone, then, agrees that ameliorating the pain of childbirth is a good
thing. The mode of expression that Joyce chooses is sinuously indirect,
an awkward obliquity that alludes to the Latinate form of pre-fertilized
English. The awkward expression also hints at the facts surrounding Mina
Purefoy's pregnancy. Certainly we are reminded of Victorian euphemism
when discussing those "in the family way." More than this, Mrs. Purefoy
has already had too many children, some of whom have died, and her husband is unable to pay the growing bills from the butcher. Throughout the
day, Bloom has noticed children on Dublin's streets without shoes, hungry, and insufficiently cared for. The nation needs to do more for them as
well. Poverty and neglect retroactively sterilize many acts of coitus.

The sentence draws its withholding economy and resistant pace from
one of Joyce's sources for "Oxen" – another backward turn – Archbishop
of Dublin Richard Chenevix Trench's tome, *On the Study of Words*. That
treatise begins:

> There are few who would not readily acknowledge that mainly in worthy
> books are preserved and hoarded the treasures of wisdom and knowledge
> which the world has accumulated; and that chiefly by aid of these they are
> handed down from one generation to another.[3]

Beginning with a way of writing that eases into its subject matter by way
of circumlocution, Trench baits and switches:

> I shall urge on you in these lectures something different from this; namely,
> that not in books only, which all acknowledge, nor yet in connected oral
> discourse, but often also in words contemplated singly, there are boundless
> stores of moral and historic truth, and no less of passion and imagination,
> laid up – that from these, lessons of infinite worth may be derived, if only
> our attention is roused to their existence. (*Study* 1)

"Boundless stores of moral and historic truth": From his earliest attention to language, Joyce had been fascinated by words and their complex
etymologies. The meaning of a single word in *Ulysses* can stop a reader
in her tracks, especially if that word brings with it an archaic aura and
formerly active significations. Just as the process of reading constantly
orients us toward what is ahead, so can word choice and citation pull
us into the near or distant past, can slow down the pace and expand the
temporal horizon of reading. In Joyce's unusual associations among fetal
growth, zoological evolution, and the history of literary style, we discover
multiple temporalities for being. The aim to discover how words testify
to moral truths and fossil history inhabits *Ulysses* as a result of Joyce's
quotation of Trench and of Trench's fertilization of the developing text.
Joyce undoubtedly favored the view that every word contains worlds and
that every style of writing opened onto a rowdy company of expressive
modes.

As he wrote *Ulysses*, Joyce increasingly recognized that the allusions he
was larding into the work and the parallels he was constructing were exerting energies of their own and setting up layers of meaning akin to etymo-
logical ones. Readily stated schematic plans had to absorb this energy by
acknowledging – in ways large and small – the narrative presence of the
semantic freight imported by those references. A given episode's development and its place within the full narrative were caught up in intertextual
cross-currents – a kind of verbal intoxication. Joyce's sources came into
the field of meaning and enlarged that field in more than just the immediate textual moment. Undoubtedly, Joyce experienced a degree of pleasure
from his ability to manage these multiple points of reference and chronologies of meaning, but he was also masochistically anxious about that
pleasure and eager to conceal some of the textual difficulties of *Ulysses* in
his explanations to friends and family.

Difficulty

As I was writing this chapter of the *Companion*, I was teaching an under-
graduate course at the University of Iowa called "Joyce and Difficulty,"
the major focus of which was *Ulysses*. From the outset of the course, we
attempted to theorize difficulty as such, making use in particular of George
Steiner's classic essay "On Difficulty" and *The Difficulties of Modernism* by
Leonard Diepeveen.[4] My opening gambit was to state the obvious: We
had to agree on what kinds of difficulty we were interested in grappling
with in relation to Joyce. Rather than charging ahead to say that the work

became harder to read as the episodes went by, we had to name the problems that flummoxed us as we encountered them.

Steiner offers a highly influential four-point analysis of literary problems. Of the four categories of difficulty he identifies (contingent, modal, tactical, and ontological), students readily affirmed that the contingencies – things to be looked up – occupied a lot of their reading time, even with the Gifford and Seidman annotations at hand and the constant presence of the Internet for informational assistance. Similarly, some were intrigued or plagued by the idea that Joyce had built in a lot of idiosyncratic tactical difficulties; his fondness for riddles, his mining of occult knowledge, his production of neologisms, and his desire to keep the professors guessing contributed to the class's purchase on the concept of the tactical obfuscation.

In addition, the modal category of difficulty found its place in our discussions. Did the work speak to us? This is the problem that Steiner organizes under the third category:

> there is a real discrimination to be made: as between our pleasure in or displeasure at something that we have thoroughly apprehended, and our reaction to, our atrophy of response towards a text whose autonomous force of life, whose *raison d'etre* in the strict sense of the phrase, escape us.... we do not feel "called upon," or "answerable to," in both of which tags the primary bonds of interaction between the poem and its listener or reader are active. ("On Difficulty" 29)

Steiner's view of our response to poetic language depends on a work's cruising the reader, meshing its sensibility with the reader's response rather than driving the reader off to check his Facebook page.

The second chapter in Diepeveen's book is called "Articulating Anxiety," and anxiety turned out to be the meat of the problem, at least as far as my class was concerned. The concerns had to do with Joyce's use of allusions to Irish history, to previous literature, to philosophy and art, and so on. How, several students asked, were they to discriminate between the materials that would prove useful later in the text and those that felt more like immediate opportunities for Joyce to show off his erudition? The issue of Joyce as intellectual competition – yet another writer bent on putting down the reader – surfaced several times. There was a stated desire to like Joyce, and class participants believed that as English majors in particular they should love *Ulysses*, but some of them were just not feeling it. Much of the antagonism and anxiety turned on questions of time. How dare a single writer compose a text that requires so much time to interpret? What right did Joyce have to bore the reader with longwinded sentences, obscure paragraphs, occult allusions, and a roster of reading trials that shifted from one episode to the next?

Anxiety over the passing of time, then, emerged as a sort of capstone issue for my students. They were willing to make the effort to read *Ulysses*; but the book is long and gets significantly harder as it goes along. In contrast to this experience of escalating difficulty, reading is often idealized as immersion. Our desire is to linger in the world of the book, to be propelled forward, not to want to close the volume or see the narrative end. But the investments in the past that *Ulysses* makes can easily halt that immersion. As readers, we have to pick up the threads of multiple chronologies and competing meaning again and again. In seizing on their own anxiety over the passing of time as they labored to read, my students acknowledged that a semester spent reading *Ulysses* means constantly reckoning up the reading gains and interpretive errors that had gone before.

Steiner foresees just this kind of complication and resistance. From his perspective, the first three classes of difficulty do not violate the basic contract between reader and writer (the terms of which are insufficiently spelled out in "On Difficulty"). But he asserts, "There is a fourth order of difficulty which occurs where this contract is itself wholly or in part broken" ("On Difficulty" 40). We cannot simply look up the information that we want, nor can we adjust our historical or cultural assumptions to get at the author's issues. Instead, these "ontological" difficulties "confront us with blank questions about the nature of human speech, about making meaning, about the necessity and purpose" of the work at hand ("On Difficulty" 41). Steiner finds the roots of ontological literary issues in late nineteenth and early twentieth century Western culture and cites in particular the cheapening of language in industrialized society. He takes things further, too: Stéphane Mallarmé revolted against the accumulated meanings of the past while also desiring to return to a moment before aesthetic magic had been undone by cultural linearity. For my purposes, it is interesting that it was Homer, Mallarmé said, who had "betrayed the primal mystery" ("On Difficulty" 43). Steiner then specifically connects this insight with Heidegger's belief that the whole of Western philosophy and poetry had lost touch with the nature of being, of our existence in the world. "In ontological difficulty," Steiner intones, "the poetics of Mallarmé and Heidegger, of the Orphic and the pre-Socratic, express their sense of the inauthentic situation of man in an environment of eroded speech" ("On Difficulty" 44).

Even though Steiner forces us to consider large philosophical matters of fundamental existence and readership, he misses out on a critical complexity in Heidegger's work that is actually quite helpful in understanding episodes 14 and 15 of *Ulysses*. For Heidegger, Time is the horizon of Being. These are complex terms, so let me say only that ontology and its temporal horizon form a crucial aspect of Joyce's most problematic episodes. In them, we learn just how deeply both Bloom and Stephen are concerned with their identity – their social being – and how their fellow Dubliners perceive them. Both men feel radically undervalued, their very personhood eroded by assumptions about being Semitic and being artistic. In Dublin, the powers that be, whether media men or an aesthetic coterie, erode the value of the unaligned individual. Both men are shunned and deprived of their keys, a fact that recasts home as uncanny and society as surreal. In the imposed dramatic format of "Circe," even the body becomes malleable, attenuated, performative, remediated, and ultimately open to an expanded sensory apparatus adrift in unmanageable layers of time.

"Circe"

Between the end of *Portrait* and Bloomsday, Stephen has learned to drink with abandon. Sorrow over his mother's death, along with newly earned funds and the company of Buck Mulligan, somewhat explain his intoxication by the evening of June 16. Stephen also seems motivated by a desire to get outside of himself, possibly to draw a line under his old way of being through bacchanalian excess. Certainly the Dionysian festivals – where alcohol and drama celebrated the Greek god – provide a model by which wine and ecstasy might free a participant's creative powers and elevate him above his peers through divine inspiration.

Although contemporary binge drinking among young adults is hardly comparable with the festivals of ancient Greece, the participants in my *Ulysses* class did know what drinking to excess looks like. Many Iowa students drink to escape their workloads; some drink to escape personal problems; some drink for something to do. No doubt a portion of Iowa students make use of illegal substances for similar reasons. My own students' observation of these social practices proved sufficient to enable a reading of "Circe" that probed the ontological problems – being and time – that the episode brings forward.

After wandering through Dublin's then-notorious Nighttown, Bloom and Stephen meet at Bella Cohen's, where Stephen breaks a lamp, careens into the road, insults a British soldier, and is knocked out. Bloom makes sure that Stephen is not taken into custody by the watch. The main line of action is relatively clear. At the same time, more than anything else,

"Circe" seems to ask the reader to sort out scenes that appear to be realistic depictions from those that are imaginative or hallucinatory. Indeed,
the single issue most often addressed by scholars dealing with "Circe" is
precisely the status of the textual depictions. Does Bloom actually become
a woman? Does he even put on women's clothing in Nighttown? Does he
converse with his long-dead grandfather, a figure who does not show up
elsewhere in the novel? Does Gerty McDowell, now a ruined woman, confront him in the late hours of the night? Are readers to believe that Bloom
really acts out his masochistic sexual desires in Bella Cohen's brothel? By
the same token, we might ask whether Stephen meets his father and suffers a dreadful vision of his dead mother. Do previously inanimate objects
suddenly caper and speak? If not, how are we to understand the drama
that Joyce wrote?

One of the most influential of early Joyce scholars, Hugh Kenner, pre-
ferred to view "Circe" as taking place on "two planes of reality."[5] Most
of the events hovered between hallucination and "irreducible naturalism,"
phantasmagoric depictions "not referable to 'real' time" ("Circe" 347, 348,
351). Because nothing was happening, Kenner questioned why the episode
found a place in the novel. For Kenner, "the only genuine hallucination
in the chapter" is the apparition to Stephen of his mother – the rest of the
events being "dramatized metaphors ... or else expressionistic equivalents
of states of feeling" ("Circe" 351–52). Most critics have enjoyed the episode
rather more and allowed more scenes to fall under the heading of hallucinations sometimes attributing Joyce's representation to a transformation
of what is actually happening to Stephen and Bloom.[6]

For example, in *Virgin and Veteran Readings of "Ulysses,"* Margot Norris
argues that the hallucinations and fantasies that beset these characters
derive from mental states but are themselves possible worlds made linguis-
tically accessible.[7] Those possible worlds, Norris argues, contain materials
that Bloom and Stephen need to encounter if they are to resolve their
conflicts and make personal progress on Bloomsday (*Virgin and Veteran*
161). In the red-light district, Stephen "has relived virtually every conflict
that has tormented him throughout his day" (*Virgin and Veteran* 169). For
Bloom, too, the world of his responsibilities and the world of his desires
come into conflict. He has concerns about his father's suicide, about
Molly's infidelity, about the anti-Semitic prejudices of many Dubliners,
and about his need for erotic fulfillment. Overall, he "wishes for an intact
and thriving family and for a progressive nation pursuing the social weal
and racial justice that would offer him a more secure sense of belonging in
the country of his birth" (*Virgin and Veteran* 170).

In contrast, John Gordon's writings have foregrounded the interpretive framework of drunkenness and drugged intoxication in "Circe."[8] In *James Joyce's Metamorphoses* (1981), Gordon rejected the idea of hallucinations, with all of the psychological overtones the word implies.[9] Instead, clearly adhering to a realist underpinning for the events in "Circe," Gordon argued that Bloom and Stephen have both come under the influence of drugs. Having focused on the "four minutes or thereabouts" in "Oxen" during which Bloom stares at a bottle of Bass (*U* 14.1181–82), Gordon carries the motif of the trance into "Circe," noting that both fatigue and the cigarettes being smoked outside Bella Cohen's – which Gordon identifies as cannabis or opium – might have produced a "contact high" for the men. He adds: "That, along with the influence of drink, tobacco, fatigue, and recent exertion, is more than enough to account for the episode's dilations, suspensions, and distortions of sensation, enough to produce the 'hallucinations' which, on one level, correspond to the 'disturbances of the eyesight and bearing'" (*Metamorphoses* 93). And Gordon thanks John V. Kelleher "for confirming that such substances could well have been around in a red light district of the period, and for pointing out that Yeats experimented with hashish while in Dublin" (*Metamorphoses* 186, n42).

Supporting Gordon's view is the fact that in the final moments of "Oxen" one of the men invokes the mildly psychoactive liquor called absinthe, and earlier in that episode "dope" (in particular, laudanum) has been mentioned (*U* 14.1533, 1024). These intoxicating substances were neither illegal nor hard to come by. Indeed, it would have been impossible for Joyce to live in Paris without coming into contact with absinthe, the effects of which are said to include precisely the sort of demented lucidity and ability to translate thought into apparent spectacle that prevails in "Circe."[10] "Oxen" has prepared the reader for these phenomena:

> There are sins or (let us call them as the world calls them) evil memories which are hidden away by man in the darkest places of the heart but they abide there and wait.... Yet a chance word will call them forth suddenly and they will rise up to confront him in the most various circumstances, a vision or a dream. (*U* 14.1344–50)

As Trench would have it, the "chance word" from different historical periods can set up eddies of significance and cross-currents of meaning that complicate and enlarge a narrative format, that pry open the regularities of everyday clock-time and release the creative power of language.

Rather than imagine that Stephen and Bloom have exorcised their demons in Nighttown or that this process has been accomplished once and for all, we might consider the whole episode a "contact high" for the reader. "Circe" is the literary equivalent of getting drunk, getting high, and exiting the theater able only to recall that this performance was long and difficult. And you cannot even remember the whole story! (Note that in "Eumaeus" very little if anything of the "Circe" text comes forward in the discourse of Bloom and Stephen.) You're not even certain that Tom and Sam Bohee haven't jumped off the Birds Eye Cigarettes pack to sing "Someone's in the Kitchen with Dinah." Your effort to escape from clock-time has expanded into a dilated time trip before returning you to regulated social temporality. Heidegger would have it that the anxiety experienced by the two men in Nighttown discloses to them that they are not and have never been at home in the world. Our being lost in the fun-house is a structural condition of our being. For Heidegger, such insights are momentary. We quickly cover up our understanding and reinsert ourselves as best we can into the lifeworld. The temporal anxieties that beset the novice reader of episodes 14 and 15 may well attest to our actual situation in the contemporary world, the pressures that modernity exerts on us, and Joyce's uncanny ability to reach out to us in the current moment.

Notes

1 John Henry Raleigh, *The Chronicle of Leopold and Molly Bloom: "Ulysses" as Narrative* (Berkeley: University of California Press, 1977), p. 131.

2 Jed Deppman, "A Chapter in Composition: Chapter II.4," in *How Joyce Wrote Finnegans Wake: A Chapter-by-Chapter Genetic Guide*, eds. Luca Crispi and Sam Slote (Madison: University of Wisconsin Press, 2007) p. 320. Further references will be cited parenthetically as "Chapter in Composition."

3 Richard Chenevix Trench, *The Study of Words* (New York: Humboldt, 1882), p. 1. Also see Sarah Davison, "Joyce's Incorporation of Literary Sources in 'Oxen of the Sun,'" *Genetic Joyce Studies* 9 (Spring 2009), http://www.genetic-joycestudies.org/GJS9/GJS9_SarahDavisonOxen.htm. Further references to the Trench text will be cited parenthetically as *Study*.

4 See George Steiner, *On Difficulty and Other Essays* (London: Oxford University Press, 1980); and Leonard Diepeveen, *The Difficulties of Modernism* (New York: Routledge, 2003). Further references will be cited parenthetically as "On Difficulty" and *Difficulties*, respectively.

5 Hugh Kenner, "Circe," in *James Joyce's "Ulysses": Critical Essays*, eds. Clive Hart and David Hayman (Berkeley: University of California Press, 1974), p. 348. Further references will be cited parenthetically in the text as "Circe."

6 Yet another group, myself among them, has been less interested in isolating the illusory than in identifying the theatrical precursors to Joyce's dramatic interlude, whether melodrama, Christmas pantomime, music hall, early

cinema, or avant-garde performance. See, for example, Cheryl Herr, *Joyce's Anatomy of Culture* (Champaign: University of Illinois Press, 1986).

7 Margot Norris, *Virgin and Veteran Readings of "Ulysses"* (New York: Palgrave Macmillan, 2011). Further references will be cited parenthetically as *Virgin and Veteran*.

8 It is worth noting that at the time of this writing, Austin Briggs, Katherine Mullin, and Finn Fordham have explored Joyce's own alcoholism and its effects on his writing See Austin Briggs, "Joyce's Drinking," *JJQ* 48 (Summer 2011): 637–66.

9 See John Gordon, *James Joyce's Metamorphoses* (Dublin: Gill and Macmillan, 1981). Further references will be cited parenthetically in the text as *Metamorphoses*.

10 See David M. Earle, "'Green Eyes, I See You. Fang, I Feel': The Symbol of Absinthe in *Ulysses*," *JJQ* 40 (Summer 2003): 691–709.

PART IV

Contemporary Theory and Criticism

CHAPTER 12

Intertextuality

R. Brandon Kershner

Ulysses is preeminent among novels that exhibit allusion or intertextuality for several reasons. For one thing, Stephen Dedalus is a dedicated esthete whose thoughts are punctuated with literary and other artistic references; and we are allowed to share his thoughts with unusual closeness. Just in the first few pages we can find possible allusions to the words of the Catholic Mass, a statement of *Romeo and Juliet*, a passage from the Maynooth Catechism, a detail from the study of classical orators, a passage from Swinburne, the Greek word for sea, and so forth (*U* 1.05–80). But *Ulysses* is by no means restricted to the realm of "high culture" in its references. Leopold Bloom's thoughts are frequently rich in reference to the popular culture of his time. In addition to this, even in expository passages there are allusions to bits of Dublin street furniture and the social life of the city, minute details that now require some research to understand. Joyce's technique allows him to name anything but to explain nothing.

The terms critics use to discuss this literary function have varied, from "allusion," "influence," "context" and "tradition" to "intertextuality," "dialogism," and even "hypertextuality." "Intertextuality" has generally replaced "allusion" in contemporary discussions that prefer not to invoke connotations of a conscious and controlling author. In place of "allusion," Julia Kristeva uses "intertextuality" in a 1969 essay written in French and translated as part of her book *Desire in Language: A Semiotic Approach to Literature and Art.*[1] In the essay "Word, Dialogue, and Novel" she introduces aspects of the thought of Russian theoretician M. M. Bakhtin that are relatively familiar to literary critics. These include the concept of dialogism, or the aspect of each utterance that is directed toward an anticipated or imagined response. Bakhtin refers to this effect as a kind of "double-voicedness," and attributes it to most utterances, since most statements are spoken within multiple contexts (the speech of one's parents or peers; the unvoiced but potential language of those who because of tradition, habit, or ideology might wish to oppose or support the speaker's point of view; and so forth).[2] In the reading process, the text is dialogical with the various possible languages of the reader; but when the text includes quotation or allusion of some sort, it is itself dialogical, and presents itself to the reader in that form. Bakhtin celebrates this state of languages, which he sometimes terms "heteroglossia,"[3] just as he condemns a "monological" state – the notion of a language that claims total authority and denies the possibility of interaction.

Since the appearance of Kristeva's essay, "intertextuality" has been used in two contexts. First, it has been a primarily theoretical term pointing to an impersonal field of intersecting texts that characterize the field of discourse. As Jacques Derrida argues, each text or utterance is a textile of signifiers whose signifieds are determined by other discourses; thus there is nothing beyond the text.[4] A great deal of the discussion of intertextuality in this mode is theoretical and seldom stoops to interpreting specific examples of texts intersecting texts; the point here is not interpretation but laying bare the logic of reference. In a second, more traditionalist context, "intertextuality" has been used as a substitute for "influence." Since the traditional kind of influence study relies on an idea of the author as a creative agent, it necessarily includes discussion of biography, psychology, history, and whatever themes or arguments might be deduced from the texts under consideration. The more theoretical version of intertextual study, however, could be seen as egalitarian in ignoring any specifics of an author's life or reputation. Kristeva's own sense of intertextuality is, however, already interpretive since any text "is a permutation of texts, an intertextuality; in the space of a given text, several utterances, taken from other texts, intersect and neutralize one another" (*Desire* 36).

Although a good deal of intertextual study of Joyce's writing has reflected the ideas of Kristeva and Derrida, up into the 1970s, nearly all of it was presented as the study of "influence" or the discussion of "allusion" in Joyce. But despite its popularity, relatively little work was devoted to an analysis of allusion itself. One of the most sophisticated (though limited) discussions of allusion is C. Perri's essay "On Alluding," which approaches the problem "semantically and pragmatically, that is, as a species of reference and as a speech act used to *do* things with words."[5] Perri dissents from the traditional definition of allusion, which specifies that it must be an "indirect" or "tacit" reference to a text, person, or cultural object. She argues that there is no distinction between literally naming a source and withholding the name. An allusion is thus

> a way of referring that takes into account and circumvents the problem of what we mean when we refer: allusion-markers act like proper names

in that they denote unique individuals (source texts), but they also tacitly specify the property(ies) belonging to the source text's connotation relevant to the allusion's meaning. ("On Alluding" 291)

Ulysses is a kind of limit-case for allusion in the novel since Joyce nearly always introduces or interpolates texts, things, or cultural references silently, without supplying the reader with a useful context. This is not a matter of neglect or inadvertence, but is instead a conscious (though often frustrating) strategy. Among the most frequently cited references on *Ulysses* is Don Gifford's *"Ulysses" Annotated*, a book whose general utility is admitted by nearly everyone.[6] Mary and Padraic Colum, friends of Joyce and enthusiasts of *Ulysses*, admit that "James Joyce writes as if it might be taken for granted that his readers know, not only the city he writes about, but its little shops and its little shows, the nicknames that have been given to its near-great, the cant phrases that have been used on the side streets."[7] And as Joyce matures, he relies increasingly on material that is borrowed, quoted, and adapted from elsewhere.

Some of this material is made of obscure high-cultural allusions such as "agenbite of inwit" (*U* 1.481), but some appear as spoken references to topics of the day (in 1904), so that non-academic Dubliners were at times inclined to dismiss his writing as simply a compilation of pub talk. To some extent they were right, but Joyce also deploys allusions of all sorts and cultural levels in *Ulysses*. Partly this has a realistic justification: Stephen's mind leaps to draw parallels between his experience and the world of literature, even when the association is somewhat strained. As early as *A Portrait of the Artist as a Young Man*, he turns his daily walk into a small library, thus transporting himself mentally from the Dublin slums to a rather baroque world of literature:

> He foreknew that as he passed the sloblands of Fairview he would think of the cloistral silverveined prose of Newman, that as he walked along the North Strand road, glancing idly at the windows of the provision shops, he would recall the dark humour of Guido Cavalcanti and smile. (*P* 176)

Even the middlebrow Bloom thinks allusively, though his stream of consciousness is more inclined to reference a few lines from *Sweets of Sin* than the spiritual meditations of Newman. In *Finnegans Wake* the writing is still more allusive because so many of the sentences are made up of warped and manipulated quotations from literature, proverbs, riddles, clichés, and other sorts of "public language," while the present-day fictional Earwicker family resonates with a series of historical and mythic figures.

Joyce, in a well-known passage, claimed that he had invented nothing and would be "quite content to go down to posterity as a scissors-

and-paste man," perhaps suggesting the figure of a newspaper sub-editor (*Letters I* 297). Poststructuralist critics are particularly fond of this quotation, because it resonates so clearly with Roland Barthes's concept of the intertextual universe – an infinite, anonymous series of texts, all interacting with others and none attached to an author exerting agency.[8] And the longer scholars study Joyce's writing, the more passages that were thought to have originated with Joyce turn out to be adapted quotations. It soon became apparent, in fact, that any passage of his writing will be vibrant with a series of more or less explicit verbal, imagistic, or thematic echoes of earlier writers. The issue for many years has been how to determine which of these echoes is significant to Joyce's text, and how. Indeed, it is not clear what constitutes an allusion in Joyce, since potential examples range along a spectrum from a unique verbal citation such as "agenbite of inwit," which was immediately identified, all the way to a broad echo of an earlier writer's themes, such as the classic discussions of epistemology that Stephen might evoke in "Proteus."

From the first, Joyce's defenders saw his dense use of allusion to classical mythology, classic literature, church fathers, and canonical literary figures like Shakespeare as evidence of his erudition and seriousness of purpose – and there was certainly need for such a defense, considering the furor that greeted some of the erotic or scatological passages in *Ulysses*. This defense evolved into an aspect of New Critical dogma perhaps best exemplified in T. S. Eliot's essay "*Ulysses*, Order, and Myth," which argued that the parallel Joyce offered between Homer's *Odyssey* and a day in 1904 Dublin constituted a literary breakthrough. He announced enthusiastically that "Instead of narrative method, we may now use the mythic method. It is, I seriously believe, a step toward making the modern world possible for art."[9]

Joyce also felt it important that his readers appreciate the complex parallels between his novel and Homer's epic. He talked his friend Stuart Gilbert into writing the study *James Joyce's "Ulysses*,"[10] which was, in part, an explanation of the book's series of allusions to the *Odyssey*, based on a series of charts that Joyce gave him. During long talks, Joyce also explained other formal aspects of the book, such as the long list of medieval rhetorical devices used in "Aeolus" and the series of imitations of major British prose stylists deployed in "Oxen of the Sun." After Gilbert's publication, readers were shown that Joyce's novel – which some early reviewers thought chaotic – had a large layer of secondary meaning that warranted study, and critics were encouraged to find subtle patterns and allusions of the kind Joyce had demonstrated he was entirely capable of making. Later on, according to Vladimir Nabokov, Joyce came to regret the whole idea of Gilbert's book (*JJII* 616, n.1). From the first he resisted all publishers' requests to identify the episodes by their Homeric names, suggesting his ambivalence about the status of the mythic superstructure.

But few of his critics felt a similar ambivalence. The first decade or so of serious explication of *Ulysses* involved tracing direct and indirect allusions to Classical writing, the Bible, and Shakespeare. This kind of criticism attempted to locate Joyce (and Eliot) within what Gilbert Highet called "the Classical Tradition,"[11] a natural heir to a position within F. R. Leavis's *Great Tradition*.[12] While there was little dispute about the fact of Joyce's allusions, arguments about their meaning and importance continue. Eliot seems to read the Homeric parallels as an indictment of modern society, treating Bloom, a middlebrow Irish Jew, as the modern degenerate version of a classical hero. Starting in the 1960s, however, a number of critics defended Bloom and the modern world with him, asserting that the Homeric parallel underlined the genuine heroic qualities of a pacifistic contemporary man who is the victim of both anti-Semitism and his spouse's unfaithfulness.[13]

The Homeric parallel can be viewed as the hidden figure in the carpet that puts the seal of meaning on the novel, but it can also be seen as nothing but a temporary scaffolding that helped Joyce in his composition while being of little significance to the reader. In his investigation of the composition of *Ulysses*, A. Walton Litz notes that many of the Homeric parallels Joyce included on his charts were never actually used in the book, while some were added very late in the book's composition, apparently as embroidery, and could not easily be called "structural."[14] Indeed, Homer's epic may be invoked purely for contrast with life in 1904 Dublin. M. Keith Booker, attributing the insight to Fritz Senn, argues that "Joyce does not use the *Odyssey* as a structural model for *Ulysses*. Instead, Joyce sets up the relatively homogeneous style and language of Homer's epic as a starting point against which he can define his radically heterogeneous text as the antithesis."[15] The thematic parallel to this formal interpretation is the ironic reading in which the world of *Ulysses* stands, for better or worse, as the antithesis of the Homeric world.

During the period in which New Critics paid special attention to Christian references in literary works that were not on the surface Christian, some were eager to discover and interpret them even in the work of an admitted apostate like Joyce, since his writing was still permeated with Biblical tags and echoes of the Church Fathers.[16] J. Mitchell Morse's *The Sympathetic Alien* concentrates on the work of Ignatius Loyola, founder of the Jesuit sect in which Joyce was raised, as well as Aquinas, Augustine, and Duns Scotus. Morse is especially useful in showing how Joyce consciously attempted to adapt Catholic rites and concepts to his basically secular work.[17] A somewhat less sophisticated work is Virginia Moseley's *Joyce and the Bible*, which painstakingly surveys Joyce's work for verbal echoes or situational parallels with the Latin Vulgate, the Douay Bible, or the King James version (which Joyce cites remarkably often for a Catholic writer).[18] Moseley argues that there is a hidden structural motif in *A Portrait* based on the yearly liturgical cycles of the Roman Catholic Church displayed in the Daily Missal. "What," she asks, "could be more ironic than the fact that the very thing from which Stephen Dedalus-Joyce seems to be escaping, the imitation of Christ ... affords the method of escape."[19]

In finding a structural motif where other critics had not, Moseley here resembles a group of critics who, once they have meditated on sources validated by Joyce himself, proceeded to find them throughout his oeuvre. One example of this is Richard Levin and Charles Shattuck's "First Flight to Ithaca: A Reading of Joyce's *Dubliners*," which ingeniously argues that the naturalistic stories of *Dubliners* conceal a series of Homeric allusions.[20] Similarly, after Joyce (by way of Beckett) had admitted that the historical cycles posited by Giambattista Vico had a structural role in *Finnegans Wake*, Margaret Church argued that Vico's thought also lay behind the structure and plot of *A Portrait*.[21] Among the early influence studies that have attracted the attention of Joyceans is Mary Reynolds's *Joyce and Dante: The Shaping Imagination* (1981).[22] This book has the advantage that Joyce on several occasions stated his admiration for the Italian writer, while it has the disadvantage that Dante was a believer who wrote in totally different genres from Joyce and at a very different time. Suggesting a theory of influence, Reynolds writes, "At an early stage [Joyce] marked out a small number of his predecessors for lifetime engagement, attaching their work to his. But this was a peculiarly loose attachment, which encroached while maintaining its distance" (*Dante* 3). "Attaching their work to his" gives the impression that Joyce is the active, even aggressive one in this literary exchange, suggesting that the work thus "engaged with" is itself changed by Joyce's incorporation of it. On the other hand, "maintaining its distance" implies that Joyce's own work remains in some way independent of the work alluded to; one might imagine that if a less original and powerful writer than Joyce were concerned here the work might be swamped by an allusion to a writer with the power of Dante. When the allusion is to a writer of the stature of Homer or Shakespeare, Reynolds claims that those two writers are "structural presences" – Homer as a model and Shakespeare as an illustration – while Dante is present only "by quotation" (*Dante* 3).

In considering Joyce's broader inheritance from the European tradition, Klaus Reichert examines the possible influence of Flaubert, Tolstoy, D'Annunzio, Ibsen, and Gerhart Hauptmann.[23] He also argues for the significance of Nietzsche in Joyce's early thought, pointing out their mutual enthusiasm for Wagner – a subject more thoroughly explored in Timothy Martin's *Joyce and Wagner*.[24] Although there may be specific allusions to many of these figures in *Ulysses* (such as Mulligan invoking Nietzsche's *Übermensch* at the end of "Telemachus"), it is nevertheless difficult to disentangle the specific influences of individual artists from the more general impact of the broad European aesthetic movements in which Joyce was a participant. The problem becomes even more acute when considering figures (such as Wagner) whose main form of expression was not literary, involving as it does the issue of comparison among different arts, in which many of the parallels to Joyce's practice are metaphorical. Similarly, Maria Tymoczko in *The Irish "Ulysses"* argues that Joyce was heavily influenced by Irish culture, including writing in the Irish language (with which he was thought to be only superficially acquainted) and writing using the same Irish mythology that obviously influenced Yeats.[25]

The study of literary influence is itself a destabilized theoretical practice. Critics may (and generally did) concentrate their attention on the writer being influenced, and the context of that attention may be directly biographical, psychological, historical, sociological, or some combination of these. Critical attention may fall upon the mechanism relating the work of the writer to an earlier writer, and this kind of study tends to be poetic, linguistic, or more generally formalist. Finally, a critic may concentrate on the effect on the reader of the passage under study, in an example of reader-response criticism. Of these possibilities, the first and third have proven the most productive. In *The Anxiety of Influence*, Harold Bloom offers a neo-Freudian reading that concentrates on the later writer's psyche as it is revealed by his practice of allusion.[26] Writers are evaluated as "weak" or "strong," and their relationship is usually Oedipal, so that in the case of two strong writers the one alluding must regard the one alluded to as a paternal figure. In Bloom's system, the beginning poet, or *ephebe*, must creatively misread his predecessor in an act of poetic misprision. In developing six kinds of misprision – which resemble both Freudian defenses and rhetorical tropes – Bloom moves his theory in the direction of literary relations rather than the psyche of the poet, and to a degree blends the two.

Walter Jackson Bate in *The Burden of the Past and the English Poet*[27] discusses the problem of "belatedness," in which earlier poets present a challenge to later ones, who are forced into innovation and rebellion. In the late 1960s, however, readings rooted in the personality of the author were displaced by the rise of Barthes's development of the concept of intertextuality. In "The Death of the Author" Barthes actually displaces two figures: the author, at least in his or her role as biographical and psychological entity, and the reader in his or her similar role. "We know now," he writes, "that a text is not a line of words releasing a single 'theological' meaning (the 'message' of the author-God) but a multi-dimensional space in which a variety of writings, none of them original, blend and clash. The text is a tissue of quotations drawn from the innumerable centres of culture."[28] Barthes claims that the reader displaces the author, but in any conventional sense the reader is also displaced:

> A text is made of multiple writings, drawn from many cultures and entering into mutual relations of dialogue, parody, contestation, but there is one place where this dialogue is focused and that place is the reader; not, as was hitherto said, the author. The reader is the space on which all the quotations that make up a writing are inscribed without any of them being lost.... Yet this destination cannot any longer be personal: the reader is without history, biography, psychology. (*Image/Music/Text* 148)

"Once the Author is removed, the claim to decipher a text becomes quite futile," contends Barthes, thus at a stroke doing away with interpretive (what he calls "Classic") criticism (*Image/Music/Text* 147). But nothing in Barthes's system puts any limit on the interacting texts – or what he terms the cultural "codes" – and much of the interpretive work he does on Balzac's story in *S/Z* is made possible by his artificially limiting those codes.[29]

Since Barthes's seminal work, a great deal of critical work in Joyce has reflected his ideas alongside those of Derrida – for instance, most of the essays in *Post-Structuralist Joyce: Essays from the French* and Eloise Knowlton's *Joyce, Joyceans, and the Rhetoric of Citation*, the latter of which is a meditation on authority and the rhetoric of quotations of all sorts.[30] Both of these reflect a more general linguistic turn. But the bulk of criticism produced by the move to poststructuralism as exemplified in Barthes and Derrida was not interpretive work focused on texts antecedent to *Ulysses*. Brilliant as some of this work was, it failed to reflect directly the general move toward history and politics that is evident in criticism of the past twenty years. Along with the rise of postcolonial criticism, this reflects the increased focus on race, gender, and class. In addition, one of the legacies of structuralist criticism was the huge expansion of acceptable objects of critical analysis from a small number of "great" literary texts worth study (as F. R. Leavis argued should be the function of criticism in society) to a virtually unlimited number of texts, including professional wrestling, Superman comics, and best-selling books.

The book that introduced the study of popular culture in Joyce's work most influentially was Cheryl Herr's *Joyce's Anatomy of Culture*, published in 1986, followed by a somewhat different but parallel approach to Joyce's use of the popular culture of his time in my own *Joyce, Bakhtin, and Popular Literature* in 1989.[31] Herr's book concentrated on the press, the stage (especially the music hall), and popular preachers while benefitting from a remarkable amount of archival study. Herr's theoretical base was in semiotics, but her discussions drew on a wealth of thinkers whose work had a historical dimension, such as Michel Foucault. My analysis was more textually oriented, dealing with books such as *Tom Brown's Schooldays* or *The Three Musketeers* and rather obscure novels with which Joyce was familiar. As the title suggested, my book relied heavily on Bakhtin's thought – which remained poststructuralist (especially in Kristeva's presentation of him) – but welcomed analysis of the ideological base of the multiple "languages" posited by Bakhtin. I discussed the ideological and rhetorical elements of the popular texts he treated and analyzed their intertextual connections with Joyce's text in all the richness of their dialogic relationships. My next book, *The Culture of Ulysses*, reflected a more general change in critical focus in its move from the intertextuality of novels (such as Marie Corelli's work) to analysis of a variety of discourses, such as Orientalism and the semiotics of body builder Eugen Sandow.[32] For Herr and for myself, some popular discourses – such as the pantomime or the daily newspaper – do work of political resistance in a way parallel to that of avant-garde writing like *Ulysses*.

Since the subject was introduced, there have been numerous books investigating aspects of popular culture alluded to in Joyce's work. Garry Leonard's work on advertising as discourse is one of the more interesting.[33] The larger move toward Foucault's style of analysis was also hospitable to the growing interest in history and how a historical analysis might illuminate Joyce's texts. Here the term "intertextuality" is sometimes stretched, but a number of critics – such as Robert Spoo in *James Joyce and the Language of History* – pursued historical allusions (especially ones to a period after 1904, such as to World War I) that were more subtle or indirect than previous commentators had allowed.[34] Some of this work was carried out under the rubric of postcolonial criticism, but no matter the theoretical slant, the dominant trend of Joycean critical investigation over the past twenty years has been historical. It has also been rooted in a broader sense of intertextuality that reflects the mutual interaction of elements of all social levels in a broad cultural whole – a style of analysis now evident in New Modernist studies.[35] Since the 1960s, interest has shifted emphatically from source studies of the allusions, to the "strong" writers of canonical modernism, to broad cultural patterns and the implication of their forms – such as the newspapers that furnish a suggestive intertext to *Ulysses*.

In 1973, speaking about the possible future of influence study, Harold Bloom asked, "And what is Poetic Influence anyway? Can the study of it really be anything more than the wearisome industry that will soon touch apocalypse anyway when it passes from scholars to computers?" (*Anxiety* 31). Neither Bloom nor any other critic over forty years ago could envision the impact (apocalyptic or not) that computers would have on literary scholarship. Most directly, computers and the availability of digitalized texts have enabled far more efficient and productive searches than were possible even to critics with the prodigious memory of Bloom. In the case of pastiche episodes such as "Nausicaa" it is fairly easy to trace sentence fragments and entire sentences back to obscure women's novelettes; the issue is to make sure the passages are distinctive enough to ensure that we are dealing with a quotation rather than a coincidence, and then to evaluate the significance of the allusion, if any. Computers and digitalized records have also made it much easier to trace the more obscure historical figures who appear in *Ulysses*, like Fred Gallaher and Philip Beaufoy. Some work of this sort is included in issues of *James Joyce Online Notes*.

The other area of significance of computers for Joyce studies stems from the realization that a full appreciation of Joyce's intertextuality leads to an understanding of how *Ulysses* participates in the mode of hypertext. Several projects have sought to produce genuine hypertext versions of Joyce's works, which would include all major textual variants and identification of the allusions about which there is general agreement, and in some projects brief interpretive passages as well. All these projects so far have foundered for reasons of copyright, but with the expiration of copyright in Joyce's works in several jurisdictions, it seems likely that at least one hypertext *Ulysses* will appear. Imagining a hyperlinked version of the book, however, returns us to some basic problems about how we determine the borderlines of allusion. For example, I have argued that the end of "Sirens," where Bloom musically breaks wind, alludes to turn-of-the-century French entertainer Joseph Pujol, known as "*le petomane*," who was able to produce musical tones from his nether orifice, to comic effect (*Culture* 14). Yet this is hardly a direct allusion, since it relies on a subtle parallel and the uncertain chance that Joyce – who never mentioned the "flatulist" – was aware of him.

The strongest effect of the rise of the computer, however, has been as a metaphor for the text of *Ulysses* itself. Unlike conventional novels, Joyce's novel is an intricate, dense web of reference: It encompasses self-reference and references to all levels of culture – from high-cultural allusions to classical writing and medieval theology, through middlebrow writers like Marie Corelli, to low-culture phenomena like the music hall and the "panto." The book offers its readers multiple levels of allusion in the guise of intertextuality, where the texts are no more exhaustible than the Internet. Like any hypertext, *Ulysses* encourages the reader to move along unpredictable paths through its words because its own logic is not simply linear. Like Borges's "garden of forking paths," *Ulysses* leads us through multiple reading experiences, so that we are now drawn out of the book, now drawn several episodes further into it, to where a theme sounded early in the book is continued. It is clear that in dealing with Joyce's prototype of a hypertext we will never be able to say that we have finished with the book.

Notes

1 Julia Kristeva, *Desire in Language: A Semiotic Approach to Literature and Art*, ed. Leon S. Roudiez (New York: Columbia University Press, 1980). Further references will be cited parenthetically as *Desire*.

2 M. M. Bakhtin, *The Dialogic Imagination: Four Essays*, ed. Michael Holquist (Austin: University of Texas Press, 1981), p. 434.

3 "Heteroglossia, once incorporated into the novel ... is another's speech in another's language, serving to express authorial intentions but in a refracted way." Bakhtin, *Dialogic*, p. 324.

4 Jacques Derrida, *Positions*, trans. Alan Bass (Chicago: University of Chicago Press, 1976), passim.

5 C. Perri, "On Alluding," *Poetics* 7 (September 1978): 290. Further references will be cited parenthetically as "On Alluding."

6 Don Gifford with Robert Seidman, *"Ulysses" Annotated*, 2nd ed. (Berkeley: University of California Press, 1988).

7 Mary and Padraic Colum, *Our Friend James Joyce* (New York: Doubleday, 1958), p. 142.

8 See, for example, Roland Barthes, *The Pleasure of the Text*, trans. Richard Miller (New York: Hill and Wang, 1975).

9 T. S. Eliot, *"Ulysses*, Order, and Myth," *The Modern Tradition: Backgrounds of Modern Literature*, eds. Richard Ellmann and Charles Feidelson, Jr. (New York: Oxford University Press, 1965), pp. 679–81.

10 Stuart Gilbert, *James Joyce's "Ulysses"* (New York: Alfred A. Knopf, 1930).

11 Gilbert Highet, *The Classical Tradition: Greek and Roman Influences on Western Literature* (New York: Oxford University Press, 1949).

12 F. R. Leavis, *The Great Tradition* (New York: New York University Press, 1948). Leavis put a greater emphasis on moral seriousness than did some of the early New Critics, who were more concerned with ambiguity and complexity. He also chose Lawrence rather than Joyce as his model of modern literary greatness.

13 See, for example, Leslie Fiedler, "Bloom on Joyce; Or, Jokey for Jacob," *Journal of Modern Literature* 1 (1970): 19–29; Marilyn French, *The Book as World* (Cambridge: Harvard University Press, 1976); William York Tindall, *A Reader's Guide to James Joyce* (New York: Farrar, Straus, and Giroux, 1959).

14 A. Walton Litz, *The Art of James Joyce: Method and Design in "Ulysses" and "Finnegans Wake"* (New York: Oxford University Press, 1961), passim.

15 M. Keith Booker, *Joyce, Bakhtin, and the Literary Tradition: Toward a Comparative Cultural Poetics* (Ann Arbor: University of Michigan Press, 1995), p. 22.

16 Buck Mulligan in the first episode of *Ulysses* makes this point when he tells Stephen, "You have the cursed Jesuit strain in you, only it's injected the wrong way" (*U* 1.209).

17 J. Mitchell Morse, *The Sympathetic Alien: James Joyce and Catholicism* (New York: New York University Press, 1959).

18 The Latin Vulgate was a fourth-century translation of the Bible into Latin that eventually became the officially promulgated Latin version for the Roman Catholic Church. The Douay Bible was a 1582 translation from the Latin Vulgate into English and was commonly used within the Roman Catholic Church. The King James version was a 1611 translation into English sponsored by King James for use in the Church of England. It is generally recognized for its literary quality.

19 Virginia Moseley, *Joyce and the Bible* (DeKalb: Northern Illinois University Press, 1962), p. 32.

20 Richard Levin and Charles Shattuck, "First Flight to Ithaca: A Reading of Joyce's *Dubliners*," in *James Joyce: Two Decades of Criticism*, ed. Seon Givens (New York: Vanguard Press, 1948), pp. 47–94.

21 Margaret Church, "A Portrait and Giambattista Vico: A Source Study," in *Approaches to Joyce's "Portrait": Ten Essays*, eds. Thomas F. Staley and Bernard Benstock (Pittsburgh, PA: University of Pittsburgh Press, 1976), pp. 77–89.

22 Mary T. Reynolds, *Joyce and Dante: The Shaping Imagination* (Princeton, NJ: Princeton University Press, 1981). Further references will be cited parenthetically as *Dante*.

23 Klaus Reichert, "The European Background of Joyce's Writing," *The Cambridge Companion to James Joyce*, ed. Derek Attridge (Cambridge: Cambridge University Press, 1990).

24 Timothy Martin, *Joyce and Wagner: A Study of Influence* (Cambridge: Cambridge University Press, 1991).

25 Maria Tymoczko, *The Irish "Ulysses"* (Berkeley: University of California Press, 1994).

26 Harold Bloom, *The Anxiety of Influence: A Theory of Poetry* (New York: Oxford University Press, 1973). Further references will be cited parenthetically as *Anxiety*.

27 Walter Jackson Bate, *The Burden of the Past and the English Poet* (Cambridge, MA: Harvard University Press, 1970).

28 Roland Barthes, *Image/Music/Text*, trans. Stephen Heath (New York: Hill and Wang, 1977), p. 146. Further references will be cited parenthetically as *Image/Music/Text*.

29 Roland Barthes, *S/Z: An Essay*, trans. Richard Miller (New York: Hill and Wang, 1974).

30 Derek Attridge and Daniel Ferrer, *The Poststructuralist Joyce: Essays from the French* (Cambridge: Cambridge University Press, 1984); Eloise Knowlton, *Joyce, Joyceans, and the Rhetoric of Citation* (Gainesville: University Press of Florida, 1998).

31 Cheryl Herr, *Joyce's Anatomy of Culture* (Urbana: University of Illinois Press, 1986); R. B. Kershner, *Joyce, Bakhtin, and Popular Literature: Chronicles of Disorder* (Chapel Hill: University of North Carolina Press, 1989).

32 R. Brandon Kershner, *The Culture of "Ulysses"* (New York: Palgrave Macmillan, 2010). Further references will be cited parenthetically as *Culture*.

33 Garry Leonard, *Advertising and Commodity Culture in Joyce* (Gainesville: University Press of Florida, 1998).

34 Robert Spoo, *James Joyce and the Language of History* (New York: Oxford University Press, 1994).

35 For a general introduction to this fundamental rethinking of modernist studies, see Douglas Mao and Rebecca L. Walkowitz, "The New Modernist Studies," *PMLA* 123.3 (2008): 737–48.

CHAPTER 13

Bodies

Vike Martina Plock

> "Among other things," [Joyce] said, "my book is the epic of the human body.... In my book the body lives in and moves through space and is the home of a full human personality. The words I write are adapted to express first one of its functions then another. In *Lestrygonians* the stomach dominates and the rhythm of the episode is that of the peristaltic movement."
>
> "But the minds, the thoughts of the characters," I began.
>
> "If they had no body they would have no mind," said Joyce. "It's all one."[1]

As the quoted dialogue with Frank Budgen illustrates, Joyce's fiction prioritises the body as a site of critical examination. In his unconventional development of literary character it is not, as Budgen surmises, the minds of his protagonists but the physical reality of their organisms that marks the starting point for phenomenological experience. For this reason – because Joyce intended to unsettle the Cartesian mind-body dualism by offering an alternative perspective on human subjectivity – bodies in *Ulysses* really do matter. But if Joyce made his characters' corporality and their physical sensations of central importance to his developing literary aesthetics, it should also be acknowledged that the bodies he presents in *Ulysses* were similarly designed to disrupt binary thinking. Hardly anywhere is the body, or any of its individual parts, constructed as an easily legible sign. Instead, Joyce's novel attempts to dismantle established notions of gender and race while developing a sustained scepticism about discourses that emphasise the singularity and wholeness of the human. Consequently, those bodies that are particularly dismantled, feeble, or grotesquely shaped obtain immense prominence in the pages of *Ulysses*.

The reader does not have to search for long to encounter bodies that are depicted in an advanced state of collapse. In the "Sirens" episode, for instance, human organisms are splintered and break up into individual parts. The barmaids' "wet lips" titter (*U* 11.76); ears have to be "unplugged" to hear (*U* 11.136); and Bloom's "dark eye[s]" pass Aaron Figatner's jewellery shop on Wellington Quay (*U* 11.149). Up to this point, this deliberate and pronounced synecdochic fragmentation of bodies marks Joyce's most radical experimentation with representing physicality in *Ulysses*. Although bodies have certainly crowded the pages of his text on previous occasions – the end of "Calypso" showing Leopold Bloom on the cuckstool is an obvious case in point – the representational techniques encountered in "Sirens" significantly develop Joyce's aesthetic recalibration of physiology and bodily functions. As readers move away from the novel's "initial style" (*Letters I* 129), in which stream of consciousness and free indirect discourse decisively and systematically interrupt the third-person, past-tense narration, Joyce's depiction of the body undergoes equally drastic changes. If the focus on the body's materiality facilitated, in the earlier episodes of *Ulysses*, the promotion of novelistic verisimilitude, then experiments such as the figurative fragmentation of human bodies in "Sirens" assist in defamiliarising the world Joyce depicts. Through the detailed portrayal of Buck Mulligan's "[s]tately, plump" (*U* 1.1) shape, Bloom's avaricious appetite for "grilled mutton kidneys" (*U* 4.4), and the impressive assembly of other physical details and physiological processes, the material reality of turn-of-the-century Dublin is, in the earlier episodes of *Ulysses*, brought closer to the reader's attention. The result is an augmentation of the novel's mimetic features.

By contrast, the alternative representation of physicality in "Sirens" underlines that human bodies are elaborate constructs. Rather than forming holistic units, they are assembled from small individual components or building blocks. As Marjorie Howes explains in Chapter 9, readers turning to "Sirens" find that the unfolding narrative fragments as well. While Joyce fractures human bodies, the awareness of the novel's constructedness is thereby sharpened, plot gives way to formal experimentation, and linguistic extravagance offsets the realist facets of earlier chapters. The innovative depiction of human bodies in *Ulysses*, in other words, is synchronised with an equally revolutionary challenge to literary conventions. In Joyce's hands, the novel becomes a living organism, one that is animated, flexible, and never static. As Joyce explained to Frank Budgen, "the words I write are adapted to express first one of [the body's] functions then another" so that the physiological processes depicted in individual parts of the novel determine and are emulated by the episodes' stylistic idiosyncrasies. By the same token, *Ulysses* purposefully moves beyond an uncomplicated use of physiological imagery for the sole purpose of strengthening the text's correspondences with the physical world. Although it serves to introduce a sense of novelistic authenticity in the first chapters, bodily imagery evolves in *Ulysses* so as to keep pace with the text's formal flexibility. As a result, the representation of the body in *Ulysses* is constantly shifting, always probing, and, very often, exceptionally perplexing.

This chapter uses the representation of physiology in *Ulysses* as a thematic nexus to discuss a selection of critical approaches that have dominated Joyce scholarship in recent decades. Beginning with Foucaultian discourse analysis, it will revisit Joyce's attempt to devise the Linati schema as a vehicle to promote a reading of *Ulysses* that uses the text's engagement with the human organism as an interpretative scaffold before discussing feminism, postcolonialism, disability studies, and animal studies. Ultimately, I will suggest that Joyce's revolutionary depiction of physiology and bodily functions – and his interest in the rebellious and unruly body in particular – defies abstraction and makes any uncomplicated alliance with generalising discourses or a particular theoretical framework exceptionally difficult.

As I have shown elsewhere, the conceptual ambiguity in Joyce's depiction of the body must be read in concert with his efforts to challenge contemporary debates about the ways in which the body was read and conceptualised. The second half of the nineteenth century saw the radical reorganisation of the medical profession and its attempts to classify and standardise bodies through the establishment of comprehensive nosological and diagnostic parameters.[2] Since the eighteenth century – as Michel Foucault argues in *The History of Sexuality* – institutional control of individuals was facilitated by a "multiplication of discourse" in newly emerging professions such as law and medicine, as well as in traditional scholastic practices such as clerical doctrine.[3] From then on, a plethora of "interlocking, hierarchized" discursive patterns resolutely established who was qualified to speak about the body, its physiological functions, and sexuality (*Sexuality* 30). When debates about the human body became institutionalised, only those individuals distinguished by expert knowledge were authorised to decide where, how often, and in which professional registers the body's physiological manifestations might become the subject of conversation.

At this point readers of *Ulysses* need only think of Gerty MacDowell's compulsion to speak about the details of her first menstruation in the confession box (*U* 13.453–59). Here is a Joycean character whose behaviour and discursive patterns are thoroughly shaped by the institutional authority of the Catholic Church. While Gerty is notably embarrassed – "crimsoning up to the roots of her hair" (*U* 13.454) when revealing uncomfortable details of her adolescent physiology – the priest's reassuring, if not patronising, response that it was "no sin because that came from the nature of woman instituted by God" (*U* 13.456–57) marks his confidence in his own authority and illustrates the power he has over Gerty, the subject who is forced to "confess" intimate information. Thus her body becomes the site of a discursive intervention that maintains the hierarchical relationship between priest and penitent. Later, in "Penelope," Molly Bloom remembers how she interrupted exactly this customary power dynamic through a purposefully performed naivety. Her confession ("he touched me father") triggers the priest's inevitable question of "where" she was touched (*U* 18.107–08). By deliberately playing the "fool" and answering with the words "on the canal bank," Molly forces Father Corrigan into taking a more active part in the ensuing dialogue: "but whereabouts on your person my child on the leg behind high up was it yes rather high up was it where you sit down yes" (*U* 18.108–10). Unlike Gerty, Molly hates "that confession" (*U* 18.107) and resents the obligatory disclosure of private information. But her strategy of deliberate evasion introduces a rebellious element into the conversational pattern and engages Father Corrigan in a mock-teasing dialogue that forces him to verbalise exactly those details that she, Molly, is supposed to reveal. This nascent defiance of making the body the subject of a public, institutionalised discourse was shared by Joyce, who noted, in a manner similar to Molly, that the discursive organisation of the body could result in the curtailing of individual freedoms. As he would have realised, in a sociopolitical environment that was unlikely to tolerate psychological, intellectual, or emotional diversity, the body became an opportune target for asserting institutional control. In response to these and similar efforts to normalise individuality and its infinite physiological manifestations, Joyce consciously resisted urges to represent bodies as easily classifiable, manageable units. Instead, he developed a fascination for bodies that are fragmented, disabled, uncontrollable, and endlessly malleable.

At the outset, though, Joyce himself suggested the human body as a defining feature that could help unlock the latent mysteries of *Ulysses*. On 21 September 1920, he sent to the Italian critic Carlo Linati a detailed schema that allocated a human organ to all but the first three episodes. In an accompanying letter he further explained that his "intention is" to allow "[e]ach adventure (that is, every hour, every organ, every art being interconnected and interrelated in the structural scheme of the whole) ... [to]

not only condition but even create its own technique" (*Letters I* 146–47). A physiological reading of the book, in other words, would not only provide the key to comprehending individual episodes, but would also explain how individual chapters operate, like the organs of a human body, in a cooperative and coordinated manner. Approximating other physiological aesthetes of his time, such as the science writer and novelist Grant Allen,[4] Joyce used the human body as a starting point to conceptualise and structure the world depicted in his book.

There is no doubt that a reading of *Ulysses* along physiological lines can generate productive interpretative results. For instance, as the organ most immediately related to speech production, the assigned body part for "Aeolus," the "lungs," corresponds neatly with the newspaper episode's thematic focus on rhetoric and political oratory. Additionally, the body's physiological processes – the rhythmical breathing in and out – are, early on in the episode, emulated by such rhetorical devices as the chiasmus and its inverted parallelism: "Grosssbooted draymen rolled barrels dullthudding out of Prince's stores and bumped them up on the brewery float. On the brewery float bumped dullthudding barrels rolled by grossbooted draymen out of Prince's stores" (*U* 7.21–24).[5] A strong associative connection can thus be established between the episode's allocated organ, its content, and its style. Additionally, a physiologically based reading of the episode can uncover Joyce's potential scepticism about language's power to generate socio-economic and political change. Like the air that is circulated in the body's lungs, speech loses its transformative energy by being endlessly repeated in clichéd rhetorical patterns. Rather than suggesting that such linguistic registers can be the expedient medium for generating political change, the lungs as the designated organ for "Aeolus" reinforce the image of inertia and stasis that, in Joyce's view, represented much more accurately the contemporary political arena in Ireland.

If "Aeolus" provides a particularly good example of an episode that productively converts physiological metaphors into interpretative strategies, other episodes illustrate the constraints that come with too-uncritical attention to the physiological imagery chosen by Joyce. His critics might question, for instance, what function – apart from being the general thematic focus – the "skin" or the "heart" take on in episodes such as "Lotus-Eaters" or "Hades." Even more reductive is the allocation of "fat" to the novel's final episode, "Penelope." First and foremost, "fat" is – unlike the heart, the lungs, or the skin – hardly an organ in the conventional sense. More problematically, the orthodox association of the episode with its assigned "organ" can, in this case, lead to a prejudiced interpretation of Molly Bloom (and the "Penelope" episode) as fleshy, parasitical surplus that might correspond to the juvenile Joyce's own assessment of woman as "an animal that micturates once a day, defecates once a week, menstruates once a month and parturates once a year" – but that denies both his female protagonist and her final monologue the intellectual activity and subversive energy located there by many readers.[6] One particularly devastating assessment of Molly and of Joyce's representation of female physiology was produced by J. B. Lyons, who, in referring to her "soiled sexuality," categorically identified Molly as an "immature and inadequate woman."[7]

Many feminists have confronted such one-dimensional and ideologically offensive readings of "Penelope" and its depiction of Molly's presumably untameable physiology. Especially since the rise of French feminism in the 1970s, a new generation of critics have contested customary representations of gender and female physiology in canonical male writing. Drawing on poststructuralist theory, French theorists such as Luce Irigaray and Julia Kristeva proposed a critical reinvention of the female body as a place of subversion and rebellion that could successfully challenge a culture of hegemonic masculinity. For Joyce scholarship, though, the work of Algerian-born philosopher Hélène Cixous represented the most significant change in the ways in which *Ulysses* and especially its representation of female physiology were read. Her 1969 doctoral thesis, *The Exile of James Joyce* (translated into English in 1976), marked an early interest in matters Joycean, but it was her 1975 essay "The Laugh of the Medusa" (English version, 1976) that proposed a radically new approach to understanding the interconnections between physiology and writing – one that also called for a critical reassessment of Joyce's own presumably reductive portrayal of femininity and the female body.[8]

Two ostensibly incompatible propositions are made in "The Laugh of the Medusa." First, Cixous argues that woman must produce a writing practice, *écriture féminine*, emanating from a conscious reliance on female body parts. "Write your self. Your body must be heard," Cixous insists (2043). This focus on female physiology will enable the woman writer to reclaim her marginalised and confiscated body. It will also produce a mode of textual composition that "sweep[s] away syntax" and all other aspects of those standardised writing practices that are the envoys of Western phallocentrism (2049). Second, "The Laugh of the Medusa" suggests, somewhat conflictingly, that both male and female writers can produce *écriture féminine*. For Cixous, however, this presumed contradiction is a fundamental aspect of *écriture féminine*. Because it aims to disregard the binary logic of Western thought, it is able to abandon the conventional distinction between male and female by offering instead a subversive model of heterogeneity, diversity, and transitional intellectual spaces. For this reason, both male and female writers can be credited with writing *écriture féminine*. In fact, Jean Genet is one writer explicitly mentioned in "The Laugh of the Medusa." Another is Joyce himself, whose final chapter of *Ulysses*, with its rebellious syntax, lack of punctuation, and explicit references to female physiology and sexuality, most emphatically embodies *écriture féminine*. In this reading, Molly's final "yes" marks a revolutionised, affirmative recognition of the female body.

Cixous's assertive, albeit controversial, intervention was instrumental in conceiving a positive reconfiguration of Joyce's representation of femininity. It overrode readings of Molly's pathological or "soiled sexuality" and it also generated a range of critical approaches that aimed to further complicate the ways in which the female body is depicted in Joyce's text.[9] Moreover, it emphasised that the body was more than a convenient metaphor for revealing the latent mysteries of *Ulysses*. If Joyce's own suggestion to read his novel alongside physiological imagery had explicitly established the body as a site for narrative experiments, Cixous enabled alternative, politically motivated readings of the body.

Another critical response to Joyce's work that came with an equally strong interest in underlining the political facets in his depiction of the body was postcolonialism, which surfaced in the 1990s as a particularly dominant strand in Joyce scholarship. Many postcolonial scholars have used the "Cyclops" episode to develop their critical readings. Set in the decidedly Irish space of Barney Kiernan's pub, this chapter focuses on colonialism, Irish nationalism, and racial xenophobia as interconnected discourses that converge in the figure of the boisterous "citizen" whose mutinous, masculine body becomes Joyce's target for parody and critique (*U* 12.151–67). Enda Duffy, for example, concludes that some of the monstrous depictions of Irish masculine physiology in circulation at the turn of the century forced writers such as Joyce to "face down the stereotypes with which the colonial native had been characterized in the minds and discourses of the colonizer."[10] In this critical construction, both the body of the citizen and the body of Joyce's text itself become contested spaces in which different political ideologies compete for prominence. But Joyce's preoccupation with colonial politics exceeds "Cylcops" and its localised account of a small group of individuals with divergent political agendas. Earlier, in "Wandering Rocks," the city of Dublin appears as a breathing, living organism – albeit one hampered by political oppression and the cultural restrictions that are the adjuncts of its colonial status. Here, as in "Aeolus," the narrative focus moves away from Bloom and Stephen, in favour of a more stratified and universal perspective that makes the city itself the episode's central character.[11] On first reading, an image of a bustling, lively cityscape might materialise, in which the paths of different characters intersect and which hosts the procession of a royal official. Despite this initial optimistic impression, Joyce, in "Wandering Rocks," nonetheless returns to an interpretation of Dublin first introduced in 1914 in *Dubliners* that presents his hometown as a paralytic colonial space and the Irish nation as a disabled and disenfranchised body politic.

This image of colonial stasis is replicated in the episode's structure. Even though the focus of "Wandering Rocks" is the streets of Dublin, its opening section concentrates on "[t]he superior, the very reverend John Conmee S. J." and follows him on his vigilant perambulation through the city (*U* 10.01). Although he would like to see himself as a benign and kind-hearted philanthropist, Conmee appears as a pompous and conceited snob, who offers blessings instead of alms (*U* 10.10) and who talks condescendingly to the Belvedere schoolboys who pass him on his way (*U* 10.40–55). It is, however, a particular Joycean narrative technique that most evidently brings Conmee's self-centeredness to the fore. Indeed, most of the forty or so paragraphs that constitute this section present Conmee himself as the acting or perceiving subject of the narrative: "Father Conmee crossed to Mountjoy Square" (*U* 10.12), "Father Conmee smelt incense on his right hand as he walked" (*U* 10.79), "Father Conmee sat in a corner of the tram-car" (*U* 10.115), "Father Conmee, reading his office, watched a flock of muttoning clouds over Rathcoffey" (*U* 10.184–85). Through Joyce's subtle narrative intervention, the progress through Dublin by a representative of the Catholic Church – one of Stephen's "two masters" (*U* 1.638) – mirrors the image with which the episode concludes and which represents with the "imperial British state" (*U* 1.643) the other of Stephen's two masters: the viceregal cavalcade on its procession through the streets of Dublin.[12] By enclosing the narratives of Stephen, Bloom, and the rest of the ordinary Dubliners that make up the majority of the "Wandering Rocks" episode in this manner, Roman Catholicism and British colonialism are identified as the two oppressive forces that hold sway over Dublin and thwart its sociopolitical autonomy, its economic progress, and the intellectual development of its inhabitants.

Already apparent in Joyce's representation of Dublin as a location handicapped by colonial politics is his predilection for considering broken, injured, and disempowered bodies in his fiction. The Irish capital emerges in *Ulysses* as a severely damaged and dysfunctional body politic, a condition that also finds expression in a variety of disabilities Joyce attributes to his characters. From the "onelegged sailor" (*U* 10.07), who cruises the streets of Dublin in "Wandering Rocks," through Gerty MacDowell with her "one shortcoming" (*U* 13.650), and Bloom's physical debilities such as sciatica (*U* 15.2782) to Dilly Dedalus's physical signs of malnourishment (*U* 10.855) – bodies in *Ulysses*, with a few notable exceptions, are shown to be in a precarious state of ill health if not in danger of irrevocable collapse. Even the "happy *accouchement*" (*U* 14.1311), the birth of Mortimer Edward Purefoy in "Oxen of the Sun," is a drawn-out event with decidedly pathological components (*U* 14.1334). The news that Mina Purefoy is "three days bad" (*U* 8.282) prompts Bloom's thoughts about infant mortality in "Lestrygonians" (*U* 8.481–82) and brings back painful memories and visions of Rudy, his infant son who died aged seven days (*U* 8.610, 11.1067, 15.4962). As a result, an event that in literary hands other than Joyce's might have been exploited as a quintessential metaphor of fertility, regeneration, and revival becomes connected to the general exploration of infirmity and frailness taking place in *Ulysses*.

Given the abundance of impaired, maimed, or handicapped bodies that fill the textual space of Joyce's novel, it is hardly surprising that scholars with an interest in disability studies would find *Ulysses* an extremely rich source. In recent years, this particular field of study has gained momentum and is now making a significant contribution to the study of English literary history, while the work of scholars such as Lennard J. Davis, Tom Shakespeare, and Martha Stoddard Holmes has brought welcome attention to the historical changes in the cultural perception of physical debility, disability, and deformity.[13] These and similar critical excavations have established that our contemporary construction of disability, which aims to differentiate between "normal" and "disabled" bodies, is a very recent invention. As Davis has convincingly shown, it is in the nineteenth century – and particularly with the rise of statistics as a modern science – that "disability" and "normality" as relational or oppositional concepts emerged for the first time.[14] Bodies were carefully measured, evaluated, categorised, and classified in order to establish firm tenets for physiological standards and norms. If the pre-Enlightenment world had set up the concept of idealised mythological bodies that compromised human physiology by deeming all non-celestial bodies insufficient and irregular, this nineteenth-century change in the understanding of human anatomy introduced the idea of corporeal norms while also setting new standards for inclusion and exclusion. From now on, physical normality was associated with social and moral competence – even with superiority – while the critical assessment of the disabled body with its physical markers resulted in disqualifying and devaluing individuals who did not comply with the standards of this new "hegemony of normalcy" ("Normalcy" 10).

In *Ulysses*, Bloom is introduced as the mock-heroic everyman, or, in Joyce's own words, the "all-round," the "complete" man (*Making* 17). At first glance, Bloom's status as an average guy seems to conform to the normative dictates of the newly established anthropometric sciences. Soon, however, it becomes apparent that Joyce's perception of a "complete" man does not measure up to expectations of normativity. On the contrary, with his peculiar culinary preferences, his unusual sexual proclivities, his complex racial background as well as the small flaws in his physical appearance, Bloom emerges as a character dynamically challenging rather than enforcing prescriptive notions of standardised physicality.[15] His is a portrait of a *"l'homme moyen,"* whose every feature contests normativity's hegemonic rule.[16] Similarly, in "Nausicaa," the novel's insistence on presenting the emotional as well as the sexual desires of a handicapped young woman once again reveals Joyce's intention to confront the regulative interventions of modern sciences of the body. Realistically, Gerty's chances of an advantageous marriage are slim; her idealising fantasies about herself and her romantic possibilities might therefore lead to patronising interpretations. The episode insists, however, that it is not Gerty's "shortcoming" (*U* 13.650) but her individual experiences and hopes that define her. In an important rebellious twist, Joyce makes the experience of presumably imperfect or disabled individuals an important representational aspect of his novel and acknowledges erotic needs in a character that would conventionally be overlooked by the romantic discourse of courtship.[17] Accordingly, in the development of such characters as Bloom and Gerty, alterity and resistance are identified as potential attributes of the unclassifiable, irregularly shaped body.

However, it is not only the aberrant bodies of the Irish citizens that attain prominence in *Ulysses*. With a view to challenging anthropocentric viewpoints, Joyce also reserves space for the representation of bodies belonging to non-human species. Bloom's first verbal exchange of the day, in fact, is not with his wife Molly but with the cat that stalks him in the kitchen while he is preparing breakfast. Right from the beginning, therefore, animals are at the forefront of the novel's conceptual agenda, and Bloom's curiosity and compassion for his feline counterpart call into question the categorical distinction between humans and non-humans – a distinction that motivates the discourses of legitimised violence and discrimination towards animals that Jacques Derrida identifies as a central strand in the history of Western humanism.[18]

Indeed, Bloom's encounter strikingly anticipates the one Derrida describes in his treatise on animal studies, "The Animal That Therefore I Am."[19] In these reflections on the relationship between humans and animals, Derrida uses the description of an early-morning encounter with his cat as the starting point for a philosophical investigation, in which he argues that the last two centuries have witnessed an unprecedented acceleration of the systematic exploitation, marginalisation, and subjugation of animal species. And what facilitates this hierarchical relationship is, according to Derrida, a central premise that has shaped Western thinking since René Descartes (1596–1650): the generic separation of man as thinking animal from the rest of the animal species. As the philosopher Giorgio Agamben explains: "*Homo sapiens*, then, is neither a clearly defined species nor a substance; it is, rather, a machine or device for producing the recognition of the human."[20] Moreover, as Derrida suggests, this binary model – which helps to reinforce man's self-understanding and his claim to privilege over the non-human world – is sustained by linguistic patterns: "The animal is a word, it is an appellation that men have instituted, a name they have given themselves the right and the authority to give to another living creature" ("Animal" 392). In order to disrupt the existing linguistic structures, Derrida coins the term "*animot*" ("Animal" 405) as an expression that points both to the categorising power of language ("*mot*": French for "word") and to an alternative perspective in which the recognition of plurality and diversity within the singular ("*animaux*": French plural for "animal") replaces a hegemonic discourse of oppression.

Like Derrida, Bloom is conscious of the cat's scrutinising gaze that turns him into the passive object rather than the constituting subject of the encounter: "Wonder what I look like to her. Height of a tower? No, she can jump me" (*U* 4.28–29). His engagement with the non-human Other encourages dialogue rather than subjugation. Although the cat becomes, at times, the object of his affectionate scrutiny – "Mr Bloom watched curiously, kindly the lithe black form. Clean to see: the gloss of her sleek hide, the white button under the butt of her tail, the green flashing eyes" (*U* 4.21–23) – his comments represent an empathic and imaginary reading but never the actual appropriation of the cat's point of view. His encounter with the cat is thus a very good example of what Donna Haraway calls "becoming with" animals – an epistemological condition that displaces the customary degradation of animal life by a shared sense of curiosity and reciprocity among "companion species."[21] Most appropriately, Bloom's

engagement with his cat can be described as one of productive and mutually constitutive amalgamation, a situation in which different species share
the same habitats and environments but not necessarily the same phenomenological experiences. In this manner, Joyce, in an early episode
of *Ulysses*, begins to question viewpoints that insist on perpetuating the
objectifying, hierarchical relationship between humans and animals.

With its description of a hallucinatory world of unfulfilled desires and
repressed memories, "Circe" also illustrates Joyce's pronounced desire
to interrupt the customary human-animal divide. Set at midnight in
"Monto," Dublin's notorious red light district, it takes place somewhere
between reality and imagination. No wonder, then, that this world of
liminal milieus and experiences is inhabited by individuals who visual-
ise, on a corporeal level, this Joycean desire to challenge anthropocentric
thinking. The novel here describes a phantasmagorical environment with
speaking objects and characters that continually change their costumes,
shapes, or identities. One of the first shapeshifters the reader encounters is
the dog that persistently trails Bloom on his route through Nighttown. In
the course of a few pages, Bloom's companion, the "*retriever*" (*U* 15.247),
turns into a "*sniffing terrier*" (*U* 15.356), is then called "*the whining dog*"
(*U* 15.577), and turns back into a "*retriever*" (*U* 15.659) before metamorph-
osing into a "*wolfdog*" (*U* 15.663), "*the munching spaniel*" (*U* 15.690), and a
"*bulldog*" (*U* 15.693). A pet cat accompanied Bloom when he made his first
appearance in the realist part of *Ulysses* in "Calypso"; Joyce, in an interesting instance of textual parallelism, now uses another animal to escort him
on his way into the fantastic dream world of "Circe."

As in previous episodes, then, some textual space is reserved in "Circe"
for the representation of animal species. This time, however, the episode's
anti-realist contours also allow for a more adventurous depiction of humans
and animals. For not only do animals, like their human counterparts,
change shape in "Circe," but some of Joyce's protagonists – such as Bloom's
father and grandfather – grow animal appendages that render them hybrid
figures with unstable taxonomic identities. Accordingly, "Circe" produces
an apparition of Rudolph Bloom who feels "*with feeble vulture talons …
the silent face of Bloom*" (*U* 15.259–60). Correspondingly, Bloom's grandfather, when delivering his lengthy discourse on female anatomy and other
luscious subjects, is accessorised with "*weasel teeth*" (*U* 15.2339), a "*yellow parrotbeak*" (*U* 15.2415), "*turkey wattles*" (*U* 15.2434), "*hunched wing-
shoulders*" (*U* 15.2460), "*a horning claw*" (*U* 15.2461), and finally a "*tail*"
(*U* 15.2630). Elsewhere, his passionate verbal outbursts at times approach
the sonic quality of different animal voices (*U* 15.2465, 2638).

No doubt in many of these cases these animalistic features are meant to transpose individual character traits into physiological markers. Because Rudolph descends like a patient yet unrelenting scavenger on his son when inquiring about his dealings in Nighttown, the "vulture talons" are more than appropriate physiological indicators of the persistent energy with which he continues to prey on Bloom's conscience. In Leopold Virag's case, some of the animal appendages have equally strong symbolic resonances, even if the unpacking of the intended symbolism is more challenging. Conventionally, turkey wattles are ornamental organs suggesting sexual competitiveness and physical fitness – personal and physiological attributes clearly at odds with the depiction of Bloom's grotesquely misshapen grandfather. Nonetheless, as an animal that represents gluttonous feasting, the turkey is still an appropriate animalistic companion for Virag, who delivers an exceptionally lecherous discourse in "Circe."

However, if animal features are nothing more than expressions of human character traits in this episode, then Joyce's cross-bred figures would be little more than an anthropomorphic appropriation of animal life drawn up to reinforce an oppositional reading of human and non-human species. But "Circe" depicts both Rudolph Bloom and Leopold Virag as liminal figures existing somewhere between such polar realms as life and death, past and present, memory and imagination. It is in this context that their transformation into hybridised creatures should be read. Both characters are intermediaries in "Circe." Consequently, their composite bodies defy clear phenotypical classification as much as their appearance in "Circe" rebels against the principles of conventional ontology. Neither humans nor animals, Bloom's ancestors emerge as textual constructs that showcase Joyce's attempt to contest notions of human existentialism as the philosophical premise that sanctions the subjugation of non-human species.

If such passages in *Ulysses* gravitate towards representations of anomalous, irregular, or unclassifiable bodies, then the novel as a whole subjects even those human organisms that are practically unscathed or "normal" to a systematic fragmentation and dismemberment. The barmaids' figurative segmentation in "Sirens" attests to Joyce's analytical interest in bodies as complexly organised biological mechanisms that resist being abstracted and pressed into fixed conceptual moulds. As much as he devised *Ulysses* as a textual misfit that defied novelistic conventions of its time, Joyce's emphasis on the unstable boundaries of the human organisms that he included in his novel opposes traditional expectations of literary character. His work, which systematically resists working towards a predictable or conventional conclusion, does not prioritise the lives and bodies of normal, virtuous and honourable characters inhabiting the world of literary texts subscribing to the realist tradition. For Joyce, the unruly, unclassifiable bodies of the disabled, the disenfranchised, the eccentric, and the unconventional were imbued with much more significance. These he observed with fascinated curiosity because they promised to fall outside essentialist nomenclatures. In his view, they could be mobilised as novelistic devices to rebel against discursive interpretations of human physiology that intended to structurally organise the modern social landscape and threatened to relegate the experience of outsiders to the realm of the pathological.

As will have become apparent, the critical approaches outlined here are not always mutually exclusive and often engage a similar set of interpretative frameworks. What they do not offer, neither individually nor collectively, is a fixed or stable theory on human physiology as it is depicted in *Ulysses*. On the contrary, the variety of different theoretical and historical constructions employed by different critics points to the variability in Joyce's conceptualisation of physiological imagery. As much as the body is never a stable category in *Ulysses*, many of its critical assessments will ultimately fall short of providing irrevocable readings. What might be perceived as interpretative shortcoming or limitation, however, should by no means be regarded as analytical impasse. Instead, it evidences the thematic amplitude in Joyce's representation of the body. And it is precisely because of the conceptual opulence of the physiological imagery *Ulysses* provides that scholars past and present have found it such a rewarding starting point for launching their critical interventions into Joyce studies.

Notes

1 Frank Budgen, *James Joyce and the Making of "Ulysses"* (Bloomington: Indiana University Press, 1960), p. 21. Further references will be cited parenthetically as *Making*.

2 Vike Martina Plock, *Joyce, Medicine, and Modernity* (Gainesville: University Press of Florida, 2010), pp. 5–24. For more criticism on Joyce's engagement with contemporary physiological and medical discourses see also John Gordon, "James Joyce, Skinside Out," in *Physiology and the Literary Imagination: Romantic to Modern* (Gainesville: University Press of Florida, 2003), pp. 147–85, as well as his *Joyce and Reality: The Empirical Strikes Back* (Syracuse: Syracuse University Press, 2004).

3 Michel Foucault, *The History of Sexuality: The Will to Knowledge*, vol. 1 (London: Penguin, 1998), p. 30. Further references will be cited parenthetically as *Sexuality*.

4 In his 1877 study *Physiological Aesthetics*, Grant Allen tried to explain "the purely physical origin of the sense of beauty and its relativity to our nervous organisation" (2). Aesthetic appreciation is here reduced to simple physiological processes. According to Sandra Tropp, Joyce drew heavily on Allen's theory when scripting the section in *A Portrait* that deals with Stephen's aesthetic theory. See Grant Allen, *Physiological Aesthetics* (New York: D. Appleton and Company, 1877); and Sandra Tropp, "'The Esthetic Instinct in Action': Charles Darwin and Mental Science in *A Portrait of the Artist as a Young Man,*" *JJQ* 45 (Winter 2008): 221–44.

5 See Andrew Thacker, *Moving Through Modernity: Space and Geography in Modernism* (Manchester: Manchester University Press, 2003), pp. 133–37.

6 Stanislaus Joyce, *The Complete Dublin Diary of Stanislaus Joyce*, ed. George H. Healey (Ithaca, NY: Cornell University Press, 1971), p. 11. For an alternative reading of fat as the organ of "Penelope," see Ellmann's essay on "Endings" in this volume.

7 J. B. Lyons, *James Joyce and Medicine* (Dublin: Dolmen Press, 1973), p. 173.

8 Hélène Cixous, *The Exile of James Joyce*, trans. Sally A. J. Purcell (London: J. Calder, 1976); and "The Laugh of the Medusa," in *The Norton Anthology of Theory and Criticism* (New York: Norton, 2010). Further references to "Laugh of the Medusa" will be cited parenthetically in the text.

9 See, for instance, Richard Brown's (editor) collection *Joyce, "Penelope" and the Body* (Amsterdam: Rodopi, 2006) for diversified critical readings of the graphic depiction of Molly's physicality.

10 Enda Duffy, *The Subaltern "Ulysses"* (Minneapolis: University of Minnesota Press, 1994), p. 95.

11 For a detailed account of this shift, see Chapter 8.

12 Trevor Williams has coined the term "Conmeeism" for the episode's depiction of the Catholic Church's oppressive force. See "'Conmeeism' and the Universe of Discourse in 'Wandering Rocks,'" *JJQ* 29 (Winter 1992): 267–79.

13 See Lennard J. Davis, *Enforcing Normalcy: Disability, Deafness and the Body* (London: Verso, 1995); Martha Stoddard Holmes, *Fictions of Affliction: Physical Disability in Victorian Culture* (Ann Arbor: University of Michigan Press, 2004); and Tom Shakespeare, *Disability Rights and Wrongs* (London: Routledge, 2006).

14 See Lennard J. Davis, "Constructing Normalcy: The Bell Curve, the Novel, and the Invention of the Disabled Body in the Nineteenth Century," in *The Disability Studies Reader*, ed. Lennard J. Davis (New York and London: Routledge, 1997), pp. 9–28. Further references will be cited parenthetically as "Normalcy."

15 Bloom's awareness of potential flaws in his appearance is made evident in the "Nausicaa" episode when he stresses that he did not let Gerty see him "in profile" so as to mask a misshapen nose or another physical blemish (*U* 13.836).

16 The term "*l'homme moyen*" ("average man") was coined by the sociologist and statistician Adolphe Quetelet in his *A Treatise on Man and the Development of his Faculties* (1835) to describe human individuals who exhibit average features

and would therefore represent the norm against which potential aberrations and abnormalities could be measured.

17 Recently, Dominika Bednarska has provided a detailed analysis of Gerty as a desiring, disabled character. See "A Cripped Erotic: Gender and Disability in James Joyce's 'Nausicaa,'" *JJQ* 49 (Fall 2011): 73–89.

18 For a detailed exploration of Bloom's engagement with the cat as well as Joyce's attempt to challenge anthropocentric perspectives, see David Rando, "The Cat's Meow: *Ulysses*, Animals, and the Veterinary Gaze," *JJQ* 46 (Spring/Summer 2009): 529–43.

19 Jacques Derrida, "The Animal That Therefore I Am (More to Follow)," trans. David Willis, *Critical Inquiry* 28 (Winter 2002): 369–418. Further references will be cited parenthetically as "Animal."

20 Giorgio Agamben, *The Open: Man and Animal* (Stanford, CA: Stanford University Press, 2002), p. 26.

21 Donna Haraway, *When Species Meet* (Minneapolis: University of Minnesota Press, 2008), pp. 16–17.

CHAPTER 14

Symbols and Things*

Paul K. Saint-Amour

> It is a suffocating, mœtic expanse of objects, all of them lifeless …
> Wyndham Lewis on *Ulysses*[1]

> Any object, intensely regarded, may be a gate of access to the incorruptible eon of the gods.
> Buck Mulligan, contemplating a Bass Ale label (*U* 14.1166–67)

Ulysses is crammed with objects. When it comes to stuff, Joyce's novel is a tackle box, a jumble sale, a museum attic after an earthquake. Even English-language novels of the realia-jammed nineteenth century can seem uncluttered and selective in comparison. A modern epic by a writer who claimed to "have a grocer's assistant's mind," the book brims not just with things but also with inventories of things (*Letters III* 304). Typically the form of the inventory presupposes that its items belong together on the same shelf of the world where they are being enumerated. The grocer's assistant stocking the storerooms of *Ulysses*, however, has other ideas about objects, order, and ontology. Here, just to reacquaint us with some of its shelves, are two of the book's shorter inventories:

> And all came with nimbi and aureoles and gloriae, bearing palms and harps and swords and olive crowns, in robes whereon were woven the blessed symbols of their efficacies, inkhorns, arrows, loaves, cruses, fetters, axes, trees, bridges, babes in a bathtub, shells, wallets, shears, keys, dragons, lilies, buckshot, beards, hogs, lamps, bellows, beehives, soupladles, stars, snakes, anvils, boxes of vaseline, bells, crutches, forceps, stags' horns, watertight boots, hawks, millstones, eyes on a dish, wax candles, aspergills, unicorns. (*U* 12.1712–19)

> They comprised astronomical kaleidoscopes exhibiting the twelve constellations of the zodiac from Aries to Pisces, miniature mechanical orreries, arithmetical gelatine lozenges, geometrical to correspond with zoological biscuits, globemap playing balls, historically costumed dolls. (*U* 17.572–75)

The first of these itemizes the haloes, ritual accessories, and vestments worn by a procession of clergy and saints who bless Barney Kiernan's pub and its denizens in "Cyclops." The second, from "Ithaca," lists instructive toys for a nonviolent kindergarten. But neither list describes actual objects in *Ulysses*'s baseline narrative world: The procession of holy folk occurs in one of the parodic interpolations in "Cyclops," and the toys are "[c]ertain possible inventions" that Leopold Bloom imagines during his postprandial reveries but has not, to date, managed to build (*U* 17.563). Most of the items in the first list are not physical objects but symbols or attributes woven into the saints' vestments. Yet the list is long enough that its items threaten to revert, in the reader's mind, from symbols back to solid objects, while several of the more worldly ones ("buckshot," "boxes of vaseline," "watertight boots") strain or rupture the holy category to which they supposedly belong.

What is true of such inventories is true of the book's general handling of objects: Far from treating them as inert props or appurtenances, *Ulysses* is deeply interested in how things are defined and perceived through their relation to other entities; in the conditions under which things become symbols; and in how both things and symbols produce meaning and the impression of a world. Rather than conjure them for walk-on parts only to discard them, *Ulysses* traces objects from pocket to pocket and episode to episode, imbuing them with detailed, sometimes obdurate materiality, while conscripting them for an enormous range of ideological roles and psychosexual substitutions. It also plays restlessly with how things travel between the literal and the figural; the particular and the universal; the mundane and the transcendental; the fictional, the factual, and the counterfactual. This broad spectrum of object-play has posed challenges for readers and scholars of Joyce's book. It also makes *Ulysses* an appealing site at which to consider questions of materiality, instrumentality, ethics, and more – both within and beyond literature.

Bowl, Mirror, Razor

First things first. Before reviewing how readers have thought, and might continue to think, about symbols and things in Joyce's book, let us look at a smaller sample of its objects – in fact, the first three that *Ulysses* names: "a bowl of lather on which a mirror and a razor lay crossed" (*U* 1.01–02). These three simple items vibrate with symbolic potential from the moment we encounter them. Forming roughly a Celtic cross – two lines intersecting within a circle – they reintroduce the Irish Catholicism that plays so important a role in all of Joyce's fictions. As utensils in a daily ritual, they stand in for the quotidian. Yet when Buck Mulligan spoofs the Mass while shaving, the bowl, the mirror, and the razor become the liturgical vessels and vestments in his mock Eucharist. We can read their first appearance, then, as setting up the crossing of sacred and mundane – the humbling of the Sacrament and consecration of the everyday – that happens throughout "Telemachus." Later moments in the episode link the razor to Stephen Dedalus, called "Kinch, the knifeblade" by Mulligan, whom Stephen thinks "fears the lancet of my art as I fear that of his" (*U* 1.55, 52). The bowl of lather finds its counterpart in Dublin Bay, whose "dull green mass of liquid" in turn reminds Stephen of the bowl of white china into which his dying mother had vomited "green sluggish bile" (*U* 1.108–09). And Stephen himself turns the mirror into the first symbol mentioned explicitly by the text: "It is a symbol of Irish art. The cracked lookingglass of a servant" (*U* 1.146). By the time the narrative leaves them, these three objects have been associated laterally with many other elements in the world of the novel as well as projected vertically into several symbolic registers. Their affiliation with the Eucharist and their role in Stephen's quip might be said to make these objects second-order symbols: They stand in for the work of standing in – for the process by which things come to mean more than what they are.

But the bowl, mirror, and razor are also objects with origins, histories, and materiality within the represented world of June 16, 1904. Even as they accrue figurative and associative meanings, these things accumulate physical detail. We learn that the bowl is made of polished nickel (*U* 1.306); that the razor is the kind that folds (*U* 1.123); that once thrust in Mulligan's pocket it makes a clacking sound against the mirror, which for its part is "cleft by a crooked crack" (*U* 1.148,135–36). In fact, it is not until the mirror is described as cracked – and as purloined by Mulligan from his aunt's "plainlooking" servant Ursula – that it becomes a workable vehicle for Stephen's "symbol of Irish art" (*U* 1.139–40). Whereas an object's symbolic function might seem to depend on its being generic or generalizable, these objects become more particular as they become more symbolically fraught. Just before descending to breakfast, Stephen observes:

> Warm sunshine merrying over the sea. The nickel shavingbowl shone, forgotten, on the parapet. Why should I bring it down? Or leave it there all day, forgotten friendship?
> He went over to it, held it in his hands awhile, feeling its coolness, smelling the clammy slaver of the lather in which the brush was stuck. So I carried the boat of incense then at Clongowes. I am another now and yet the same. A servant too. A server of a servant. (*U* 1.306–12)

Here the shavingbowl becomes a symbol of Stephen's "forgotten friendship" with Mulligan since the latter has begun playing lackey to the Englishman Haines; in carrying down the abandoned bowl, Stephen will feel himself to be no longer Mulligan's friend but "a server of a servant." But the passage insists that the bowl is not only a symbol. It is also a prompt to association (as Mulligan's mock-liturgical use of it seems to conjure the image of incense boats in real Masses), and thus to memory ("So I carried the boat of incense then at Clongowes") and to a recognition of the self's stability and flux in time ("I am another now and yet the same"). And it is a singular object endowed with physical traits (coolness, weight, texture, contents with a particular smell) worth tarrying over for their own sake. The tenderness of Stephen's communion with the shavingbowl may be the most surprising thing about the passage, as if in going to the bowl and holding it, feeling it and smelling its lather, he was taking up Mulligan's forgotten friendship – not with Stephen, but with the object.

What does a reader interested in *Ulysses*'s first three objects gain by consulting the schemata that Joyce circulated in 1920 and 1921, which identified "Symbols" for most of the book's episodes? Not much. For "Telemachus," the Linati schema lists "Hamlet, Ireland, Stephen" and the Gilbert schema gives us simply "heir." These are figures, not objects, and they seem unconcerned with mirror, bowl, and razor unless we strain for equivalences (Ireland = mirror? Hamlet = razor? Stephen = bowl?). Where the schemata list objects, the emphasis falls not on the objects' particularity but on their enchainment in a theme or epic correspondence – thus, the symbols for "Lotus Eaters" in the Linati ("Host, penis in the bath, froth, flower, drugs, castration, oats") index the theme of narcosis synced to the Homeric episode. Accordingly, the most influential early commentators on *Ulysses* tended to treat its objects as secondary, subordinating them either to the book's Homeric lattice or to its supposed universality. Claiming that Joyce's innovative "mythical method" provided "a way of controlling, of ordering, of giving a shape and a significance to the immense panorama of anarchy and futility that is contemporary history," T. S. Eliot put *Ulysses*'s objects among the chief targets of its rage for order, components of the modern chaos that myth would put straight.[2] Ezra Pound was more circumspect about the book's Homeric parallels, calling them "chiefly [Joyce's] own affair, a scaffold, a means of construction, justified by the result, and justifiable by it only."[3] But he insisted no less strenuously than Eliot on the secondariness of its historical particulars: "The details of the street map are local but Leopold Bloom (*né Virag*) is ubiquitous. His spouse … exists presumably in Patagonia as she exists in Jersey City or Camden" (*Pound/Joyce* 198). Wyndham Lewis, as ardent in disparaging *Ulysses* as Eliot and Pound were in defending it, confirmed their views of the book's project even as he condemned it for failing to impose order on its materials, failing to bring historicity to the heel of the universal:

> [I]t lands the reader inside an Aladdin's cave of incredible bric-à-brac in which a dense mass of dead stuff is collected, from 1901 toothpaste, a bar or two of Sweet Rosie O'Grady, to pre-nordic architecture.... The amount of *stuff* – unorganized brute material – ... slows it down to the pace at which, inevitably, the sluggish tide of the author's bric-à-brac passes the observer, at the saluting-post. (*Time* 89)

All of which leaves us in a strange place with regard to our three objects. The Homeric parallel imposes no discernible order on them, which would seem to relegate them to the status of "unorganized brute material" – of excess batter dripping, burnt, down the side of myth's waffle iron. Yet if mirror, bowl, and razor seem to fall outside the grid of Homeric correspondences, they clearly have a place within the novel's Catholic imaginary and, by dint of Stephen's "symbol of Irish art" remark, within its colonial problematic. This is to observe that *Ulysses* is endowed with more than one organizational framework, and that these may be in conflict with one another – that what one framework sees as "dead stuff," another might place near the center of a symbolic system. What's more, neither Eliot nor Pound nor Lewis seems interested in grappling with the materiality of the book's objects, despite the pains *Ulysses* takes to establish that materiality. Notwithstanding the differences among these statements by Joyce's contemporaries,[4] they share several articles of faith: that the literary object's historical and material particularities are utterly distinct from its symbolic function; that particular objects are among the "raw materials" of a work, at once preceding it and requiring transformation; and that a work's coherence and universality depend on its subduing those objects, whether it be to myth, satire, or objective spatial form.[5]

But can't an object in *Ulysses* have equally weighted symbolic and material functions? Robert Martin Adams thought so, and concluded that the way to understand the co-presence of these functions was first to distinguish more clearly between them – to separate "surface" ("the things which were put into the novel because they are social history, local color, or literal municipal detail") from "symbol" ("the things which represent abstract concepts of special import to the patterning of the novel").[6] Adams sketched a methodological process of elimination:

> When we know what part of the book is mainly literal Dublin detail, we can give more, or at least different, weight to what is palpably symbolic. When we know what basic materials Joyce started with, we may be able to estimate his artistic intent from the changes he imposed on them, the selection he made among them, his omissions. (*Surface* xvii)

For Adams, surface was not simply the raw material out of which symbols were produced; surface was itself produced through the transcription and alteration of historical materials (e.g., persons, places, events), and those compositional processes were therefore worth following. The book's symbolic level, meanwhile, was not what justified or organized its objects but was in a sense their remainder – what was left over after "social history, local color, [and] literal municipal detail" had been traced to their sources. Adams's work helped license at least two approaches to Joyce's novel that remain vital today: historicist readings that compare and contrast *Ulysses*'s Dublin to the historical Dublin preserved in archives, libraries, museums, and the actual city's built environment; and genetic studies that track Joyce's compositional processes in the attempt to fathom his sources, his decisions, and his priorities. Still, Adams's model breaks down at the scale of our sample objects. Although mirrors, folding razors, and nickel bowls presumably existed in 1904 Dublin, *Ulysses* doesn't describe these household objects with either the specificity (e.g., brand, place of manufacture) or breadth (e.g., indications of their role in social history) that would qualify them as "literal Dublin detail." The result: Our three objects are again stranded in the "symbol" column, with no additional light shed on their materiality, their historicity, or just how they "represent abstract concepts of special import to the patterning of the novel" beyond what we knew at the outset.

So far we have treated the distinction between *Ulysses*'s symbols and objects as an interpretive toggle switch. That is, we have sorted objects into either surfaces or symbols. Even when something partakes of both, we have tended to privilege symbol as the site of the novel's "patterning" energies, the place where it bestows meaning on historical content. It is possible, though, to see *Ulysses*'s Homeric structure (to choose one of its several organizational frameworks) as an *object* of interpretation rather than a privileged *mode* of interpretation – as something we should make sense *of* rather than make sense *with*. Here I am paraphrasing the Marxist critic Fredric Jameson, who has called for a "radical historization of the form itself," adding that "what is to be interpreted is then the historical necessity for this very peculiar and complex textual structure or reading operation in the first place."[7] According to Jameson, the book's Homeric grid attempts belatedly to impose what late capitalism has already taken away: a sense of meaning, plenitude, coherence, and comprehensibility in our relations with one another and with the object world. Our experience only *seems* alienated and arbitrary, the Homeric structure would reassure us, adding that every *thing* is also a symbol, every putatively random event deeply undergirded by a timeless universal narrative. Yet the modernism of *Ulysses*, Jameson continues, lies not in the reassurances offered by its mythic architecture, but in its refusal of them. That refusal he sees as one of the central lessons of modernist form:

> I believe that today, whatever our own aesthetic faults or blinkers, we have learned this particular lesson fairly well: and that for us, any art which practices symbolism is already discredited and worthless before the fact. A long experience of the classical modernisms has finally taught us the bankruptcy of the symbolic in literature; we demand something more from artists than this facile affirmation that the existent also means, that things are also symbols. But this is very precisely why I am anxious to rescue Joyce from the exceedingly doubtful merit of being called a symbolic writer. (*Modernist Papers* 140)

That any writer, let alone Joyce, might need rescuing from symbolism may seem counterintuitive. But for Jameson, *Ulysses*'s contribution lies not in the vertical operations of symbolism but in its restoring certain broken horizontal links: between commodities and the human labor that produces them, and among humans whose social relations with one another have become mediated – even supplanted – by relations with and among things. By these lights, the great affirmation of Joyce's book is neither its elevation of the everyday through myth nor Molly Bloom's final "Yes" (*U* 18.1609). Instead, says Jameson, it's to be found in "Ithaca," where the water from the Blooms' tap is traced back "less to its origins in Nature, than to the transformation of Nature by human and collective praxis deconcealed" (*Modernist Papers* 151). Such an approach understands Joyce's novel as incarnating, not transcending, historical necessity. This *Ulysses* insists on its own status as a made thing, on a level with the objects it describes.

Soap, Potato

To think more about turning away from mythological or symbolic readings of objects, let's set down our mirror, razor, and bowl and take up two other things to which we are introduced in a less portentous manner: the bar of lemon soap Bloom buys at Sweny's druggist in "Lotus Eaters" and the potato he carries in his pocket throughout the day. These objects will eventually be singled out when, in "Circe," the Daughters of Erin invoke them as intercessors: "Wandering Soap, pray for us ... Potato Preservative against Plague and Pestilence, pray for us" (*U* 15.1946, 1952). But they are also carefully tracked throughout the text, endowed with particular locations and origin-narratives as well as with multiple functions. The book's attentiveness to such commonplace objects has privileged them in *Ulysses* scholarship. Reactivating some of that work here will help us think about the kinds of analysis both enabled and impeded by the exemplarity of potato and soap in discussions of the book's objects.

Traveling a complex route from impulse-purchase through Bloom's various pockets to a speaking role in "Circe," the bar of soap has become for many Marxist scholars *Ulysses's* touchstone commodity fetish – the cardinal example, that is, of the commodity misrecognized under capitalism as autonomous, self-creating, and magically capable of entering into social relations with persons and with other commodities. Discussing advertising's role in fetishizing the commodity, Franco Moretti writes:

> It is no accident that one of advertising's favourite rhetorical flourishes is a metaphor in which – pathetic fallacy indeed – the product emerges as a "force of nature." The commodity must visibly take on independent, natural, and even human properties: "We're a capital couple are Bloom and I; / He brightens the earth, I polish the sky." So sings Bloom's notorious soap, rising as the sun in the "Circe" chapter.[8]

It is largely because of the soap's performance in "Circe" that Moretti dubs the episode "still the unsurpassed literary representation of commodity fetishism" (*Signs* 185). More recently, critics have mapped all of the novel's soap references to Marx's writing on use-value, the commodity fetish, and capital; insisted on how commodity fetishism operates differently in an occupied colonial city; and traced the salvific powers that arise from the soap's association with Milly and Molly Bloom (and hence with the *moly* flower that saves Odysseus from Circe's magic).[9] With the exception of the last, these discussions follow Jameson in adhering to the political economy of 1904 and in steering clear of Homeric readings. Yet there is an echo of those supposedly discredited mythical or symbolic readings in critical treatments of the soap as commodity fetish par excellence. Much as the Homeric reading uses mythic correspondence to imbue a contemporary object with meaning, the commodity reading locates the significance of the soap within a Marxist epistemology – an analytic system that is implicitly deeper and more authoritative than the surface it decodes. Additionally, by emphasizing the commodity form and the scenes of the soap's advertising, purchase, and consumption, these analyses mostly forbear to reconnect it to the laborious conditions and agents of its production.[10]

The potato Bloom carries as memento and talisman has been a marquis object in *Ulysses* criticism at least since Hugh Kenner used it to exemplify what he called the "aesthetic of delay," Joyce's way of dripfeeding information about a person, event, or thing into the text so dispersively that only a perfectly retentive reader – or one equipped with a perfect search engine – could gather it all.[11] Collating the book's many references to it, we learn that Bloom's wizened spud is a lucky charm of his mother's, which she believed had the power to absorb pestilence. It reminds him of her; it is also a relic of the 1845–47 famine. The potato and the bar of soap, compounded into *"potatosoap"* when Bloom pats himself down to see if he's had his pockets picked (*U* 15.243), seem otherwise set up as contrasting types of object. Where the soap is fabricated from multiple ingredients (including beef tallow, as "Hades" reminds us) through industrialized processes, the potato is the simpler yield of agricultural production.[12] It is unbranded, unpriced, and inherited, whereas the "lemonflavoured" soap is purchased on account for fourpence and, as we learn in "Ithaca," made by Barrington's (*U* 17.231–33) – a firm whose real-world counterpart was owned by a Dublin family of Quaker chandlers who did business out of Great Britain Street. Yet both of these objects have the magical ability to ward off danger – to be in excess of their materiality, to be fetishes in at least the anthropological sense. That the potato has some protective function in Bloom's mind, at least, is confirmed when his temporary loss of it to the sex-worker Zoe Higgins triggers some of the most extreme scenes in "Circe" – from messianism and calumny to Bloom's bondage, transgendering, and sexual abuse at the hands of the trans-madam "Bello." Bloom's loss of the potato, writes Mark Schechner, "is a symbolic castration and separation from *amor matris* [love of and for the mother]. His momentary unwillingness either to struggle to get it back or to relinquish it manfully is a tacit submission to pornocracy, government by whores."[13] In this psychoanalytic reading, the potato stands in for Bloom's phallus, and its detachability and loss are signs of his castration anxiety – his fear that he will be unmanned for his wayward desires by a paternal figure or by a phallic mother such as Bello. Suzette Henke has linked this castration anxiety to the dysfunction in Bloom's sexual relations with his wife, suggesting his fear of seeing his penis "disappear" into Molly's vagina explains the couple's not having had intercourse to completion since the death of their son eleven years earlier.[14]

Such readings of Bloom's potato have the virtue of accounting for the text's vigilance toward it and for the magical powers it seems to possess: If the potato is indeed placed in a psychosexual circuit with Bloom's phallus, no wonder it sparks with significance. Still, as with commodity-fetish readings of the soap, the psychoanalytic take on the potato bestows emblematic importance on the object partly by downplaying its material particularity, with the implication that an object becomes worthy of critical attention in proportion as it overflows its mere thingliness. We could say that the favoritism scholars exhibit toward objects such as *Ulysses's* soap and potato amounts to a second-order fetishism: the singling-out of a few objects in a crowded textual field on grounds that they incarnate an abstract form (e.g., the commodity fetish, the sexual fetish) important to the critic. Such biases may not be totally eliminable, may even be a condition of reading. But it is worth asking what sorts of attention they eclipse, and to what sorts of objects. Recently a cluster of approaches known as "thing theory" has emerged out of impatience with abstract and vertical readings of the object – with readings of literary objects as either "standing for" some allegorical or symbolic meaning in another register of the text or as incarnating abstractions such as the commodity form. Thing theory suggests that these abstract or vertical readings of the object cause us to ignore whole dimensions of its materiality that we can recapture by taking objects more literally: by understanding them to figure, chiefly, themselves.

One major strain of thing theory begins by distinguishing between two terms that I have so far treated as synonyms: *objects* and *things*. The object it understands as compliant and manipulable; as "ready-to-hand" in Heidegger's terms – that is, as so thoroughly assimilated to its instrumental function, its use as a means to an end, that we do not theorize it and may not even notice it. The thing, by contrast, is an obstinate, broken, or recalcitrant object, one that becomes "present-at-hand" by dint of having jumped the tracks of its instrumentality. As long as they're amenably permitting you to see, your eyeglasses are objects; but when they break and you're blindly trying to fix them with tape, your eyeglasses become unruly things. As thing theorist Bill Brown puts it, we look *through* objects but *at* things.[15] You use but barely notice the furniture in your house – until a family member moves it while you're gone; the sideboard, once a trusty object, is suddenly a thing when your head encounters it unexpectedly in the dark. In making the jump to thinghood, an object appears to assert itself and therefore to lay some claim to agency, even a kind of subjectivity. In its unruliness, the thing seems to commandeer some of the agency and subjectivity of the person it hinders, injures, or surprises. Things expose the poverty of the subject/object geometry by which we instrumentalize everything we deem nonhuman, a vast category that can include inanimate objects, the environment, the nonhuman animal, and the person whose humanity we deny.[16]

You might expect *Ulysses* to have played a prominent role in the development of thing theory. After all, the examples I just gave are from Joyce's book: In "Circe," we learn that Stephen broke his glasses on June 15 and has been without them since, and in "Ithaca" Bloom whacks his head on a walnut sideboard Molly has moved earlier in the day, possibly with the help of Blazes Boylan (*U* 15.3628–29, 17.1274ff). "Signatures of all things I am here to read," thinks the visually hampered Stephen as he walks on Sandymount Strand, bereft of the cracked eyeglasses of a scholar (*U* 3.02). Yet thing theory has so far been remarkably uninterested in reading the signatures of things in *Ulysses*, and at least one book-length study of modernism's excessive objects has all but done without Joyce.[17] Nor do I think this is the result of scholarly oversight so much as it is a telling silence. Here let me offer a proposition: *Ulysses*, for all its many objects, contains very few things.

Such a claim may seem to fly in the face of Stephen's broken glasses and Bloom's repositioned sideboard, to say nothing of singing soap and periaptic potato. But in the first instance, *Ulysses* seems to look away from its few unruly objects rather than at them. We never actually encounter Stephen's glasses in *Ulysses*, only evidence of their absence. Bloom's sideboard goes pointedly undescribed after his head strikes it: Only the contents of its drawers are listed, and then only pages later. The talismanic roles of both potato and soap are uses to which those objects are put by a human subject. Rather than providing evidence of their recalcitrance, such uses of these objects contribute to a sense of their docility in being repurposed for errands beyond the pale of their design. As we've already seen, the more roles these objects play, and the more extravagant their roles, the less in focus they are as resistant and singular entities. "Circe," with its dozens of speaking and animated objects, seems as if it would be the swarming-ground of upstart things in the novel. But when the bells of St. George's church say "Heigho! Heigho!" (*U* 15.1186) or the quoits of the Blooms' bed say "Jigjag. Jigajiga. Jigjag" (*U* 15.1138); when the wreaths of smoke from the sex workers' cigarettes say, "Sweet are the sweets. Sweets of sin" (*U* 15.655), and Baby Poldy's bronze buckles say "Love me. Love me not."

Love me" (*U* 15.2009); even when the soap sings or when Bella Cohen's fan speaks on her behalf, what we're encountering is a world of objects not run amok in nonhuman agency but instrumentalized all the more through the trick of ventriloquism. For what they have to say is always ancillary either to the human actors around them or to the prefabricated language of the marketplace. Thus, when the soap speaks, it adapts language from a Brooke's Monkey-Brand soap ad.[18] Even when the nymph from *Photo Bits*, descended from her frame over the Blooms' bed, upbraids Poldy for his erotic attentions to her, she does it in a Nausicaan jumble of fashion-mag argot and purple romance prose. It's as if the object world had been given voice solely for the purpose of renewing its vow of subservience to human agents or to capitalism's project of channeling all materiality down commodification's slick funnel.

Old Clothes, Sardines

Yet we make a mistake if we read either the commodity form or commodity fetishism as the final word on objects in *Ulysses*. Objects in the novel are at their least autonomous when they are at their most animated; if anything, they reveal rather than conceal the human social relations that subtend them. In addition, most of the prominent objects in "Circe" are making at least their second appearance in the novel. Where we'd expect the commodity fetish to speak most bewitchingly in the moments of first encounter that precede the act of consumption, in "Circe" the speech of objects requires their being in a condition of return, recirculation, and repurposing. This points us to an undertheorized region of *Ulysses*: its universe of used objects that includes Stephen's secondhand breeks, boots, and other hand-me-downs from Mulligan; the used copy of Chardenal's French primer his sister Dilly buys for a penny from a cart where Stephen half expects to see his "pawned schoolprizes" (*U* 10.840); the "left off" or secondhand clothes once bought and sold by the Blooms (*U* 11.496); and all the other pre-owned objects that circulate in a colonial economy where the supply of new commodities vastly exceeds the buying power of the populace. There is, in fact, an emerging social history of the secondhand that looks to address the consumption and biography of used objects. According to the editors of one anthology, this new line of inquiry sees

> consumption [as] pliable, a practice of consolidating past owning as much as purchasing something new. [It emphasizes] the tempo or periodicities of consumption [and recognizes that] the relationships between people and things have life-histories of their own, dominated by use and reuse,

frequency of purchase, disposal and dispersal, gifting, storage and lending, pawning and circulation, renewal or lifestyle changes.[19]

This description of an emerging field in the social history of consumption sounds like a prescription for *Ulysses*. One thing it reveals is that we've been so busy tracing the book's recycling of *language* – its allusions and appropriations, its intertextual linkages and its intratextual repetitions and variations – that we haven't thought to read *Ulysses* as capturing the multiple lives of objects, and thus as an immanent critique of the commodity fetish as a universal theory of the object.

But other books draw their readers' attention, if less intently than Joyce's novel does, to the secondhand. This essay concludes with a kind of object construction that is more unique to *Ulysses*, in particular to the oscillating distance between its stylistic and material worlds and to the lateral transfer of affect between persons and objects. Early in "Oxen of the Sun," the narrator describes the food being consumed in a lounge in the Holles Street maternity hospital by "many that sat there at meat," a rowdy group of medical students and their friends (*U* 14.124). Transposed into the terms of 1904, the fare – bread, wine, and a tin of sardines – seems modest, but in the fourteenth- and fifteenth-century idiom of Mandeville and Malory, the featured dish makes the narrator gape with amazement:

> And there was a vat of silver that was moved by craft to open in the which lay strange fishes withouten heads though misbelieving men nie that this be possible thing without they see it natheless they are so. And these fishes lie in an oily water brought there from Portugal land because of the fatness that therein is like to the juices of the olivepress. (*U* 14.149–54)

Stuart Gilbert links these sardines to the fish caught by Odysseus's men off the coast of Thrinakia before they slaughter and eat the forbidden cattle of Helios (*Joyce's "Ulysses"* 258). But that trivial moment in Homer is exceeded by the marvel and humor of the "Oxen" passage, which effects a re-enchantment essentially without myth. A re-enchantment without fetishism, too, in that the magic here is irreducible to wayward desire or to the commodity form. Studying 1904 canned sprat ads or the economics and geopolitics of the sardine industry could illumine but not exhaust this passage, whose strangeness results from a kind of anachronism particular to *Ulysses* – one in which a pre-modern style is made to describe, and thus to marvel at, an early-twentieth-century industrial object that would have been miraculous to Mandeville and Malory.[20] If the passage has any truck with symbolism, it is of a horizontal kind achieved through a connection to an earlier passage, in "Sirens":

– The wife has a fine voice. Or had. What? Lidwell asked.

. . .

– Very, Mr Dedalus said, staring hard at a headless sardine.

    Under the sandwichbell lay on a bier of bread one last, one lonely, last sardine of summer. Bloom alone.

– Very, he stared. The lower register, for choice. (*U* 11.1209, 1219–22)

There may be no stranger object in *Ulysses* than this headless lone fish, laid out like a dead princess under glass and bound to Bloom through the lyrics of a song ("'Tis the last rose of summer / Left blooming alone"[21]). Much as the nickel shaving bowl is both more and less than a symbol of "forgotten friendship," the sardine here acts as a confederate or emissary of Bloom's affect – his aloneness, his loneliness – without losing its particularity. No wonder Simon Dedalus, in his moment of captivation, stares hard at this surreal funereal object.

As readers of *Ulysses*, we stare over Simon's shoulder at the sardine, following its cultural and personal associations, its absurdity and eros and pathos, its being joined by the prose of "Sirens" in a metonymic chain with both a cuckold's isolation and a zaftig soprano's bottom range ("The lower register, for choice"). We are asked to fall for a series of jokes about the miracles of canning and oil-packing as cognate with those of loaves and fishes, but also to take seriously the loneliness of the last sardine. We might also find ourselves wondering what sort of object a sardine is and how it gets coded as a marvel rather than as merchandise, or as an object rather than as the remains of a being. In tracking the migrations of other boundary-crossing objects in *Ulysses*, we witness how the novel both enacts and catalogs means of re-enchanting the contemporary – means that include but are not limited to the vertical endorsements of myth and symbol, the abstracting power of the commodity, the animate magnetism of the fetish, and the historical dislocations of style. And we grow acquainted with the book's way of alternately rewarding, shattering, and transforming our critical optics. Whether we grope our way through *Ulysses* for the first or fortieth time, we are just beginning to read the signatures of all its liminal things.

Notes

* This essay is dedicated to the participants in the 2012 National Endowment for the Humanities Summer Seminar, "James Joyce's *Ulysses*: Texts and Contexts," and to my friend and co-director, Kevin J. H. Dettmar. My thanks to Michael Rubenstein, Sean Latham, and Christian Howard for their helpful comments on an earlier draft.

1 This essay is dedicated to the participants in the 2012 National Endowment for the Humanities Summer Seminar, "James Joyce's *Ulysses*: Texts and Contexts," and to my friend and co-director, Kevin J. H. Dettmar. My thanks to Michael Rubenstein, Sean Latham, and Christian Howard for their helpful comments on an earlier draft. Wyndham Lewis, *Time and Western Man*, ed. Paul Edwards (Santa Rosa, CA: Black Sparrow Press, 1993), p. 89. Further references will be cited parenthetically as *Time*.

2 T. S. Eliot, "*Ulysses*, Order and Myth," in *Selected Prose*, ed. Frank Kermode (London: Faber, 1975), p. 177.

3 Ezra Pound, "*Ulysses*," *The Dial* 72:6 (June 1922): 623–29, reprt in *Pound/Joyce: The Letters of Ezra Pound to James Joyce, with Pound's Essays on Joyce*, ed. Forrest Read (London: Faber and Faber, 1968), p. 197. Further references will be cited parenthetically as *Pound/Joyce*.

4 On the differences between the Pound and Eliot readings of *Ulysses*, see Joseph Brooker, *Joyce's Critics: Transitions in Reading and Culture* (Madison: University of Wisconsin Press, 2004), esp. chs. 1 and 3.

5 Stuart Gilbert differed from all three in holding out the possibility that *Ulysses*'s coherence might arise from its harmonizing, rather than taming, its materials "in such a way that, without losing their vitality and integrity, they yet fit together and form a concordant whole." See Stuart Gilbert, *James Joyce's "Ulysses,"* rev. ed. (Harmondsworth: Peregrine, 1963), p. 21. Further references will be cited parenthetically as *Joyce's "Ulysses."*

6 Robert Martin Adams, *Surface and Symbol: The Consistency of James Joyce's "Ulysses"* (New York: Oxford University Press, 1962), p. xvii. Further references will be cited parenthetically as *Surface*.

7 Fredric Jameson, "*Ulysses* in History," in *James Joyce and Modern Literature*, eds. W. J. McCormack and Alistair Stead (London: Routledge and Kegan Paul, 1982), reprt. in Fredric Jameson, *The Modernist Papers* (London: Verso, 2007), pp. 139. Further references will be cited parenthetically in the text as *Modernist Papers*.

8 Franco Moretti, *Signs Taken for Wonders* (London: Verso, 1983), pp. 195–96. Further references will be cited parenthetically as *Signs*.

9 See, respectively, Daniel Moshenberg, "The Capital Couple: Speculating on *Ulysses*," *JJQ* 25 (Spring 1988): 333–47; Enda Duffy, *The Subaltern "Ulysses"* (Minneapolis: University of Minnesota Press, 1994), pp. 151ff.; and Mark Osteen, *The Economy of "Ulysses": Making Both Ends Meet* (Syracuse, NY: Syracuse University Press, 1995), pp. 128–31.

10 Moshenberg notes that when the funeral cortege in "Hades" is stopped by a drove of cattle and sheep in the road on their way to the slaughterhouse, Bloom thinks, "Dead meat trade. Byproducts of the slaughterhouses for tanneries, soap, margarine" (*U* 6.395–97). Yet he reads the passage as allegorizing alienated labor generally rather than as hauntingly reminding the reader of one source of the soap that Bloom has purchased. See Moshenberg, "Capital Couple," p. 339.

11 See Hugh Kenner, "*Ulysses*," rev. ed. (Baltimore and London: Johns Hopkins University Press, 1987), ch. 8.

12 On "Hades" and the animal content of soap, see endnote 10.

13 Mark Schechner, *Joyce in Nighttown: A Psychoanalytic Inquiry into "Ulysses"* (Berkeley: University of California Press, 1974), p. 109.

14 See Suzette A. Henke, *Joyce's Moraculous Sindbook: A Study of "Ulysses"* (Columbus: Ohio State University Press, 1978), pp. 225–26.

15 Bill Brown, "Thing Theory," *Critical Inquiry* 28 (Autumn 2001): 4.

16 For a particularly rich discussion of the relations among machines, humans, and nonhuman animals, see Maud Ellmann, "*Ulysses*: Changing into an Animal," *Field Day Review* 2 (2006): 74–93.

17 In *Solid Objects: Modernism and the Test of Production* (Princeton, NJ: Princeton University Press, 1998), Douglas Mao refers to "Joyce's obtrusive catalogues of urban detritus and household debris" but focuses on the work of Virginia Woolf, Wyndham Lewis, Ezra Pound, and Wallace Stevens (13). Catherine Flynn, in her fine "A Brechtian Epic on Eccles Street: Matter, Meaning, and History in 'Ithaca,'" *Éire-Ireland* 46 (Spring/Summer 2011), makes a point of avoiding Bill Brown's distinction between objects and things on grounds that "alienation gathers around all domestic objects in 'Ithaca'" (p. 76, n23). Otherwise, critics reading Joyce in some relation to thing theory have tended to focus on works other than *Ulysses*. Lisa Fluet's "Stupidity Tries: Objects, Things, and James Joyce's 'Clay,'" *Éire-Ireland* 46 (Spring/Summer 2011): 194–223, mounts a subtle reading of that *Dubliners* story by considering the relations between stupidity and materiality. Patrick W. Moran argues that hoarding, of the sort both described and undertaken by *Finnegans Wake*, transforms objects into things by compounding their excessive significance through sheer superfluity of number; see his "An Obsession with Plenitude: An Aesthetics of Hoarding in *Finnegans Wake*," *JJQ* 46 (Winter 2009): 285–304.

18 "We're a capital couple, the moon and I / I polish the earth, she brightens the sky / And we both declare, as half the world knows, / Though a capital couple, we won't wash clothes." See Hye Ryoung Kil, "Soap Advertisements and *Ulysses*: The Brooke's Monkey Brand Ad and the Capital Couple," *JJQ* 47 (Spring 2010): 417–26.

19 Jon Stobart and Ilja Van Damme, "Introduction," in *Modernity and the Second-Hand Trade: European Consumption Cultures and Practices, 1700–1900*, eds. Jon Stobart and Ilja Van Damme (Basingstoke: Palgrave MacMillan, 2010), p. 2. I'm indebted to Heidi Smith for calling my attention to this and other scholarship on secondhand objects.

20 A few pages later, in a section that mashes up Defoe with Hakluyt, Goldsmith, Sterne, and several others, the tinned fish are again praised, this time by Lenehan: "There's as good fish in this tin as ever came out of it and very friendly he offered to take of some salty sprats that stood by which he had eyed wishly in the meantime and found the place which was indeed the chief design of his embassy as he was sharpset" (*U* 14.548–51).

21 See Don Gifford with Robert J. Seidman, *"Ulysses" Annotated: Notes for James Joyce's "Ulysses"* (London: University of California Press, 1998), pp. 309, 292–93.

Abbreviated Schema for Ulysses

Although we now typically refer to the individual episodes of *Ulysses* using names taken from scenes and characters in the *Odyssey*, such titles appeared nowhere in either *The Little Review* or in any editions of the book approved during Joyce's life. Joyce regularly used these titles on some of his manuscripts as well as in his private correspondence, but they appeared first in an organized way in a pair of "schemas" – one in Italian and the other in English – that were privately offered to friends and collaborators writing about *Ulysses*. These two documents differ from one another in important ways, although both make clear that by the time of their creation (quite late in the composition process) Joyce envisioned a deep structure for *Ulysses* based not just on Homer's epic, but on a variety of other symbolic elements as well, including color, art, time, and the body. In addition, each episode is assigned what Joyce first calls a "tecnica" then a "technic," an unusual word now generally taken as a synonym for narrative technique.

Here you will find a modified version of the "Gilbert" schema, which appeared first in Stuart Gilbert's *"Ulysses": A Study* when it was published in 1930. This table is redacted and included here only as an initial point of reference. Full versions of both schemas are now readily available online. For a detailed comparison and analysis of the differences between the two schemas, see the Appendix to Richard Ellmann, *Ulysses on the Liffey* (Oxford: Oxford University Press, 1972).

	Title	Scene	Hour	Organ	Symbol	Art	Technic
1	"Telemachus"	The Tower	8 AM		Heir	Theology	Narrative (young)
2	"Nestor"	The School	10 AM		Horse	History	Catechism (personal)
3	"Proteus"	The Strand	11 AM		Tide	Philology	Monologue (male)
4	"Calypso"	The House	8 AM	Kidney	Nymph	Economics	Narrative (mature)
5	"Lotus-eaters"	The Bath	10 AM	Genitals	Eucharist	Botany, Chemistry	Narcissism
6	"Hades"	The Graveyard	11 AM	Heart	Caretaker	Religion	Incubism
7	"Aeolus"	The Newspaper	12 noon	Lungs	Editor	Rhetoric	Enthymemic
8	"Lestrygonians"	The Lunch	1 PM	Esophagus	Constables	Architecture	Peristaltic
9	"Scylla and Charybdis"	The Library	2 PM	Brain	Stratford, London	Literature	Dialectic
10	"Wandering Rocks"	The Streets	3 PM	Blood	Citizens	Mechanics	Labyrinth
11	"Sirens"	The Concert Room	4 PM	Ear	Barmaids	Music	Fuga per canonem
12	"Cyclops"	The Tavern	5 PM	Muscle	Fenian	Politics	Gigantism
13	"Nausicaa"	The Rocks	8 PM	Eye, Nose	Virgin	Painting	Tumescence, detumescence
14	"Oxen of the Sun"	The Hospital	10 PM.	Womb	Mothers	Medicine	Embryonic development
15	"Circe"	The Brothel	12 midnight	Locomotor Apparatus	Whore	Magic	Hallucination
16	"Eumaeus"	The Shelter	1 PM	Nerves	Sailors	Navigation	Narrative (old)
17	"Ithaca"	The House	2 PM	Skeleton	Comets	Science	Catechism (impersonal)
18	"Penelope"	The Bed		Flesh	Earth		Monologue (female)

Further Reading

Few works have generated more critical commentary in the last century than *Ulysses*. There are now at least five peer-reviewed journals dedicated to Joyce, hundreds of scholarly monographs, and scores of guides, introductions, casebooks, and companions. In addition, there are four volumes of Joyce's correspondence (with more now in preparation), several major biographies of Joyce and his family, a sixty-three-volume collection of his unpublished work, and – thanks to the patchwork expiration of copyright protections in various jurisdictions – a growing number of editions of *Ulysses* itself. For those first attempting to make their way through the book, such a mass of material can prove as daunting as the novel itself.

To provide some companionable guidance to such readers, I offer here a toolbox rather than a bibliography: a collection of resources essential to novice readers that provide overviews, historical contexts, and incisive interpretive aids. In addition, each of the essays in this volume contains a useful bibliography that will gradually lead interested readers to some of the many pathways through *Ulysses*.

General Introductions

Blamires, Harry. *The New Bloomsday Book*. 3rd Edition. New York: Routledge, 1996. A detailed paraphrase of each episode of the novel that essentially retells the story in lucid prose. Very useful if you find yourself losing track of the narrative's events, but treats style as utterly distinct from content.

Gilbert, Stuart. *James Joyce's "Ulysses": A Study*. 1930. New York: Vintage, 1955. The earliest introduction to the book, containing the first published schema as well as summaries of the episodes that focus on the Homeric parallels. Contains a great deal of summary and quotation. Still a useful guide, despite its age.

Kenner, Hugh. *Ulysses*. Revised Edition. Baltimore, MD: Johns Hopkins University Press, 1987. A general introduction from perhaps the very best close reader of the text. Devotes chapters to major topics while also tracking the plot of the book.

Kiberd, Declan. Ulysses *and Us: The Art of Everyday Life in Joyce's Masterpiece.* New York: Norton, 2009. A chapter-by-chapter study of the book that emphasizes Joyce's engagement with the mysteries of everyday life and the importance of the novel's Irish contexts.

Lawrence, Karen. *The Odyssey of Style in "Ulysses."* Princeton, NJ: Princeton University Press, 1981. A useful counterbalance to Blamires that focuses on the changing styles of the book, tracking the way the story shifts its focus from character to language and form.

Reference Works

Fargnoli, Nicholas, and Michael Gillespie. *James Joyce A–Z.* New York: Oxford University Press, 1995. An encyclopedia with listings covering Joyce's life as well as the characters, symbols, and references in his work.

Gifford, Don, and Robert J. Seidman. *"Ulysses" Annotated.* Berkeley: University of California Press, 1988. The most widely used reference book in Joyce studies, it provides detailed annotations of individual passages and references. Should be used cautiously by first-time readers, because its level of detail can quickly cloud the movement of the narrative.

Gunn, Ian, and Clive Hart. *James Joyce's Dublin.* New York: Thames & Hudson, 1975. A mapping project that tracks the events of Bloomsday through the streets and interiors of 1904 Dublin.

Norburn, Roger. *A James Joyce Chronology.* New York: Palgrave, 2004. A year-by-year annotated list of events in Joyce's life. Although it lacks narrative structure, it does provide a clear timeline that can sometimes be difficult to extract from the major biographies.

Joyce's Life

Bowker, Gordon. *James Joyce: A New Biography.* New York: Farrar, Straus, and Giroux, 2012. Although lacking the level of scholarly detail and citation Ellmann offers, this recent study provides an informative narrative account of Joyce's life.

Budgen, Frank. *James Joyce and the Making of "Ulysses."* 1934. Bloomington: Indiana University Press, 1960. Although somewhat breezily written, this early biography was prepared under Joyce's supervision and is thus packed with fascinating information about the writer's creative process.

Ellmann, Richard. *James Joyce.* New and Revised Edition. New York: Oxford University Press, 1982. One of the most famous biographies of the twentieth century, this massive volume remains the standard scholarly account of Joyce's life and work. The revised edition features a detailed index.

Joyce, James. *Letters and Selected Letters.* 4 Volumes. Stuart Gilbert and Richard Ellmann eds. New York: Viking Press, 1966, 1975. Together, these four volumes contain a wide array of Joyce's correspondence and are very well indexed. These contain only a portion of Joyce's letters, however, and a new collection of unpublished correspondence will appear starting in 2016.

McCourt, John. *The Years of Bloom: James Joyce in Trieste 1904–1920.* Madison: University of Wisconsin Press, 2000. Focuses on the years Joyce spent in the city where *Ulysses* took its initial shape. Although lacking Ellmann's scope, it does attend carefully to the city's unique culture and its effect on Joyce's imagination.

Manuscripts and Early Versions

This is not an exhaustive list of archival sources for *Ulysses*, given that manuscript and other pre-publication materials are spread among numerous libraries in Ireland, the United States, and the United Kingdom. Listed here are some of the major resources that might provide a starting point for those interested in Joyce's composition process. With the exception of Gabler, different editions of *Ulysses* itself are not provided because these have now become numerous.

Groden, Michael, Hans Walter Gabler, David Hayman, and Danis Rose with John O'Hanlon, eds. *The James Joyce Archive.* 63 Volumes. New York: Garland, 1977–79. A facsimile edition that collects much of the pre-publication material for all of Joyce's works, including notesheets, notebooks, drafts, and placards. The material relating to *Ulysses* is concentrated in volumes 12–27. Must now be supplemented with additional materials, especially the items available online at the National Library of Ireland.

Joyce, James. *Ulysses: The Critical and Synoptic Edition.* 3 Volumes. Hans Walter Gabler ed., with Wolfhard Steppe and Claus Melchior. New York: Garland, 1984. This three-volume edition of *Ulysses* provides a somewhat controversial reading text, which became the basis of the 1986 *Ulysses: The Corrected Text* (the text cited throughout this companion). For scholars, its real use resides in its careful recording of the numerous textual variants. Interpreting Gabler's system for recording these variants, however, is a difficult task.

The Joyce Papers c.1903–1928. National Library of Ireland. http://catalogue.nli. ie/Record/vtls000194606. Accessed April 2014. Digital reproductions of more than 700 pages of manuscript and pre-publication material, including several drafts of episodes from *Ulysses.* The online finding guide provides detailed information about the various items and a useful overview is offered by Luca Crispi, "A First Foray into the National Library of Ireland's Joyce Manuscripts: Bloomsday 2011," *Genetic Joyce Studies* 11 (2011); www.genetic-joycestudies.org/.

Major Critical Studies and Collections

Adams, Robert Martin. *Surface and Symbol: The Consistency of James Joyce's "Ulysses."* Oxford: Oxford University Press, 1962. An early and lucidly written study of the novel that explores the productive tension between the book's simultaneous commitment to realist detail and symbolic abstraction.

Attridge, Derek. *James Joyce's "Ulysses": A Casebook.* New York: Oxford University Press, 2004. Features twelve major essays on the novel covering a range of perspectives. A useful place to go after finishing this *Companion.*

Davison, Neil. *James Joyce, "Ulysses," and the Construction of Jewish Identity.* Cambridge: Cambridge University Press, 1998. A study of Joyce's engagement with the major debates of his day surrounding Jewish identity and the ways these shaped his construction of Leopold Bloom.

Devlin, Kimberly and Marilyn Reizbaum, eds. *"Ulysses" – En-Gendered Perspectives: Eighteen New Essays on the Episodes.* Columbia: University of South Carolina Press, 1999. A widely cited collection of essays on Joyce and feminism. It functions as a kind of counterpart to Hart and Hayman.

Duffy, Enda. *The Subaltern "Ulysses."* One of several major studies that helped initiate postcolonial readings of the novel by attending carefully to its distinctly Irish contexts. Readers interested in these issues should also look at books and essays by Emer Nolan, Vincent Cheng, and Declan Kiberd.

Gibson, Andrew. *Joyce's Revenge: History, Politics, and Aesthetics in "Ulysses."* Oxford: Oxford University Press, 2002. A detailed historical reading of *Ulysses* that considers the way Joyce's book resists and critiques British imperial practices in Ireland.

Groden, Michael. *"Ulysses" in Progress.* Princeton, NJ: Princeton University Press, 1977. A still foundational study of the way Joyce created *Ulysses*; it tracks the development of the book from a handful of notebooks through it numerous drafts and revisions. Although some of the information has been superseded by more recent manuscript discoveries, its basic outline of Joyce's writing process remains essential reading.

Hart, Clive and David Hayman, eds. *James Joyce's "Ulysses": Critical Essays.* Berkeley: University of California Press, 1977. Eighteen essays by major figures in mid-century Joyce studies. Each focuses on a single episode of the novel and offers a close, often influential reading of the text.

Norris, Margot. *Virgin and Veteran Readings of "Ulysses."* New York: Palgrave Macmillan, 2011. A masterful and clearly written study of the book that focuses on its narrative elements including plot, character, suspense, and resolution.

Pearce, Richard. *Molly Blooms: A Polylogue on "Penelope" and Cultural Studies.* Madison: University of Wisconsin Press, 1994. A collection of essays that reconsider not only the final chapter of the book but Molly Bloom more generally from a variety of critical perspectives including feminism, cultural studies, and postcolonialism.

Other Resources

James Joyce Quarterly. The international journal of record for Joyce studies, it publishes articles, notes, reviews, images and "entertainments" on all aspects of the author's life, work, and afterlife. It also features the "James Joyce Checklist" in each issue – a comprehensive survey of work by and about Joyce published throughout the world.

James Joyce Checklist Online, http://norman.hrc.utexas.edu/jamesjoycechecklist/. A digital compilation of the *JJQ*'s quarterly bibliography of Joyce criticism. It can be searched by topic, title, and author, making this the richest, most efficient place to begin researching any topic in Joyce studies.

International James Joyce Foundation. The central organization devoted to Joyce studies, it hosts a biennial symposium, offers graduate student travel fellowships, and publishes a regular newsletter.

Joyce Studies Annual. This journal publishes long-form scholarship on Joyce in addition to journal-style articles.

Dublin Joyce Journal. Published at University College Dublin, this relatively new publication features articles on Irish aspects of Joyce's life and writing.

James Joyce Broadsheet. Offers reviews and short commentaries as well as notes on Joyce-related events throughout the world.

James Joyce Literary Supplement. A biannual publication of book reviews with occasional short articles.

Hypermedia Joyce Studies, http://hjs.ff.cuni.cz/. An online annual originally founded to publish scholarship on Joyce that might leverage the critical potential of hypertext. Now largely publishes critical essays.

Genetic Joyce Studies, www.geneticjoycestudies.org. A digital journal published annually that focuses on Joyce's writing process and the development of his works from notes to published texts.

Modernist Versions Project: Ulysses, http://web.uvic.ca/~mvp1922/. A digital edition of the 1922 *Ulysses.* Part of a larger project, it will eventually allow readers to compare different versions of the text.

Joyce Images, http://www.joyceimages.com/. A rich collection of historical images from 1904 Dublin, all linked to individual episodes of *Ulysses.* As a whole, the site offers a terrific sense of the visual culture from which the novel emerged.

Index

Cambridge Companions to...

TOPICS

Printed in Great
Britain
by Amazon